THE AMAZING BOOK OF EVERYTHING

YOUR COMPLETE
GUIDE TO PERSONAL SUCCESS,
WEALTH, HEALTH AND HAPPINESS

THE AMAZING BOOK OF EVERYTHING

YOUR COMPLETE GUIDE TO PERSONAL SUCCESS, WEALTH, HEALTH AND HAPPINESS

COMPLETELY REVISED AND UPDATED BY
THE PERSONAL & FINANCE CONFIDENTIAL RESEARCH TEAM

EDITED BY IAIN MAITLAND

Published by Agora Lifestyles Ltd
Registered Office: 103 New Oxford Street, London WC1A 1QQ
Telephone: 0171 447 4018

Registered in England No: 3303666 VAT No: GB 629 7287 94

ISBN No: 1 899964 95 9

Printed in Great Britain by MPG Books, Ltd, Bodmin, Cornwall

CONTENTS

INTRODUCTION

Dear Friend,

Welcome to *The Amazing Book of Everything, Your Complete Guide to Personal Success, Wealth, Health and Happiness.* It's packed full of little-known secrets and tips that your *PFC* team has uncovered for you from around the UK and all over the world. My name is Iain Maitland, I'm the editor of *PFC*, and it's my job to choose the very best tricks of the trade to go into each month's issue. I only select those that will enable you to become more successful, wealthier, healthier or happier! I use all of these insider secrets myself – and they've brought about huge changes in my own life. Now they're going to do the same for you.

DO YOUR WORK IN HALF THE TIME

Whilst editing *PFC*, I receive hundreds of documents from your team of experts, insiders and contacts around the world. All of them vying for my attention with another 'must-include' hint or secret strategy! I have to read every one of them – just to make sure I don't miss out on that one piece of information that might change your life forever. To begin with, I didn't do anything but read all day, everyday, and yet my in-tray still got fuller and fuller. But one of your inside contacts then told me about photo-reading, an amazingly simple technique that allows you to process twice as much information in half the time! You can learn about it on page 105. Now, I deal quickly with all the letters, faxes and e-mails, leaving me more time to compile *PFC*. And I've also got time to play with my three children in the evening!

ALL TYPES OF GOODS – AT 10% OFF HIGH STREET PRICES

If you came into my office, you'd ask me about the expensive high-tech equipment I use to edit *PFC* for you. I always have the latest computer and software packages, a top-of-the-range scanner, a marvellous fax machine and a host of other gizmos that look as though they've come straight out of a NASSA space station. And I know exactly what you'd say. 'They must have cost a fortune!' That's what everyone says. Then they guess how much everything cost me. '£3,000, £5,000, more than that?' Wrong! I paid less than £500 for the whole lot. How? I go to government auctions where the seized and liquidated stocks of failed businesses are sold off at next-to-nothing prices! Take a look at page 113 – and you'll find out how you too can pick up all types of incredible bargains at rock-bottom prices.

FIVE-STAR HOLIDAYS – AT TWO-STAR PRICES

PFC has a team of specialists and inside contacts all across the world; in Europe, the US, Asia, and even as far away as Australia! The net is cast far and wide to ensure that you're brought the most useful, least-known news and information every month. The one thing that all these insiders have in common is that they're the best in their field, they're high-flyers, and they travel the world. On page 3, they share one of their favourite secrets with you. Now you can be in the know and stay in top five-star hotels all over the world – but only ever pay two-star prices! I'm now halving my hotel bills and enjoying a luxury lifestyle with this canny trick of the trade.

AMAZING SECRETS REVEALED TO YOU

This book contains hundreds (or even thousands) of sensational secrets and shortcuts to success. Want to get up to 50% discounts on home improvements? Turn to page 59. Trying for a baby? You can choose your baby's sex – check out page 108! Do you want to know how to spot a home-working scam? The con-artists' shabby secrets are exposed on page 219! And why should you put haemorrhoid cream on your face? Or cat litter? You'll find out on pages 226 and 233. And would you like to earn money reading a book? All is revealed on page 233.

AND THERE'S MORE

There's more to *PFC* than secrets and shortcuts – much, much more! As a welcome new subscriber, you're guaranteed to discover the secrets that the large corporations, official bodies, and governments don't want you to know about. And you'll also receive little-known share tips each month – the up-and-coming companies to invest in, and the ones to avoid at all costs. The latest medical advances from hospitals and research centres around the world will be brought straight to you – often before they've even become public. And you'll be alerted to the scams and scandals that are taking place across the UK and on the internet – and offered the very best advice for avoiding them. Plus, you'll hear news of the latest top products and services available now and coming soon – and how you can benefit from them.

MUCH, MUCH MORE!

There's more? Of course there's more!! I personally promise that you'll be offered at least six, tip-top give-aways in each and every issue of *PFC*. Guides, books, CDs, audio-tapes, video-tapes – they've all been selected carefully and approved as best-buy products; except they're free to you! They're all yours in *Freebies on Request*. You'll also receive details of little-known organisations and self-help groups in your regular *Helplines* section. These tried-and-tested phone-lines bring you practical, specialised and independent advice on a wide range of topics, from student tax dilemmas, through consumer rights to getting the best pension for your retirement years.

AND STILL THERE'S MORE

Last – and hopefully not least! – there's me. I'm not one of those editors who sits at a desk and hides away from readers behind an army of secretaries, researchers and contributors. I'm here for you – so if you need further information on any topic, call me and I'll ensure it features in a future edition of *PFC*. And I will do my best to answer your questions. If I don't know the answer, I'll pass it on to *PFC*'s UK Panel of Experts; you'll meet them on pages xv to xix. And if they can't answer your question (and from personal experience, I know that's unlikely), they'll know someone who can – because they've each got inside contacts around the world. So phone me - my direct line is 01394 210085. Or you can fax me on 01394 210254, or e-mail me at Imaitland@aol.com If you prefer pen and paper, write to me at *PFC*, Agora Lifestyles Limited, 103 New Oxford Street, London, WC1A 1QQ.

I look forward to hearing from you soon.

Kindest regards,

Iain

Iain Maitland

Iain Maitland

PFC Editor

PS. Do read and enjoy all of this sensational book. You'll find page after page of insider secrets and clever tricks of the trade that will help you to become healthier, wealthier and more successful in everything you do. I personally guarantee it.

PPS. And do you know a little secret you could share with your fellow subscribers? Earn yourself some money by sending in your tip for the regular *Treasure Trove* section. You'll find this on page 250 of this book. And if I publish your idea, I'll personally send you £20.

MEET YOUR EXPERTS

PFC's UK panel of experts comprises leading specialists from all over the country. They have three main aims. One, to uncover the most up-to-date and very best information for you from around the world. Two, to present it to you in the most concise and accessible format. Three, to offer practical and personalised advice to you on request. If you have any questions, you can contact any of your experts through your editor, Iain Maitland.

Want to know more about **ALTERNATIVE MEDICINE**? And find an effective, safe cure for your condition? Then you'll want to be introduced to Dan Hennessy, the managing director of the renowned Frank Roberts Herbal Dispensaries Limited. This West Country firm supplies herbal medicines to customers all across the world. Dan is an active member of the British Herbal Medicine Association, and will bring you 29 years' of know-how and research in the field of herbal medicine.

Learn how to fast-track your **CAREER DEVELOPMENT** with Angela Edward. Angela is a policy adviser at the London-based Institute of Personnel and Development, the UK's leading authority on personnel issues. She is responsible for setting the standards of good practice which are implemented by organisations across the country. Her extensive knowledge of today's working environment and the needs of employers will bring you the best possible career guidance.

Make sure your **FINANCIAL PLANNING** generates the best returns via Saran Allott-Davey, the managing director of Heron House Financial Management, the all-female, high-profile IFA firm. In addition to being the Chair of the Institute of Financial Planning in South Wales. Saran is a financial expert who has achieved the very highest financial planning qualifications, so she has amassed a lot of expertise to pass on to you. Saran broadcasts regularly on BBC Radio about financial matters – and looks forward to including you among her confidants.

Interested in **FITNESS**, and keeping your body fit and young? Let Kristin Centofanti share the knowledge she's gained as a research consultant at Ultratone Limited. Kristin lectures worldwide on health, fitness, sport and beauty issues. Her father introduced and pioneered domestic muscle stimulators in the UK; and Kristin now trains people in their use.

Fancy a flutter? And winning a tax-free sum too? Nick Daws is acknowledged as one of the UK's top **GAMBLING** experts, and is your *PFC* gambling guru. He also edits *British Gambling News* and writes extensively on horseracing and other sports for the national press. Let Nick introduce you to the top tips that will help you beat the bookies!

Stay in good **HEALTH** with Dr Jeremy Sims, who works at hospitals around the United Kingdom. Jeremy is also responsible for bringing news of the very latest medical developments to the attention of the national and international press – and plans to deliver these to you first.

Do you need to be guided through the minefield of **INVESTMENTS**? Nigel Bolitho, an independent financial adviser at BV Services in Cambridge, will lead you safely through his areas of expertise. Nigel will also provide you with expert advice on school fees planning and higher education funding.

Get the answers to the trickiest **LAW** problems from Peter Walker, a barrister and a financial accountant working in commerce and industry. As *PFC*'s legal specialist and the author of numerous successful books both in the UK and overseas, Peter will guide you through the UK law system – and drop you one or two little-known tips on legal loopholes!

Looking for **LOVE**? Pat Jones is the founder of Local Links, the UK's fastest growing introduction agency. With Pat's advice and contacts, hundreds of couples have found lasting happiness together. Maybe you too will find that special friend or lover you've been seeking.

If you need professional advice on **PENSIONS**, David Holland, the managing director of R.K. Harrison in London is your man. David will offer you his expert advice on savings and pensions, and may let you in on one or two personal and corporate money-spinning secrets as well.

Build up your **PERSONAL DEVELOPMENT** skills through Gordon Veniard, the founder of one of the UK's leading personal development agencies – Veniard's Communication Works! Gordon presents training events and seminars on a broad range of self-development topics for both business and personal life. He will help you get motivated in goal setting, improve your negotiating tactics and perk up your selling techniques!

If you like **PHOTOGRAPHY**, you'll want to know Steve Barham – *PFC*'s award-winning photographer. As a member of the British Institute of Professional Photography and the Master Photographers' Association, Steve will share his professional secrets with you. Steve has won both the Kodak Family Portrait Photographer of the Year and the Agfa Wedding Photographer of the Year – which makes him the ideal person to pass on a clever trick or two.

Buy and sell **PROPERTY** more successfully with Alison Rollé, a founding member of *Loot*, the newspaper for DIY property sellers across the United Kingdom. Alison is well positioned to advise you on every aspect of property dealing, and all those little tricks of the trade you'd love to know about.

Do you work from home or are you thinking of doing so? You'll profit from the **SELF-EMPLOYMENT** advice of Sophie Chalmers, editor of *Better Business*, the UK's top monthly magazine for self-employed people working alone or from small offices. Sophie will provide you with the advice and knowledge that has made her magazine hugely popular with Britain's increasing number of home-based workers.

Have better **SEX** with the help of Angela Gray, the former UK editor of *Mind, Body, Soul* magazine. Angela now writes extensively on personal, sexual and relationship issues for the national press, and brings her sound advice and sympathetic understanding to all *PFC* subscribers.

Are you a budding **SHARES** investor? Or an experienced pro? Either way, you'll discover some red-hot tips from Tom Winnifrith, the editor of Tom Winnifrith's *Red Hot Penny Shares*. Tom will tell you where to invest, and why. He'll also monitor shares, and advise you when to sell, or buy more. All you need to do is invest, and cash in on his expertise!

Increase your **SPORTS PERFORMANCE** with Harald Øyen, the highly regarded, UK-based expert in human performance enhancement. Harald has developed many innovative and effective techniques for increasing individual and team performance in sports techniques. Harald's advice will enable you to revitalise your performance.

Need help in sorting out your **TAX**? Gerry Hart is at hand to assist you. A former national president of the Chartered Institution of Taxation, Gerry now heads The Tax Team – the UK subsidiary of the world's largest tax return preparers, H&R Block International. Gerry is also a member of the editorial board of the prestigious publication *Tax Journal*, and intends to share his tax know-how with you.

Interested in **TRAVEL** and **OVERSEAS WORK**? Mark Hempshell, the UK editor of *International Job Finder* is the adviser for you. He is the author of numerous books on working and living overseas, including *How to Find a Job Abroad* and *Your Own Business in Europe* and is the editor of the *Guild of Wealth* for the Anglo Wealth Alliance. Mark is well placed to offer the canniest advice on successful and lucrative foreign work placements.

Thinking about investing in **UNIT TRUSTS**? Accept the help available from Pascal Matic, an independent financial adviser at UNITAS in Lincolnshire. He specialises in worldwide unit trust investments – and offers you hands-on guidance in this tricky investment area.

Maximise your **WEALTH** with Bruce McWilliams, a former Citibank vice-president in London, Zurich and New York City. His international expertise and personal investment success are at your service. As editor of *Wealth Builder* and the author of the best-selling *Picking the Right Unit Trust with PEP Secrets*, Bruce will bring the secrets of his investor conferences and unit trust success direct to you!

Are you concerned about your family's **WELLBEING**? David C. Harcombe is a freelance community pharmacist in the North of England, and he reports regularly to *PFC* on many health and medical developments. If you want to cure a sniffle, know more about the medicine you're taking, or learn how to get better quicker, David has the answers you need to know.

Surf the **WORLDWIDE WEB** with Patrick Jones, head of WWW-Net Design. As *PFC*'s computer and internet specialist, he will introduce you to all of the latest technology and developments with simple, jargon-free explanations. Patrick's the best man to take you into cyberspace and beyond!

THE AMAZING BOOK OF EVERYTHING

YOUR COMPLETE GUIDE TO PERSONAL SUCCESS, WEALTH, HEALTH AND HAPPINESS

SPEND A NIGHT IN A FIVE-STAR HOTEL – PAY ONLY TWO-STAR PRICES

You can stay in the very best hotel room anywhere in the world, and pay less than you would for the most basic, lowest-priced room. Here's how:

1. **Avoid travelling at the busiest times.** Examples: midsummer, during trade fairs and conferences. Why: except for a few busy weeks each year, there are always more rooms available than guests. So: by travelling at quieter times, you boost your chances of a great deal. Tip: check the dates of conferences and exhibitions with the local tourist office before travelling. Vital: don't reserve your hotel room in advance when you book your flight and/or car hire. Reason: travel agents, airlines and car hire firms are paid on commission. It's in their interests to sell you the most expensive room they can. Also: they don't care how grim the room is because they're unlikely to take the blame for it. Instead: book direct through the hotel.

2. **Identify a range of five or six hotels in the same grading category.** Why: this number enables you to play off one against the other. Tip: don't waste your money on expensive travel guides for that region – you can get all the information you need from the local tourist office – free of charge.

3. **Call each of the hotels in turn and ask for the room rate.** Important: whatever the quoted price, reply with "But I thought you had a special offer on at the moment?" This simple question is the ideal come-on for a discount. Reason: hotels always have special offers on all of the time – but they won't declare these unless asked. Bottom line: even if they're not running a special offer, they'll probably arrange one on the spot rather than lose your custom.

4. **Be bold.** Essential: say "But the Hilton Hotel has just offered me £XX a night. Surely you can beat that?" Note: most hotels are hugely competitive and hate to be beaten by their rivals – so they'll do everything they can to snatch business from under their competitors'

noses. Remember: this hotel is unlikely to know what price you may (or may not) have been offered a few minutes earlier.

5. **Always book a mid-priced room in the hotel.** On arrival, say "I'm a frequent guest of your hotel/this chain. Can I have a courtesy upgrade?" Fact: it costs a hotel very little more to accommodate you in an executive suite than it would in the mid-priced room. If such a room is available they'll almost certainly upgrade you to keep your custom. Note: by booking a mid-priced room, you'll have priority for upgrades over those people who have booked a standard room.

6. **As an alternative, turn up at the hotel of your choice; and negotiate on the spot.** This is often the best way of getting a great deal. Why: if you don't take the room, the chances are that nobody else will. Request: a single room to double room upgrade and/or meals to be included in an all-inclusive price. Aim: to be shown to a beautiful, executive room or even a suite, and all for less than the full price of the cheapest room in the hotel.

(Source: Mark Hempshell is a PFC expert, and has written numerous handbooks on travelling and working overseas. The original version of this feature first appeared in PFC February 1998, No. 17.)

A SIMPLE TRICK TO MAKE YOUR CHILDREN TAKE THEIR MEDICINE

***PFC* tip:** take an ordinary ice cube and rub it over your child's tongue. Why: this 'freezes' their taste buds for a few seconds – and lets them swallow their medicine without having to taste it.

(Sources: PFC *health and medical specialists.)*

EAT MORE – BUT WEIGH LESS

Many people stick to a calorie-controlled, fat-counted meal plan for months, but eventually return to their old eating habits – and find the pounds pile back on again. But it doesn't have to be like this if you adopt a different approach. Here are the do's and don'ts for success:

1. **Eat more high carbohydrates – bread, potatoes, pasta, rice and cereals.** These provide starch and fibre. Base your diet around these low-fat foods and fill up on them – but avoid smothering them with butter, cream sauces and/or mayonnaise. And: fruit and vegetables are often low in calories and high in vitamins, minerals and dietary fibre. Vegetables should be eaten raw or cooked lightly to retain their nutrients. Also: eat more protein – most concentrated in meat, fish, poultry, nuts, beans, lentils and peas. White fish is particularly nutritious and low in calories; include it three times a week. Avoid fattier meats, or trim off all the fat. Plus: dairy products are the main source of calcium although many have a high fat content. Choose lower-fat options – cottage cheese, yoghurt, skimmed milk. Helpful: water is an essential part of any diet. It works as a diuretic, flushing toxins out of the body. And if you have a glass of water before a meal, it can stop you over-eating by making you feel full sooner. Tip: fizzy mineral water helps satisfy cravings for sugary drinks.

2. **Eat less fat.** Substitute high-fat dairy products for low-fat alternatives – change from full cream milk to skimmed or semi-skimmed versions. Use low-fat cooking methods – grilling, boiling, steaming. Reduce your sugar intake – from pastries, chocolate and sweets. Eating sweet things only after meals is helpful. Cut back on salt – your body requires only small amounts. Adding salt to our food can mean that we are taking in as much as 1000% more than the body needs; and can lead to high blood pressure. Avoid salting your meals, and cut down on processed foods, which contain a high amount of salt. Alcohol has no fat, but contains lots of calories. Health Authority guide: half a pint of bitter has 90 calories, ordinary strength lager has 85; a measure of spirits has 50; a glass of wine has 75 calories.

3. **Change your lifestyle.** Amending lifelong habits takes time and patience. So: introduce new foods on a step-by-step basis. Idea: even eating a small piece of fruit a day, going without cream on strawberries, or grilling when you used to fry, is a positive beginning. Next: examine

your lifestyle. Question: do you work long hours? If so, you could be snacking on high-fat foods – so start by choosing fast food that is low in fat, such as bananas or popcorn. Question: are you stressed at work? It's likely that you could be overeating to compensate – being aware of this is a good start. Question: do you have to entertain people at work? You might be eating two big meals a day, instead of the usual one. Miss out one of the lunchtime courses and choose healthier options from the menu. Try new recipes out on your family; but note that children need more fat in their diets than adults do.

Bottom line: once you've started your healthy eating plan, you'll soon realise that the food is really delicious. Idea: follow the Mediterranean cuisine of southern Italy, France and Spain; those countries that are famous for their culinary expertise and with diets that consist primarily of bread, pasta, rice, and vegetables. Most of their recipes are easy-to-follow and quick-to-produce. And the reduced rates of heart disease and strokes in those countries are thought to be due to the local diets.

(Sources: Judith Wills, Slim for Life – Six Simple Steps to Successful *and* Lasting Weight Loss, *Pamela Westland,* Low Fat Cooking, *Hilaire Walden,* Mediterranean Cooking.*)*

WIN YOUR DREAM JOB WITH A SIMPLE 'PS'

***PFC* tip:** add a 'PS' to your letter of application, using it to highlight the key benefit of employing you. Reason: after reading your introduction, most recruiters go straight to the signature and the name to see who sent the letter to them. And: they will then look down at that PS!

(Source: PFC *careers experts.)*

REVEALED – THE LITTLE-KNOWN INVESTMENT THAT'S THE ULTIMATE IN ANONYMITY

The Eurobond market offers a completely anonymous investment that's open to UK residents and pays interest gross of tax – it's the ideal way of keeping your money away from the Inland Revenue.

Background: although the Eurobond market is familiar on the continent, it is almost unheard of by the average UK investor – because exchange controls prevailed in this country for 40 years after the outbreak of the Second World War. Details: Eurobonds are similar to offshore gilts – they're issued in a variety of currencies such as US dollars, Swiss francs, and Japanese yen by sovereign states and multinational companies; their credit standing should be undoubted. The bonds are 'bearer' securities which means that they are completely anonymous. 'Eurobonds' can be purchased perfectly legitimately by UK citizens and declared on their annual tax returns. Interest on these bonds is always paid gross of tax; which leaves the buyer to settle his or her own tax affairs. Eurobonds are a favourite investment for the world's black economy operators who wish to build up offshore nest eggs. Typical: such buyers open bank accounts in overseas tax havens such as Switzerland and pay the dividends from the bonds into these accounts.

(Source: PFC *financial specialists in Europe.)*

ENJOY GREAT SEX – WHATEVER YOUR AGE

Great news: a recent US study of 50 to 70-year-old men and women shows that the vast majority of those who had partners remained sexually active. Typical: there are age-related changes that need to be dealt with – it may take longer to become aroused, erections may not be as firm, and you may need more time before you're ready for sex again. But: you can still have a terrific sex life! Here are the ins and outs of successful sex:

1. **Keep making love.** Fact: if men continue to have sex regularly, they boost their potency – those that go without sex for long enough face an increased risk of becoming impotent. And: women who have frequent sex keep their vaginal tissues more elastic and have improved vaginal lubrication. Regular sex also reduces stress and helps you to sleep. One Swedish study shows that older people who are sexually active have more vitality, greater intellectual ability and a better memory than

those who don't engage in sex. Wise: don't compare your sexual appetites and performances with those of other people; we're all different – and many people exaggerate. Important: what is 'normal' for someone else may be too much or too little for you. It doesn't matter. Bottom line: whatever you're comfortable with is fine; as long as you're happy and feel good about it.

2. **Ask your GP about any drugs that you're taking; some can interfere with your sex life.** Note: many doctors feel uncomfortable discussing sexual matters with their patients and won't volunteer information about a drug's side effects on your sex drive. Remedy: they may be able to lower the dosage that you're taking, or could substitute the drug for another medicine.

3. **Ask your GP to refer you to a gynaecologist if you're suffering from vaginal dryness associated with the menopause.** Why: they may be able to prescribe a hormonal treatment that will help. Alternative: speak to your pharmacist; there are various over-the-counter preparations available from your pharmacy. Consider hormone replacement therapy (HRT) if hot flushes and thinning vaginal tissues are affecting your libido. Idea: you may want to try taking oestrogen, which is usually combined with progestogen, another female hormone. Sensible: start with the lowest possible dosage – it will often be all that's needed. And ask about adding androgens to the oestrogen mix. Tip: some doctors are discovering that adding the male hormone to the standard oestrogen replacement regimen can boost sexual desire, although it is not common practice yet.

4. **Have your DHEA levels checked by a doctor operating on a private rather than an NHS basis.** Definition: dehydroepiandrosterone (DHEA) is a hormone in both men and women that declines with age – and can affect your sex drive. But: this hormone can be prescribed privately or is available via the internet; taken, it can restore your DHEA and libido. Contact: Optimal Health Centre, 114 Harley Street, London, W1N 1AG. Similar: testosterone levels can drop as you get

older, with comparable effects on your sex drive. Helpful: injections of testosterone can be very effective – often, only one shot is needed and sexual powers are restored straightaway. Or: Viagra improves staying power in 70% of men; again, this may be available on a private basis or purchased over the internet – although it should only be taken as the final option as it is for impotence rather than recreational use.

5. **Cut the fat from your diet.** Details: a University of Utah study found that eating fat-laden foods may decrease the production of testosterone. Also: eating fatty foods puts more fat onto your body – and US researchers have discovered that the more body fat a man has, the less testosterone is likely to be generated. Fat also clogs up arteries including the ones pumping blood into your penis, and this can lead to impotence. Tip: try a pseudo-vegetarian diet. Why: some people find that a three month 'pseudo-vegetarian' diet works wonders on their sex lives. Contents: this diet allows you to eat fresh fish and free-range chicken. Minimum: if you don't want to give up meat altogether, eat organic meat. Plus: add vitamin E to your diet. This vitamin is extremely important for sexual function – no one really knows why. Best: the easiest way to accomplish this is to take vitamin E supplements.

6. **Go easy on alcohol**. Although alcohol may put you in the mood for love, your body is less likely to respond if you have too much of it in your system. Alcohol impairs sexual performance. And: stop smoking. Worldwide studies have shown that men who smoke heavily are far more likely to be impotent than those who have never smoked or who have given up. Bottom line: smoking is known to contribute to the hardening of the arteries and will lead eventually to impotence. Vital: take some exercise. Being aerobically fit enhances your sexual performance. Cause: strenuous exercise may increase testosterone levels in men and improve the blood flow to all parts of the body, including your genitals. Bonus: becoming physically fit improves your self-esteem and makes you feel more attractive to your partner. Learn to meditate or do relaxation exercises as well. Anything that reduces stress helps your sex life.

7. **Remember romance.** Don't: underestimate the effectiveness of candles, mood music, and sexy underwear. Discover what works for you and your partner; and go for it! And: consider an aphrodisiac. Fact: there isn't a scientifically proven magic pill available yet, but various medicinal herbs are known to help you. Chinese, Japanese, and Indian Ayervedic specialists recommend certain herbs – winter cherry, liquorice, molucca bean, Indian kudjer and Indian gooseberry. Also: watch a romantic and/or erotic film.

8. **Schedule a sex session.** Note: there is no sense in trying to make love after a long and stressful day. Wise: try to have sex in the morning or afternoon; and when you're not mentally and/or physically exhausted. Or: get away for a weekend free from distractions. The absence of interruptions is often the best aphrodisiac of all. Plan for privacy. Distractions are the equivalent of a cold shower. Idea: some couples set their alarm for the early hours of the morning. Be creative – try something new, such as making love in another room, massage, or taking a shower or bath together.

(Sources: PFC *health and personal development experts, plus research into world-wide studies on sexual health and behaviour.)*

THE FREE SERVICE THAT ALMOST GUARANTEES TO FIND A LONG-LOST FRIEND OR RELATIVE

Contact your long-lost friends and relatives – get in touch with the DSS. How: write down everything you can remember about the particular friend or relative. Best: full name, maiden name, date of birth, last-known address, national insurance number, spouse's details. Then: send a letter with this information to DSS, Longbenton, Newcastle-upon-Tyne NE98 1YX – and ask them to pass it on to that person. Bottom line: they're not obliged to – but sometimes do.

(Source: Elaine Wellman, a PFC *subscriber from Herfordshire.)*

HOW TO PASS EXAMS – THE SECRETS OF SUCCESSFUL REVISION

If you're about to start revising for examinations, you'll want to remember everything you need to get 'A' grades. Here's what to do:

1. **Obtain the course syllabus from your tutor, and study it.** Fact: the majority of students sitting examinations never read the whole syllabus. Result: they cannot revise properly. Tip: internal examinations set and marked by the college do not always have a formal syllabus. Wise: use topic and sub-topic headings from lecture notes and handouts to build up the full picture.

2. **Take a sheet of paper for each subject and list the principal topics and sub-topics in columns down the page.** Next: use your own symbol system to indicate the amount of 'interest', 'knowledge/understanding', 'ease/difficulty of learning' and 'importance' of each. Example: 'iii' very interested, 'ii' quite interested, 'i' not interested.

3. **Establish your priorities.** Beginning: topics with positive symbols for both 'interest' and 'knowledge/understanding' are a good starting point, as learning these will be easiest; thus boosting your confidence. Have a trial period of one week to make sure your schedule feels right for you. Then: mix in more topics with negative symbols as your confidence grows. Important: vary subjects and topics to keep your interest going – it's your enthusiasm that will carry you through.

4. **Spot likely examination questions.** Internal: pay attention to topics that have been emphasised by the tutor and set during the course. Your tutor may be responsible for writing the examination paper. External: in many papers, a core of topics will appear with some variation from year to year. Typical: one topic will be included three or four times in a five-year period.

5. **Tackle various questions on the same topic – you'll improve your flexibility and readiness.** How: list past exam questions, grouping

them by type and emphasis. Add: any related questions raised during the course; plus others you can think of. Tip: check to see which questions occur most frequently on past papers. Try to identify that 'banker' question.

6. **Streamline your course notes.** Original: class and book notes, handouts, assignments, essays. Cut: to 'key word revision cards' – brief outline notes written onto postcards. Aim: to use the minimum number of words necessary to highlight the key points of a subject. And: 'spider diagrams' – a visually creative way of remembering important points. How: draw a circle (the spider's body) in the middle of a page with the topic name written inside it. Add lines (the spider's legs) highlighting one key point per line. Useful: these can be reproduced quickly at the start of an examination.

7. **Set clear and specific revision targets and timescales.** Bad: 'I must do it.' Good: 'I must do it by the last day of this month.' Revise tasks that are sufficiently demanding. Verify your success in learning a topic by testing yourself. Example: write an essay under examination conditions – then mark it. Useful: many examining boards sell past papers and marking schemes. Generate a feeling of accomplishment after learning a topic. It raises your interest and enthusiasm. Personal example: record your revision tasks in pencil on a large sheet of white card and rub them out as and when completed.

(Source: David Acres is a learning support tutor specialising in study skills, training and development. He is the author of How to Pass Exams Without Anxiety *published by How To Books Limited. For further details about the book, call the publishers on 01865 793806. This feature first appeared in* PFC *March 1998, No. 18.)*

THE SUPERMARKET CHECKOUT SCANDAL THEY DON'T WANT YOU TO KNOW ABOUT

***PFC* tip:** you can save as much as £100 every year on your supermarket shopping simply by watching your purchases being scanned and recorded on the checkout display. How: items that are held over the bar code scanner for too long can register twice – customers rarely have time to notice this, and don't always check their receipt line-by-line afterwards. And: 'two-for-one' offers don't always register the second item as a freebie. Important: don't go through checkouts that are staffed by students – they're more likely to make errors. Also: avoid weekend visits when supermarket checkouts are at their busiest and mistakes are made more frequently. Bottom line: don't start packing until you've seen everything has been scanned correctly – and remember to double-check by referring to your till receipt before leaving the store.

(Sources: Mary Johnson, a PFC *subscriber from East Anglia, plus additional* PFC *research.)*

BE £1,000s RICHER – THE SECRETS YOUR MORTGAGE LENDER WON'T TELL YOU

For most people, buying their own home will cost them about three times its value. Typical: they will pay around £200,000 for a £70,000 house. Why: the interest payments alone will add up to about twice the price of the house. Instead: you can pay off your mortgage years ahead of time and save thousands of pounds in interest payments. Redeeming your mortgage early and paying less is easy. All you have to know is how the system works; and how to beat it.

The system: whatever type of mortgage you choose, you'll have to pay interest, and accumulate enough capital to repay the original amount. This interest is the big addition to the cost of your home – and is where you can save the most money by making payments that reduce the capital on which future interest payments are calculated.

Beating the system: simply pay more than you have to each month. This reduces the effects of compound interest on your original loan. Write to your lender, indicating that you wish to increase your payments. Ask for this to be agreed in writing and request a breakdown of how these overpayments will affect your mortgage and what your new redemption date is. Alternative: ask your lender to work out how much extra you will have to pay each month to reduce your mortgage term by a specified number of years. And: paying more than you have to acts as an insurance policy – it allows you to miss one or two payments later when your budget may be stretched without; and all incurring penalties.

Example: to illustrate the effects of paying extra each month, consider this scenario based on a repayment mortgage at 10% interest over a 25 year term. Amount borrowed: £60,000. Contractual payment: £501 per month. If you increased monthly payments to £540, your revised mortgage period would be 20 years, and you'd save £20,700. Pay £612 a month, and the mortgage period would be 15 years, and the savings would be £40,140. If you paid £771 a month, the mortgage period would be 10 years; and you'd save £57,780 – on that £60,000 mortgage.

Caution: be aware of how mortgage lenders make money from borrowers. Some lenders leave overpayments in limbo until their year-end, when the extra amount is set against your mortgage. In effect, you're giving your lender an interest-free loan. Remedy: put the extra payments into a high-earning, savings account where it will earn interest – then transfer it across to your mortgage account just before the lender's year end. And: many mortgage and financial advisers suggest it is better to adopt this method and overpay your mortgage once a year; including interest on your savings. Also: overpayments to building societies are normally deducted from the outstanding capital once a year; usually on 31 December. Make sure your annual repayment is made just before the appropriate date, not immediately afterwards which would mean you'd have to wait a whole year before obtaining the benefits. Important: some lenders charge a penalty for early or extra repayments – check this and ask your lender to provide written details to compare the benefits with the charges levied. And: many lenders set minimum thresholds for overpayment; between £250 and £1,000.

Tip: when interest rates drop, don't be tempted to reduce your monthly payments – continue making payments at the higher level. Try to repay as much as you can when interest rates are low to achieve even higher savings. Also: endowment mortgage holders should review their policy and investment performance at regular intervals to be sure that it keeps pace with the amount outstanding on the mortgage. And: re-arrange your policy to ensure it matures at the same time as the amended repayment date for your mortgage.

(Sources: PFC *financial and investment specialists.)*

HOW TO MAKE YOURSELF LOOK GREAT IN PASSPORT PHOTOGRAPHS

***PFC* tip:** get a good passport photo from a booth by lowering the seat so that the camera is just above the level of your nose – this reduces eye shadows and strengthens your jawline. Next: raise your head – this makes your nose look smaller. Finally: smile – this transforms your face, and makes you look terrific.

(Sources: PFC *photography experts.)*

SIMPLE EXERCISES FOR PERFECT EYESIGHT – AT ANY AGE

Many eye-related problems are caused by eyestrain. How: when the eye strains to see something, the muscles surrounding it become tense and rigid. These then put pressure on the eyeball and distort its shape. Good news: we can train ourselves to relax these muscles completely and make related eyesight problems disappear. Here is a simple and easy-to-follow series of regular exercises designed to help the eye muscles relax – they should be performed without glasses or contact lenses.

1. **Eye lines:** keeping your head relaxed and still, allow your eyes to move up and down six times. Avoid any strain or effort. Repeat this three times, with a few seconds of rest in between. Then repeat – this time moving the eyes from left to right and back again. This exercise

helps relax the stiff, strained muscles around the eyes.

2. **Palming:** sit in a comfortable chair and gently rest the palms of both hands over your closed eyes. Remain like this for about ten minutes. Remove your hands and open your eyes. Now try to pick out objects of one particular colour, choosing a different colour for every day of the week.

3. **Butterfly blinking:** blink quickly for a few seconds, then gently squeeze your eyelids shut for a moment. Repeat the exercise for up to a minute. This exercise shifts the point of focus of the eye, and also helps to lubricate the outer surface by stimulating the tear ducts.

4. **Tracing shapes:** imagine there is a pencil extending from the tip of your nose. Use this to trace the outline of various objects about you, some near and others further away. This exercise helps to strengthen the ability of the eye to focus on objects at different distances. Vary the exercise by tracing figures of eight in the air.

5. **Swinging:** this should be practised standing up, but can be done sitting down. Relax your neck, and gently swing your head from side to side, backwards and forwards. Swinging is designed to relax the neck and shoulder muscles and improve the blood supply to the eyes. Note: it is important that all of these exercises are performed in a relaxed and rhythmical way, without any strain or jerkiness. Helpful: put on relaxing music while you are doing them. To gain most benefit from the exercises they need to be performed regularly; at least once a day.

Bonus: combine these five natural exercises with other ways of improving your eyesight. Diet: to ensure your eyes are nourished properly, eat plenty of fresh fruit, vegetables and high-fibre foods (wholemeal bread, nuts, fruit), and cut down on fatty foods, sugar and salt. If you suffer from poor vision at night, try increasing your vitamin A intake – from fish, carrots, tomatoes and spinach. Exercise: this stimulates your blood flow, bringing more oxygen and fuel to the eyes and taking away waste products. And: it is a proven way of reducing stress and helping you to relax. Lighting: eyes thrive on natural daylight. When reading or doing close-up work, position yourself near to a window. Avoid wearing dark glasses indoors or in normal daylight, unless they have been prescribed for a medical condition. And: if you have to work in artificial light, try to avoid fluorescent strip lighting, especially when it flickers. Ordinary light bulbs are better. Full spectrum strip lights and artificial daylight bulbs are best.

Bottom line: laser eye surgery is becoming increasingly popular. The most common procedure is called Photorefractive Keratectomy (PRK) and involves reshaping the outer surface of the eye with surgical lasers. Note: lasers are computer-calibrated and directed with pinpoint accuracy; and their beams do not penetrate beyond the surface of the eye. So: surgery is safe, and painless! Suitable: people with mild to moderate short-sightedness. Unsuitable: people with long-sight and anyone under 21 years – their eyesight is still changing. Note: there is no upper age limit for the treatment, although it may be inappropriate for people with certain medical conditions. Always: check with your GP before applying for laser eye surgery.

How: initially, you will be asked to attend a consultation for a thorough eye examination and a discussion about the operation with the surgeon. Later: on the day of the operation, the eye will be anaesthetised with drops; no injection is required. Then: the operation itself takes only a few minutes and is pain-free. After: there may be some discomfort as the outer surface of the eye heals. But: side effects normally last for no more than a few days. Note: eyesight can take a few weeks to stabilise fully – and driving a car or operating machinery is strictly forbidden during this time. Also: as PRK involves removing part of the outer surface of the eye, your eyes may always be a little more sensitive than they were before. Example: it may no longer be possible to wear contact lenses (if you still need them) after the surgery. The more short-sighted you are, the greater the chance of such side effects arising. Crucial: ask specifically about these potential dangers before the operation is carried out.

Important: laser eye surgery is performed on one eye at a time; the other eye will be treated three to six months later. Many people no longer need glasses after the operation. Others experience an improvement, but still need glasses some or all of the time. The exact results cannot be predicted; much depends on how your eyes respond to the treatment. PRK will not reverse the normal effects of ageing, in particular the need for reading glasses in older people. Note: this type of surgery is not normally available on the NHS, so you will have to pay a fee. Some clinics charge around £1,500 per eye, but others offer the operation for as little as £500. Clinics advertise in local and national newspapers; your GP and optician should be able to help you make your choice. Always: contact several different clinics, and speak to people who have been treated there before reaching a decision.

(Sources: Peter Mansfield, The Bates Method, *Harry Benjamin,* Better Sight Without Glasses, *Dr Marilyn B. Rosanes-Berrett,* Do You Really Need Eyeglasses?, *The Eyecare Information Service, 0171-357 7730, The Association of Optometrists, 0171-261 9661.)*

WARNING! THOSE YOU TRUST COULD SWINDLE YOU OUT OF YOUR INHERITANCE

***PFC* tip:** ask to see a copy of any will in which you're named as a beneficiary. Why: full receipt of your inheritance depends upon the honesty of the executors; and your vigilance. Fact: there are no automatic safeguards in place to ensure you receive any inheritance due to you. Sensible: executors should provide copies of the will for all interested parties, along with accounts of all financial transactions conducted to finalise the deceased person's affairs. Bottom line: if you think you might be a beneficiary of someone's will and want to check it without referring to the executors, obtain a copy from York Probate Sub-Registry, Duncombe Place, York YO1 2EA. Give the deceased person's name, date of death and last known address; and include a cheque for

£2.00 made payable to 'HMPG'.

(Sources: PFC *financial and legal specialists.)*

SEVEN TOP TIPS FOR INVESTMENT SUCCESS

You can make big profits from stocks and shares without knowing anything about business – simply apply these techniques that are based on human nature, common sense and timing:

1. **Spread your money between different sectors and companies.** How: choose different sectors and then scatter funds over a large number of companies. Outcome: if you rely on just four enterprises and one collapses, it's serious. Invest in ten or more, and you can live with one or two losses.

2. **Look for slow but steady risers that rarely falter.** Fact: these tend to be shares in fairly unknown firms that are not in the public eye and do not attract press attention. Tip: study the financial pages for equities that rise a penny or two on a daily basis without comment from financial analysts. Possible causes: a big investor may be buying stock gradually to avoid attracting attention, a bid may be in the offing, or the annual report day may be approaching and big profits are to be announced. Wise: get in now at the start of the ascent.

3. **Never buy on a rumour.** Why: the City hums with rumours all of the time – and many have no basis in fact. Exception: some shares at the centre of a takeover rumour often adopt an 'up, down, up further and down for good' pattern which can be milked profitably. How: buy when the share has risen on two consecutive days. Ride the share until the first fall and sell half. Wait for the momentum to gather again – and sell the rest when the share price just beats its earlier high.

4. **Buy into a company when its competitors are doing badly.** High-flying investors relish the crash of a large firm – they know that its customers will have to buy elsewhere. So they pump money into its

rivals, and make a profit. Warning: if a firm crashes because it makes a particular product which the public no longer wants, then the competitive firms are also likely to fail. Essential: inspect the products and services on offer before investing. Key question: is the core product or service provided a fad or something with an exhilarating future?

5. **Get into firms with a low share price compared to rivals in the same sector.** All investors look for good value – top-notch shares at low prices. Hint: the professionals calculate what's known as a company's price-to-earnings (p/e) ratio, which is the ordinary profits after tax divided by the number of shares in issue. The lower the company's p/e, the better value its shares are in relation to others in that sector. You can discover a company's p/e by looking at the share listings pages of the Financial Times. If you find one with a p/e lower than other enterprises in the same field, it should be worth a punt.

6. **Don't be greedy.** If a share has done well but has run out of steam, don't hold on to try and make a few more pence. Sell up now before wholesale profit-taking sets in. Best: decide in advance how high a particular share price is likely to go, and sell when it reaches that level. And: set a low figure too, based on how much you're prepared to see a share slump before selling it. For example, if it drops to 10% less than your buying price, take the money and run.

7. **Never act on just one tip.** Fact: sometimes, investment specialists seem to contradict each other – this is inevitable if you gather together a galaxy of ideas from an army of experts, all with different personalities and methods. Wisest: look at a range of tips from a wide variety of specialists; identify common areas of agreement – and then act.

(Source: Malcolm Stacey, Radio 4 reporter and author, Armchair Tycoon, *published by Robson Books Limited. Call Robson on 0171-323 1223 for more information about the book. The full version of this feature first appeared in* PFC *February 1998, No. 17.)*

DON'T LOSE YOUR TEETH TO THE DISEASE THAT AFFECTS 50% OF THE POPULATION

Follow these two simple instructions to dramatically cut your chances of suffering from gum disease. 1: Treat your teeth to a deep clean at regular intervals to reach and destroy the inaccessible bacteria missed by normal, everyday brushing. How: wet your toothbrush in hydrogen peroxide. Dip its bristles into a baking soda and salt mixture. Brush this over your teeth and gums, making sure that you include the spaces between your teeth. Leave the mixture to soak in for two minutes. 2: Rinse thoroughly. Top up your calcium intake whenever you can; a deficiency of this vital mineral can weaken your teeth and increase the chances of gum infection. Sources: low-fat milk, green leafy vegetables, legumes, salmon, low-fat yoghurt.

(Sources: PFC *panel of health experts.)*

STAND ON YOUR HEAD TO GET PREGNANT

If you're trying to conceive, don't waste your time and money on expensive and unnecessary body temperature charts, ovulation prediction kits, cervical fluid monitoring and the like. Instead, follow our top tips for getting pregnant:

1. **Make love at the right time.** To become pregnant, you'll need to make love around the time of ovulation. When: ovulation usually takes place about 14 days before the menstrual cycle is due. Example: with a menstrual cycle of 28 days, ovulation occurs on day 14. Note: with cycles of differing lengths, ovulation will still normally take place 14 days before the next menstrual cycle begins. Fact: after intercourse, sperm can survive for up to five or six days. But: after ovulation, the egg rarely lives longer than one day. Conclusion: the best time to make love if you want to conceive is the five or six days up to ovulation and the day of ovulation itself.

2. **Have a healthy diet.** Your fertility will be improved by good health – and this requires a well-balanced diet. Sensible: eat plenty of

fresh food, especially fruit and vegetables. Important: vitamins A, B, C and E and the trace metal zinc are the most beneficial for both male and female fertility. Women: vitamin A helps to produce more fertile cervical fluid at the time of ovulation. Men: there is some evidence that the amino acids L-arginine and L-carnitine improve sperm production and their condition. These are the building blocks of protein, and are used extensively in sperm manufacture. Essential: if necessary, change your diet – or at least take multivitamin preparations that include zinc.

3. **Keep fit.** Hand in hand with a good diet is the need to keep fit. Women: three thirty-minute sessions of moderate exercise each week leads to optimum fertility. Swimming is ideal. Warning: don't overdo it. Too much exercise can delay ovulation or even cause the loss of ovulation in a cycle. Men: again, moderate and regular exercise is best to maintain fitness. And: watch your weight – this is particularly important for women. Too much body fat can lead to irregular monthly ovulatory cycles due to the excess oestrogens associated with being overweight. Acceptable body fat levels as a percentage of body mass are 22-27% for women, 20-23% for men. But: avoid crash dieting though – this can disrupt the hormonal balances required for optimum fertility.

4. **Cut down on alcohol, caffeine and tobacco.** In men, these all reduce sperm count and damage the remaining sperm, and it is believed that they affect female fertility too. Alcohol: have no more than four drinks a week, and no more than two on any given day. Caffeine: you can drink up to two cups per day. Tobacco: give up altogether. There is evidence that women who smoke have less mature, viable eggs. Smoking inhibits normal egg maturation.

5. **Wear boxer shorts and baggy trousers.** The best way for a man to improve his fertility is to keep his testicles as cool as possible. Reason: testicles need to be kept cooler than body temperature for successful sperm manufacture and storage. Fact: briefs and tight trousers keep the testicles pressed closer to the body, thus raising their temperature. Better: boxer shorts allow testicles to hang free and maintain coolness. Similar:

avoid hot baths and showers too – sperm production falls markedly in temperatures above 92–93 degrees. Wise: have short, warm showers rather than long, steamy baths; and avoid direct spraying of the testicles.

6. **Make love more often.** If you have sex more frequently with your partner, the chances of conceiving are that much greater. But: many couples seem to overlook this! Recommendation: make love every day in the lead up to the day of ovulation to maximise the opportunities for conception.

7. **Do it in the morning.** The best time to make love if you're trying to conceive is in the mornings. Why: male hormone levels are highest at that time, as are sperm counts. Outcome: you'll increase the chances of conception.

8. **Make love in the missionary position.** This is the best position for getting sperm close to the cervix, and for keeping it there rather than exiting from the vagina. Because: the position allows gravity to work in your favour – the sperm are pushed downwards towards the female reproductive tract, thus boosting the possibility of meeting the egg and fertilising it.

9. **The woman should orgasm after the man.** Research has shown that conception is more likely if the woman has an orgasm during or soon after her partner's climax. Reason: on orgasm, the cervix dips into the semen pool and helps to propel it into the uterus, therefore retaining more sperm. This can best be described as a 'sucking effect'. Also: female secretions increase with orgasm – and these help to carry semen.

10. **Lie down after making love.** After sex, women should lie down with their legs and hips up for 20 to 30 minutes. Why: lying horizontally reduces the leakage of sperm, aids its movement towards the uterus (with the help of gravity), and maximises the flow of semen around the cervix. Useful: put a pillow under your hips or place your feet on an elevated surface such as the bed's headboard. This speeds sperm to the egg by letting them swim downwards with gravity. Standing on your

head has a similar effect!

Bottom line: many lifestyle changes require time to affect fertility; especially in men. Examples: diet and fitness. And: it takes 70 to 80 days for new sperm to develop and mature. So: any steps you initiate today will take some time to make a difference. Guideline: 90% of women who have regular unprotected sex become pregnant within one year. But: don't set yourself deadlines and targets – just be together, and have fun. Enjoy making love – and you'll get pregnant.

(Source: Dr Jeremy Sims, your PFC *medical expert. The full version of this feature first appeared in* PFC *March 1998, No. 18)*

THE LITTLE TRICK THAT WILL SPEED UP YOUR TAKEAWAY ORDER

***PFC* tip:** save time when ordering a takeaway – just give a simple name such as 'Smith' or 'Jones'. It saves you having to pronounce and spell your own name.

(Source: PFC *panel of specialists.)*

DANDRUFF – A TROPICAL HAIR TREATMENT THAT REALLY WORKS

Clinical tests have revealed that a traditional peanut oil and lemon juice remedy is a more effective dandruff treatment than those specially-formulated shampoos. First: rub a small quantity of warm peanut oil into your scalp – wait for two minutes to enable the skin and hair to absorb it. Next: apply the juice from a freshly squeezed lemon. Then: wait again, for about five minutes. And: shampoo your hair thoroughly. Important: repeat the treatment on a weekly basis. Reason: the mixture brings proteins to the surface of the scalp, hardening and protecting it. *(Source: the Dermatology Department, New York State University, USA, plus additional* PFC *research.)*

THE HIDDEN REASON WHY YOU SHOULDN'T ASK FOR TOO MANY MAIL ORDER CATALOGUES

***PFC* tip:** don't send for mail order catalogues too often. Why: some catalogue companies conduct credit searches before an order has been placed even though credit terms may never be requested. So: your credit status may be damaged – lenders are reluctant to provide finance to people who appear to have made repeated credit applications; it makes them seem desperate for money. Similar: be wary of paying for car and home insurance policies by instalments – again, credit searches may be recorded on your file. Wise: check your credit reference agency files every six months, and add notices of correction, where appropriate.

(Sources: PFC *research plus information from the UK's leading credit reference agencies, Equifax Europe, 0990 783783 and Experion, 0115 9768747.)*

A COMPREHENSIVE GUIDE TO FINDING A JOB ABROAD

Working overseas has never been easier. Why: 14 countries in Europe offer free access to job hunters from the United Kingdom. And: there are many opportunities in other countries around the world. Here's a step-by-step guide:

1. **Choose the right country for you.** Think carefully about your choice of country; and find out as much as you can about as many as possible before making your decision. Caution: there's a huge difference between holidaying in a country in the summer and working there in the winter. Good: those countries and regions which are less popular with expatriates offer excellent career potential because they are short of experienced, qualified people. Examples: Eastern Europe, Far East.

2. **Consider the lifestyle.** Only one-third of your day is spent at work – so take account of the accompanying lifestyle. Some countries

offer excellent job prospects but a poor quality of life. Examples: Middle East countries. Others provide modest employment opportunities but an excellent, unhurried lifestyle with fine weather. Examples: Spain, Portugal. Remember your family too – your partner's job prospects and your children's education. Essential: try to make at least one non-holiday trip to a country before accepting any job offer.

3. **Examine permit requirements.** Your chances of getting a work permit and a visa depend on where you are going, who you are and where you're coming from. Fact: sometimes these are granted readily; on other occasions they are almost impossible to obtain. Note: some countries such as America grant them only if the employer can prove local people are not available to do the job. But: European Union citizens don't need a work permit or a visa to work in EU countries.

4. **Select the right type of job.** It's easy to regard working overseas as a completely fresh start, but this is not a good idea. Reason: most of the opportunities available are for people with significant, relevant experience to offer. This is especially true for well paid jobs. Tip: find a better post more easily by applying for the same job you're doing now.

5. **Contemplate a job transfer.** Working abroad needn't mean resigning your current position and starting again. Wise: look at transferring overseas within your organisation; to other branches or subsidiaries. Alternative: consider getting a job with your company's foreign suppliers or customers. Always: use your network of contacts to find work. The vast majority of all vacancies are filled in this way in both the United Kingdom and overseas.

6. **Exploit your qualifications.** Do: find out if they are accepted in the appropriate country and check the procedure to have them recognised there. How: for professional qualifications, consult the issuing body. Also: the Europe-wide network of National Academic Recognition Information Centres can provide advice on the acceptability of academic qualifications in the European Union. Contact: UK NARIC, 01242 260010.

7. **Refine your language skills.** These are the most important attributes required to find a job abroad. Even in those countries where English is spoken in the business world, you'll get a job far more easily if you can speak the local language. And: you'll need this skill for day-to-day living as well. Tip: invest in a language course before emigrating – it's money well spent.

8. **Use appropriate newspapers and periodicals.** Spend time in a library to discover which UK and foreign publications contain vacancies relating to the work you want to do. *PFC* recommendation: *The European* newspaper is always a good starting point. If you have access to the internet, visit their website at **www.the-european.com**

9. **Use employment agencies.** Many employment and recruitment agencies handle overseas vacancies. See the *FRES Yearbook*, published by the Federation of Recruitment and Employment Services. This should be available in larger libraries. Also: the European Employment Services (EURES) network exists so that vacancies which have been notified to the state employment service in one EU country can be accessed through the state employment services in all of the others. Contact your local Job Centre.

10. **Apply direct to relevant organisations.** Why: this is done by 60% of successful expatriate job seekers. How: write, fax or e-mail prospective employers abroad asking about posts, and outlining your suitability. Do: send a CV with a covering letter to the (correctly named) individual responsible for recruiting in that firm. Best: write in the local language – but only if your command of it is good enough to impress. Useful: build a network of contacts from your own personal knowledge, international *Yellow Pages* and trade directories published by Chambers of Commerce. Try the internet too.

(Sources: Mark Hempshell, one of your PFC *panellists. This feature first appeared in* PFC *November 1997, No. 14.)*

SEVEN WINNING FRUIT MACHINE SECRETS THAT WILL HELP YOU CRACK THE JACKPOT

1. **Play at the right time.** Fact: today's fruit machines are controlled by sophisticated programs which must ensure that the overall payback to punters is maintained at the legal minimum of 70% of takings. Tip: watch a machine before playing it – and move in when previous players have been losing. It's time for a win.

2. **Look for newly installed machines.** Why: these are often set to give a higher than normal payback for the first week or so; it attracts punters. Bonus: a newly installed machine must also pay out quickly to reach that 70% minimum return.

3. **Listen carefully when you insert a coin.** Tip: if it falls a long way, the coin tubes from which winnings are paid are probably full, and additional coins are being diverted to a lower part of the fruit machine. Outcome: if the machine is full, it suggests a win is on the way – so keep playing.

4. **If you win any type of skill bonus and need some time to work out what to do, press the cancel button.** Reason: this usually slows things down, and gives you time to make decisions.

5. **If you get two holds in succession, have another go.** Note: most machines then offer a third hold – and the symbol that you need for a winning line always seems to fall into place third time around.

6. **When you win a nudge but don't have a winning line, nudge two matching fruits onto the winline.** Wise: if the next play produces a hold, spin all three reels – and the win should come in.

7. **If you have a win above the winline and the machine gives you a hold, always hold all three reels together** – they should then all nudge down as one; and give you that winning line, and even the jackpot.

(Source: PFC *gambling expert Nick Daws. The original version of this feature first appeared in* PFC *December 1997, No. 15.)*

WAKE UP WITHOUT A HANGOVER

***PFC* tip:** the best way to handle a hangover is to prevent it happening in the first place. Fact: alcohol is a diuretic – it flushes away the water in your body and causes you to dehydrate. But: you lose the body's natural supply of water-soluble vitamins and minerals too. And: it is this mixture of dehydration and vitamin and mineral deficiency that makes you feel so awful. Alternative: avoid drinking on an empty stomach, have an occasional glass of water when you're drinking alcohol, and drink lots of water before going to sleep. Plus: take a dose of vitamin C and a vitamin B complex or brewer's yeast tablets or multivitamin supplements – and stop a hangover in its tracks. Note: the best drinks to order to avoid a hangover are gin and vodka.

(Source: PFC *health and medical experts.)*

UNDERSTAND THE MYTHS OF SELF-EMPLOYMENT – THEN GO ON TO START YOUR OWN SUCCESSFUL BUSINESS

If you're thinking of setting up your own venture, you'll want to know what it's really like. Here, we shatter three of the greatest myths, and tell you how to become a successful start-up:

Myth: small is beautiful. Reality: small can be extremely difficult. Fact: running your own business requires great effort and the casualty rate is high; a small firm is much more vulnerable to a recession than a larger organisation. Example: to a big firm, the loss of a major contract is upsetting but not disastrous – to a small concern, it can make the difference between being (just) solvent and going bankrupt. Remember: the vast majority of start-up businesses close within the first year, many with horrendous debts. You need to get the right mix of ingredients together before you begin. And: be sensible, have another source of income for the first year or two.

Success: the people who are best placed to succeed are those who have spent some years working for someone else in their chosen field – you need to know what you are really up against. The highest failure rate is among those people who go into areas they know nothing about. Examples: they've shopped in a store or been in a nightclub many times and think it looks easy. Also: pick the right associates – this is often overlooked. People go into business with family and friends, usually not the right people at all! A business must have a good balance of talents: an ideas person, a manager, a sales director, a first-rate accountant.

Myth: banks know best. Truth: a local branch manager knows something about their community, and will have their own personal views on the scope of a potential business, based mainly on previous cases they have dealt with. But: they rarely have any of the specialist knowledge required for success in a particular field. And: if significant amounts of capital are involved, they will need to consult with a regional or head office – and these people have even less expertise on how businesses are run. Reason: they are money-lenders, not business experts. Ideal: you will know much more than the banker – prove it, and you will usually get your money.

Success: to raise business finance, understand the nature of the lender, and lending. Fact: commercial loan decisions are based heavily on the impression made by the entrepreneur – the financially literate and articulate borrower has a huge competitive advantage. Requirement: a well-prepared business plan – the banker may not understand this, but it shows you have done your homework. Expect: questions about the key assumptions behind your figures. Also: you need to score highly on the five 'Cs' – character of borrower, capacity to repay, conditions (product, industry, economy), capital provided (debt/equity ratio) and collateral.

Myth: gurus have all the answers. Reality: most gurus contradict each other with maddening regularity. Why: most of them have never actually owned their own business, let alone managed one. Example: Peter Drucker, the doyen of gurus, admits he has never run a business or worked as a manager. Important: be selective about who you turn to for help and advice – watch for: gurus with a passion for fancy jargon, convoluted theories and incomprehensible diagrams. Because: it often turns out to be pretentious waffle. Latest: 'downsizing' and 're-engineering' – ugly words for sacking people.

Success: take advice from those people who have 'been there, done that' before you – they are most likely to offer the best and most relevant guidance. Tip: the best theorists stimulate thought and provide genuine insights – people like Sir John Harvey-Jones, who bases his views on what he learned as head of ICI.

(Source: William Davis, a self-made millionaire and author of more than 40 books, including Great Myths of Business *published by Kogan Page. Call the publishers on 0171-278 0433 for details of the book. The full version of this feature first appeared in* PFC *April 1998, No. 19.)*

HOW TO PREVENT THE LITTLE-KNOWN DISEASE THAT AFFECTS 33% OF THE POPULATION

Candida albicans is the little-known but major disease of the 20th century. Symptoms: drowsiness, frequent infections, skin problems, feelings of anxiety and irritability. And: cravings for chocolate, sugary cereal, bread and/or alcohol, digestive problems, weak muscles, mood swings or depression, pains in the chest, dizziness and/or urinary infections. Warning: you'll be particularly susceptible if you've taken lots of antibiotics in the past – over-prescription is the major cause of the disease. Preventative measure: always make sure that any treatment is absolutely necessary before you agree to take any course of antibiotics – you may be able to transform your health simply by reducing your intake of antibiotics.

(Source: Agora Lifestyles Limited – call 0500 523 499 for your free copy of the latest issue of any of their newsletters.)

MASTER ANOTHER LANGUAGE AND EARN WHILE YOU LEARN

Most of us can speak only one language. But with two or more, we can communicate more widely with prospective business contacts, employers, even lovers. The more languages we learn, the better our chances of becoming more successful; whether in business or in life. Here are the best ways to learn a new language:

1. **Attend courses run by native speakers.** Best: look for a tutor who adopts a flexible approach to your requirements. Example: someone who is prepared to take you to a foreign language film at the cinema and discuss it afterwards in that language.

2. **Find a learning partner – someone that you can help with your language; and vice versa.** Ideal: look for a person with a similar outlook and interests to your own, and who can become a good friend. Wise: bring as much variety as possible to your sessions – read newspaper and magazine articles to each other and discuss them, go to the cinema and theatre together, introduce each other to speciality foods from your respective countries. Core skill: make sure you switch regularly between talking in your own language and the one you're learning so that you both get equal practice.

3. **Take in paying guests – foreign students and business people here for college courses, conferences and so on.** How: talk to your guests, translating difficult English words and expressions, and looking at books and magazines they've brought with them. And: ask and learn about their home town and country.

4. **Join a social club.** Idea: if you live in or near to a large town, find out if there are any social clubs or associations for people who speak the language you're learning. Reason: these are ideal places to meet people

informally and practise your conversational skills, as the majority of the members will be native speakers.

5. **Get a pen-friend.** Tip: when writing, look constantly for ways to improve your progress. Examples: alternate between writing in English and your penfriend's language, and suggest they do the same so that you get equal practice with writing and reading. Ask them to point out any recurring mistakes you make and to use words and phrases you're familiar with and have learned recently. Wise: ask them to introduce three or four new words and/or phrases into each letter so that your knowledge expands steadily.

6. **Think direct.** Important: whether writing or speaking, try to avoid translating automatically into English or your mother tongue, even if it does mean using very simple sentences to start with. Stopping to translate a complicated sentence you've constructed in English will interfere with your fluency and may discourage you.

7. **Spend time in the country.** Note: the most effective way to learn a language is to be in the country where it is spoken – even a couple of weeks living with the language all around you will be worth months of classes. How: try to communicate in the foreign language first, rather than assuming that everyone you meet will understand English. You'll feel more fulfilled – and will find that people are friendlier and more willing to help you. Note: use a phrase book sparingly. Reason: you need to develop your own fluency – repeating stock phrases will hinder your thoughts and development of the language. Important: don't worry if you don't understand everything that's going on around you. Because: research has shown that people who go for the 'gist' of what's being said make more rapid progress than those who try to understand every word.

(Sources: Robert J. di Pietro, author of Strategic Interaction, Learning Languages Through Scenarios, *and Amorey Gethin and Erik V. Gunnemark, authors of* The Art and Science of Learning Languages, *plus additional* PFC *research.)*

CLAIM PRIZES AND WINDFALLS YOU DIDN'T KNOW YOU'D WON

It is estimated that UK financial institutions have more than £1 billion waiting to be claimed by their customers. Why: premium bonds, savings plans and pensions are abandoned and/or forgotten about over the years. And: people change jobs, move away, and cannot be traced easily when any payouts fall due. What to do: check all of your old accounts and policies to see if any payments might be due – then write to the appropriate financial institutions, outline the key details and sit back to collect the cash.

(Sources: PFC *financial and investment specialists.)*

SURGERY-FREE FACELIFTS AND TEN VALUABLE TIPS TO COMBAT THE EFFECTS OF AGE

Growing older is inevitable, but there are many ways of holding back time and looking your best. You can appear ten years younger by following these *PFC* facial tips – and you'll feel fitter and healthier as well.

1. **Cleanse and moisturise your face daily with products which are suited to your skin type – men should do this too**. Why: your facial skin is only around 0.12mm thick and very delicate; it takes a constant battering from dirt and dust. It needs to be treated with respect at all times. Essential: don't forget to use a rich moisturiser on your neck – this area is most prone to crinkly skin which is an instant age giveaway.

2. **Drink lots of water each day.** Fact: about 70% of the body is made up of water; and it's vital to your skin's wellbeing. Minimum: drink at least one litre a day to help keep your face looking fresh and radiant.

3. **Stay pale.** Important: protect your facial skin every day with a UVA sunscreen – even in the dullest weather. Why: without this protection, ultraviolet radiation will cause wrinkles and make you look older.

4. **Treat your face to a good diet.** Eat: lots of fresh fruit, vegetables and whole grains. Why: these will provide your skin with all the vitamins and nutrients it needs to stay healthy. Avoid: caffeine, white sugar and convenience foods that damage your skin.

5. **Give up smoking immediately.** Reason: the evil weed uses up valuable vitamin C in the body. Consequence: your skin will have more wrinkles than non-smokers' and will look yellow.

6. **Go without make-up every now and again.** This gives your skin a chance to breathe. And: combine this with a brisk walk or cycle ride in the fresh air to bring a healthy glow to your cheeks.

7. **Invest in an electronic muscle stimulator for a surgery-free 'face lift'.** How: EMS machines work by stimulating muscles to contract and relax as they do during normal exercise. It's painless and convenient – the machine does all of the exercising for you.

9. **Enjoy yourself.** Smiling and laughing exercises your face with minimal effort, and keeps it taut and healthy. And: a smiling face always appears more attractive than a sullen or worried-looking one.

10. **De-stress your life – this will help your face to cut down on its worry lines.** It's a fact – happy people look younger! And: make sure you get enough beauty sleep. Why: this gives your skin cells a chance to regenerate.

***PFC* beauty secrets:** a lightly beaten egg white mixed with two teaspoons of cornflour makes a cheap and effective face mask. Alternative: mix together a mashed-up banana with a tablespoon of honey, and apply for 20 minutes. Egg white is also a good treatment for open pores. Adding sunflower oil to warm water can help to soften your skin. Treat tired eyes by holding a peeled and grated raw potato against them. Or: use cold, wet teabags for a similar rejuvenating effect. Petroleum jelly removes mascara well, and also thickens eyelashes.

(Sources: Tracey Hollom, a beauty expert who has been involved in the health and fitness industry for many years, plus additional PFC *research. The original version of this feature first appeared in* PFC *November 1997, No. 14.)*

HOW TO BE THE LIFE AND SOUL OF EVERY PARTY

From ice breakers to party entertainments – here are our favourite party games that will make you the toast of any party. Simple to arrange and play, these fun games will guarantee that your name will appear on the guest list of every party for years to come!

WHO AM I?

Equipment: Paper, pen, and pins

Preparation: A list of famous people – anyone from Tony Blair to Lily Savage or Bart Simpson!

As your guests arrive, pin one name from your list on each of their backs. Each guest must then find out who they are by asking the other players questions such as "Am I an actor? Am I a comedian?" The only answer that can be given is "yes" or "no", and each guest may only ask three questions before moving on.

It doesn't matter if some guests figure out who they are long before the others. The rules ensure that your guests must talk to many different people – making this game an excellent ice-breaker.

UP JENKINS

Equipment: Coin

Preparation: None

This is an ideal after-dinner game – and is liable to get very silly. The table must be divided into two teams who face each other. The members of Team One then pass a small coin to each other, under the table. The object is to confuse Team Two as to who has the coin. At any point the leader of Team Two may call "Up Jenkins". At this point, all the members of Team One must put their closed fists above the table. The leader then calls "Down Jenkins" and all the Team One members must slap their palms face down on the table. Team Two has to guess who holds the coin.

If they get it right, the teams swap roles.

THE IDENTITY PARADE

Equipment: A large sheet with a small hole in it, pencils, paper

Preparation: None

Assemble half your guests behind a large sheet. Each of the hidden players takes it in turn to poke his or her nose through a hole in the sheet. The players on the other side write down which nose they think belongs to which person. This is not as easy as it sounds, particularly if your guests have only just met! The winner is the person that has the greatest number of correct guesses.

INSANE DELUSIONS

Equipment: None

Preparation: Think of as many 'insane delusions' as you can for your guests. Example: thinking they've got a ferret down their trousers, or that they've seen aliens landing, or they're the Queen.

Send one of the guests out of the room and assign delusions to everyone else. Invite the outsider back into the room to play the role of a psychiatrist. They must discover everyone's delusions by asking questions and watching their behaviour. This is another great ice-breaker which will rid guests of their inhibitions.

DICTIONARY/CALL MY BLUFF

Equipment: Pens, strips of paper, dictionary
Preparation: None

Fans of television's *Call My Bluff* will love this game. Player One chooses an unusual word from the dictionary and writes its definition down on a strip of paper. They then reads the word (but not the definition) aloud to the other players.

Each of the players then writes down a definition for the word – it can be imaginative, mundane, silly or serious.

Player One then collects and shuffles the strips of paper with the true definition and reads each one aloud. The other players then have to guess which is the correct definition. A point is awarded for each correct guess. A point is also given to each player whose definition is mistaken for the correct one by another player. The dictionary is passed to the player on the left, until everyone has had a go. The player with the highest points at the end of the round wins.

THE DRAWING GAME

Equipment: Pens and paper

Preparation: None

Guests are split into two teams, and each team then writes a list of places, people, events, quotations – for example, Prince Charles, the Millennium Dome, "to be or not to be" etc. Each player in turn is then given a word to draw for their team. The team that guesses the greatest number of words correctly wins.

The only rules are that the artist can only answer "yes" or "no" to questions and cannot use numbers or letters in their drawing. A game guaranteed to relax even the most reserved guest!

THE LIMERICK GAME

Equipment: Pens and paper

Preparation: None

Each player writes the first line of a limerick and passes it to the person on their left. The next players in turn all add a line to the limericks they have been passed until they are complete. The limericks are then read aloud – with hilarious results. Alternatively, the first person may write the first line, and pass it to their left. The second player then writes down a word that must be included somewhere in the rest of the limerick, which the third person must complete.

SPOONS

Equipment: Pack of cards, one spoon less than you have players

Preparation: Make a list of fun forfeits – for example, the loser must wash the dishes, sing a song or share an embarrassing secret!

As this is not a sedate card game, you may wish to remove all wine glasses from the table before you begin.

If you have ten players, make sure you have ten cards of each suit in your pack (e.g., Ace to ten of Hearts, Clubs, Spades and Diamonds). If you have six players you will need six cards of each suit in your pack, and so on.

Put the spoons in the middle of the table. Shuffle the deck and deal out all the cards. On the call of "Go!" everyone passes one card to the person on their left and takes one from the person on their right. The first person to collect four of a kind shouts "Spoons!" – this is the cue for everyone to grab a spoon from the middle. The loser is the person without a spoon – and they must do a forfeit.

CHEAT!

Equipment: One or more packs of cards

Preparation: None

The aim of cheat is to be the first to get rid of all your cards – by fair means or foul.

Deal all of one or more of your packs to your players. Judge for yourself how many packs you need – though your players really need at least ten cards each. It doesn't matter if some players have one more card than others.

The player to the dealer's left puts any number of cards face down in the middle of the table, saying what they have played (two fives for example). They may tell the truth – or lie. The next player must lay down a greater number of fives, or some sixes. Again, they can lie if they want – calling four fives but actually putting down three twos and a four.

Players can miss a turn if they wish.

At any point in the game the player who has just called may be accused of being a "cheat," by one of the other players. They must then reveal the cards they have just played. If they have cheated they must pick up the entire pack. But if they have not cheated, their accuser must pick up the pack.

(Source: PFC *personal development experts, plus additional UK and US research.)*

THE FEMALE CANCER THAT CAN STRIKE MEN

***PFC* alert:** breast cancer affects both women; and men. Typical: males over the age of 60 years experience more problems than younger men. Fact: the identification and treatment of breast cancer in men are similar to those for women. Wise: men should examine themselves regularly – at least once a month. Bottom line: see your GP if you notice a lump or any changes in and around the chest area.

(Sources: PFC *medical experts.)*

NINE INSIDER SECRETS THAT IMPROVE YOUR CHANCES OF GETTING YOUR BOOK PUBLISHED

Making a success of writing is much easier if you adopt a realistic, businesslike approach. Here's what you need to do to get into print:

1. **Know your category.** Fiction and non-fiction bestsellers fall into many categories. Examples: crime, thriller, fantasy, travel, cookery and health. Each are distinctive in terms of length, subject matter and cover illustration. Note: generally, publishers are not interested in books that break the category rules, or cross category boundaries.

2. **Understand your readers.** Readers of each category have specific

needs. Examples: crime readers like puzzles but detest explicit violence; fantasy fans want lots of details about everything but the real world; romance fans love the implication of red hot passion but shy away from the messy reality of it.

3. **Sell your wares.** Publishers and agents are so inundated with manuscripts that success comes only to those who know how to sell successfully. Essential: covering letters should be brief; manuscripts, neat, tidy and error-free; synopses and story outlines should be tight and clear. Important: you need to express the concept of your book in less than 200 words. Recommendation: André Jute's *Writing Proposals and Synopses That Sell* is an excellent read.

4. **Establish a work routine.** Fact: half an hour's writing a day produces more words over a year than two hours a week, or a weekend a month. Find out when you write best and most productively and build your writing time around it. If you are a morning person, that's when to write.

5. **Find a place of work.** It helps if you can create your own writing space because its familiarity triggers you into work mode. Always: guard this space well and exclude anything that distracts you from your writing work.

6. **Set realistic targets** for the amount of words to write each day and chart your progress to keep yourself at it. Average: less than 400 words a writing day is too little to get a flow going; more than 2,000 is difficult to maintain.

7. **Take regular breaks.** Writers get stale on a daily, weekly, monthly and annual basis, so build regular breaks into your routines. Exercise and diet help, as do mental and physical challenges. Also, your writing probably began with a curiosity and excitement about life: you owe it to yourself and your readers to maintain it.

8. **Distrust publishers.** Fact: the history of publishing reveals that some publishers are liars and cheats. Also: they are hopeless at

communicating with authors, and slow to pay what they owe. They are fickle too. If you accept all of this from the outset, you will suffer less grief and are far more likely to be able to negotiate your book through the system and into publication.

9. **Learn from others.** Listen to other writers talk, and ask them how they work. Useful: writers' courses are a good way of meeting would-be and successful authors. Arvon Foundation courses (01422 843714) are the best known in the United Kingdom. Tip: book early as they fill up fast. Helpful: the Society of Authors (0171-373 6642) caters mainly for published authors, but is lenient with the nearly-published. An annual subscription of £65.00 gives you many opportunities to meet fellow authors and the right to expert advice on contracts and other matters. Plus: devour material by writers on their trade. Recommendation: Celia Brayfield's *Bestseller* shows you what to do, and is an excellent read. Seek out trade magazines such as *The Bookseller* – your nearest library should keep copies of these. Use writers' annuals like *The Writers' Handbook* and *Writers' and Artists' Yearbook*; old copies should be available in the library, although it's worth buying the latest copies.

(Sources: William Horwood, author of the two best-selling trilogies about the moles of Duncton Wood, plus additional PFC research. This feature first appeared in PFC October 1997, No. 13.)

MONEY IN A FLASH – HOW YOU CAN SELL YOUR PHOTOS

Your camera can form the basis of a profitable part-time business. All you need is determination and commercial savvy and you'll find plenty of money-making opportunities for good semi-professional photographers. Here are four money-spinners:

1. **Property photography.** Using your local *Yellow Pages*, telephone all the estate agents in your area. Aim to get a regular order to take photographs of all of the houses the agency is trying to sell. Tip: to

clinch the deal, offer to photograph the first five houses free of charge. How: when you arrive, decide how to show the property in the best way. Example: if the house next door has old cars parked in the drive, closed curtains, or rubbish piled by the front door, you'll want to exclude these. Typical: most estate agents want at least one large photograph for their window display and 50 smaller prints for their written particulars. Good photographic shops can supply adhesive-backed 'stickiprints' for easy insertion onto printed particulars. Tactic: a good way to boost business is to suggest that slow-selling properties should be re-photographed regularly. Example: a photograph of a house in December will be less attractive than one taken in the spring.

2. **School photography**. Contact every school in your area by letter or telephone call; you'll find a complete list in the *Yellow Pages*. Tip: get in touch with independent schools as well. Aim to photograph every pupil in the school individually. And: offer to take brother/sister photographs, class and year photographs and school teams photographs as well. When you get your photographs developed, negotiate a bulk discount with a photograph shop or a mail order photographic processor. Ideal: the best size for a portrait photograph is 8"x 6". Mount photographs inside a neat cardboard frame; and enclose them within a clear PVC case to keep them clean – these items are available from photographic shops. The school is responsible for distributing the photographs to parents and collecting the money. Photographs are offered on a sale or return basis. Basic: you will find that the profits from sales more than cover the cost of returns. Average: the typical response rate is 65% sales to 35% returns. Usual: you would expect to have to give 20% of the sale price received as commission to the school. Always contact schools once every year to arrange to photograph the whole school again.

3. **News photography.** Approach local newspapers, local offices of national newspapers and news agencies to offer your services. Contacts can be found in *The Writer's Handbook* and/or *Benn's Media Directory* – you'll find copies of these in major libraries. Helpful: your chances of being employed will be improved if you have a selection of newsworthy

photographs ready to show the news editor. Best: photographs of people, places and events. If a newspaper agrees to use your services don't wait for them to call you. Better: keep your camera with you at all times, take photographs of any newsworthy event, and call the editor immediately with details. Examples: a traffic accident, a demonstration, or an agricultural show. Note: as you build up relationships with newspapers, they'll call you out on assignments. Payment: most editors will pay you for any photographs used rather than on an hourly rate basis. But: this can be much more profitable for you. Rates vary from £30 for a run-of-the-mill photograph, up to hundreds of pounds for a really newsworthy photograph; perhaps at a demonstration. Bonus: if you have a photograph of a major incident, you might be able to sell it to national newspapers; and earn several thousand pounds from it.

4. **Landscape photography.** Take photographs of famous buildings, local scenes and attractive landscapes, and produce a range of framed photo-prints from them. Best: widely admired sights that are popular with local people and tourists. Ideal: beauty spots, cathedrals, churches and stately homes. Plan the best place and time to take your photographs. Tip: buildings and landscapes look better when it is sunny. Take at least ten photographs, then have them developed and choose the best shot. Have five or six copies of this printed and framed. You can save money by doing this yourself using ready-made frames purchased from a framing shop. ten by eight inch photographs are the most popular size. Offer them to local shops on a sale or return basis. Home furnishings and craft shops are ideal sales outlets for you. And: you can arrange to display your pictures in local pubs and restaurants to sell them to customers. Important: check the prices of similar photographs in your area to settle on an appropriate price. Average: a good framed photograph will cost around £3 to produce using ready-made frames, and sell for about £15-20. Offer a commission of 10-15% to shops, pubs and restaurants that sell your photographs.

(Sources: PFC *photography specialists plus additional information from the British Institute of Professional Photography (BIPP), 01920 464011.)*

CHANGE YOUR DIET AND CHEER YOURSELF UP

***PFC* tip:** mounting evidence shows that depression and even schizophrenia can sometimes be caused by nothing more than dietary deficiencies or food allergies. Details: an Italian study revealed that almost all of the 331 depressed people taking part in the test had extremely low levels of cholesterol in their body. Evidence shows that very low-fat diets can cause depression. And: insufficient levels of B vitamins, high intakes of sugar and caffeine, and gluten or milk allergies have all been shown to cause or aggravate mental illness too. Fact: your doctor won't tell you that other common triggers for depression include some prescription drugs such as antihistamines, antibiotics, drugs for high blood pressure, nasal decongestants and heart drugs. Warning: the last thing you want to deal with when you're suffering from depression is an episode of ill health. But: that's exactly what you can experience with many common depression drugs. Tricyclic antidepressants can cause delirium, fatigue, excessive sweating, the dangerous lowering of blood pressure, and even strokes and heart attacks. Prozac has brought on vomiting, diarrhoea, anxiety, insomnia, sexual problems, muscle, bone, ear and eye pain and even suicide in some people.

(Source: Agora Lifestyles Limited. – call 0500 523 499 for a free copy of the latest issue of any of their newsletters.)

FIVE KEY QUESTIONS YOU MUST ASK YOUR INDEPENDENT FINANCIAL ADVISER

You can find the right IFA for your needs by asking five key questions:

1. **Who regulates you?** Make sure they are registered with a regulatory body such as the Personal Investment Authority (0171-538 8860) or the Securities and Futures Authority Limited (0171-378 9000). Note: you will also be covered by compensation schemes run by

the regulatory body – although there is no protection against investments which just do badly. That's why you should ask these additional questions:

2. **What are your qualifications?** Check their business card for one or more of these abbreviations. CeFA, CIP, IAC, MLIA (Dip), ITC. Important: see if they have also passed relevant Financial Planning Certificate examinations in those areas that they're advising you about. Fact: obtaining advanced qualifications shows an understanding of more complex financial issues, such as inheritance taxation. Look for these abbreviations: AFPC, PIC, AIFP, ALIA (Dip), FLIA (Dip), MSI (Dip), AMSI (Dip), MSFA, ACII. Top qualifications: FCII, FSFA, FIFP, FIA, FFA.

3. **What are your personal areas of expertise and experience?** Tip: few IFAs can offer quality advice on all aspects of personal finance; the majority of them specialise in one or more areas. Warning: be wary of any IFA who promises advice on all conceivable topics. Better: look for a firm that contains a mix of advisers who cover topics of relevance to you. Note: newly qualified advisers may be keen, but are unlikely to be as good as someone with several years of experience behind them. Wise: pick an experienced IFA; and one with clients who are similar to you.

4. **How do you receive your income?** Sensible: negotiate a fee for advice in advance – commission-only payments tend to be higher; and they encourage some IFAs to recommend products which generate the most commission for them. Typical: (high-commission paying) endowment mortgages are suggested instead of (low fee-paying) repayment mortgages. Important: if you decide to buy a product that includes a commission payment to the IFA, ask for a proportion to be paid back to you. Ideal: the difference between what you would have paid as a straight fee and the total commission involved in the transaction.

5. **What ongoing services do you provide for clients?** Essential: your financial adviser should be chosen on a long-term basis. Tip: avoid

someone who is just starting out – they may move on shortly. And: don't pick someone who is approaching retirement. Best: pick an IFA of similar age and circumstances to you – they'll have a better knowledge and understanding of your situation, may share the same sort of views and opinions, and can work with you as your circumstances change through to retirement.

(Sources: PFC *financial experts.)*

HOW TO AVOID HAVING YOUR INSURANCE CLAIM REJECTED

There's one thing insurance companies don't tell you when you're arranging an insurance policy – they're not going to pay out unless they have to. But you can make sure that your claim is settled in full if you learn the main tactics employed by insurance companies to avoid settling claims – and beat them at their own game.

'Incorrect information was provided by the policy holder'. Example: a lecturer stated he was a 'teacher' – and it invalidated a subsequent claim. Important: always be honest with insurers – disclose convictions and previously refused or cancelled policies. Note: insurers do share data like this with each other.

'Material facts were not disclosed'. Definition: anything that might cause the insurer to view you as a greater risk, and charge a higher premium. Problem: it's almost impossible to know what these might include. Example: one insurance claim for a car theft was refused simply because the policy holder did not disclose they lived near to a youth club; which allegedly increases the risk of car theft by joyriders. Always: volunteer potentially relevant information, even if you're not asked about it.

'That cover is not provided by the policy'. Example: one household policy covered the cost of consequential damage resulting from a burst pipe, but not for replacing the pipe – which was far more expensive. Why: most policies do not cover everything, even so-called 'comprehensive' ones. If something is not stated in the policy, it almost certainly isn't covered. Do: ask for written clarification when necessary. Warning: verbal assurances count for nothing when it comes to a claim unless you can prove what was said.

Do's and don'ts: ignore the advertisements. Fact: advertisers often push the law to the limit, implying that the advertised policy gives you complete cover, but it doesn't. Essential: study the policy, not the marketing hype. Buy insurance only from those insurers who belong to the Association of British Insurers (0171-600 3333). And: check that the insurance company also participates in the Insurance Ombudsman Scheme (0171-928 4488). Important: you can then appeal if a claim is refused – most insurers will settle relatively minor claims (£1,000 or less) to avoid this time-consuming procedure.

Fill out the proposal form yourself; or check it has been completed properly. Why: an incomplete or incorrectly completed form may invalidate the policy – but they won't tell you that until you claim. Never: rely on a broker or intermediary to do it for you. Remember: reveal all the facts – anything that might be of any relevance. Read the small print – and check you've got the cover you want. Motto: if it's not included, it's excluded. Clarify in writing if necessary. Example: 'new-for-old' cover normally needs clarification. Why: it usually applies only if goods are lost or destroyed completely. If they can be repaired, the insurance company may insist on this. Do: make sure you understand exactly what each term and phrase means.

Notify changes. Example: if you take in a lodger, this can affect your household cover, and even invalidate any subsequent claim. Also: acquiring a pet can do the same if it's not covered by the policy. Keep proof – retain copies of everything from the advertisement through the proposal form to the insurance policy and letters of clarification. Don't: rely on the insurer to provide you with any evidence in the case of a claim. Make realistic claims – the majority of these will be settled without query. Vital: avoid inflating claims to make up for any inconvenience caused to you. Note: these are more likely to be queried, and the whole claim rejected.

(Sources: PFC *editor Iain Maitland spoke informally to claims investigators at insurance companies, and talked off-the-record to other relevant people within the industry. The original version of this feature first appeared in* PFC *October 1997, No. 13.)*

HOW TO GET 48 HOURS OUT OF EVERY DAY

If you've been struggling to get everything done, you'll want to know how to manage your time more effectively. Here are the secrets of success:

1. **Use a 'to do' list that sets out everything you must, should and could do that day, week or month.** How: give each item a priority code. Examples: 'A' for essential tasks, 'B' for those to do tomorrow, 'C' for activities to do this week, and 'D' for anything that you'd like to do. Do prioritised tasks in that order and cross them off your list. Important: go through your list every day and re-organise priorities.

2. **Always do essential tasks first and leave other activities until later.** Warning: it is satisfying to cross off completed tasks; and you may be tempted to do easy but unimportant C's and D's first. If you find yourself doing trivial tasks, work out why. Typical: some people don't want to start a particular task because they don't think they'll be able to finish it to perfection. Resolution: remember that 80% of the value comes from 20% of the work. So, unless that final 20% produces the high value, it doesn't matter if the final polish is lacking. Also: other people don't like starting a large activity because its size and complexity are daunting. Answer: break the job into separate, smaller tasks, prioritise and cross them off your list on completion.

3. **Maximise your most productive time.** How: keep a record of your daily cycle; when you feel bright and alert, and dull and tired. Then: organise your day around these times. Tip: do regular tasks at the

same time each day. By turning them into a habit, they'll seem less demanding.

4. **Minimise time-wasting activities.** Ideal: only handle each piece of paper once – preferably when you receive it. Example: deal with your post as you open it. If you can't reply or react immediately – and you usually can by writing a brief reply on it, photocopying it and putting it in an envelope – place it in one pile for tackling later, another for filing, or simply put it straight in the waste paper basket. Essential: get into the habit of doing everything systematically and having a place for all of your paperwork. Result: you'll know what you've done, are doing, and where to find documentation.

(Sources: Kate Keenan, The Management Guide to Making Time, *Marek Getlin,* Making Time Work for You, *plus additional* PFC *research.)*

THE SIMPLE TAX TACTIC THAT WILL ADD 40% TO YOUR ANNUAL BONUS

***PFC* tip:** increase your annual bonus by as much as 40% by using a tax-boosting tactic known as a 'bonus waiver'. Example: an employer proposes to pay a bonus of £10,000 to an employee. Cost to employer: £10,000 bonus plus £1,000 National Insurance contribution – a gross cost of £11,000. Received by employee: £10,000 minus £4,000 income tax (assuming the employee's income is subject to higher-rate tax at 40%) – a net receipt of £6,000. Alternative: if the employee waives their right to any bonus, the employer can pay this sum into an occupational pension scheme as a lump sum. Note: the normal 15% restriction on member contributions is overcome because it is an employer contribution, rather than the employee's. And: this tactic will not at present attract an employer's National Insurance contribution on the payment, so the employee's benefits from the gross contribution are paid into their pension fund.

(Source: PFC *contributor, David Holland, R.K. Harrison Financial Services.)*

ENJOY A FABULOUS HOLIDAY – ABSOLUTELY FREE OF CHARGE

***PFC* tip:** the easiest way to arrange a free holiday is to swap your home for a comparable property. The exchange is free, apart from the minimal cost of finding someone who wants to trade with you. How: place an advertisement in an international publication such as '*International Living*', (0171-447 4018). That two-minute call could get you free accommodation in a luxury villa in the Caribbean, a charming apartment in Rome, or a rambling ranch house in Mexico! Alternative: contact a home-exchange organisation. These companies publish directories several times a year detailing those people who are interested in swapping homes, when they want to travel, where they wish to go, and so forth. Useful contact: Homelink International, (01344 842642).

(Source: International Living *newsletter published by Agora Lifestyles – phone 0500 523 499 for a free copy of the latest issue.)*

UNDERSTANDING DREAMS – UNCOVER THE TRUTH ABOUT YOURSELF

If you read the messages of your unconscious mind, you'll find it easier to identify and deal with your hopes and fears – and can go on to become a happier and more fulfilled person. Here's what to do:

1. **Record your dreams.** When: you'll remember them most when you wake up, so have a pen and paper beside the bed. Tip: before you go to sleep, start a new page in your dream notebook and put the next day's date on it – this lets your unconscious know your intentions in advance. Outcome: knowing that you are going to take its messages seriously, your unconscious will make greater efforts – and you will be more likely to remember what you dream.

2. **Don't interpret a single dream.** Why: it will produce misleading results. Best: record a body of information about your dreams; and analyse a wider range to produce more accurate assessments.

3. **Eliminate (parts of) dreams that are not of a symbolic nature.** Example: re-runs of that day's events. But: ask yourself why your unconscious has replayed those events – you may wish to subject them to a more detailed investigation. Also: ignore any event that seems to be a response to a physical stimulus. Typical: thirst or the desire to urinate may impinge upon your dreams. Ignore: those dreams that refer simply to you and your own desires; wish-fulfilment and anxiety dreams.

4. **Interpret the remaining dreams: they represent messages from your unconscious mind.** Symbolism: parts of the mind specialise in visual understanding and communicate through pictures or symbols. Often, symbols work by analogy. Example: if a blind person appears in a dream, then your unconscious mind may be pointing out some blindness in yourself; some obvious truth that your conscious mind is choosing to ignore. Note: symbols might seem bizarre and nonsensical, but could still contain an important message. Example: during a conversation, you're transformed into a flying seagull – your unconscious might be suggesting that you should 'fly away' from such conversations in future. Alternative: the message might be that something you've learned in that conversation could give you a new freedom – as symbolised by the seagull in flight. Bottom line: the meaning of a symbol depends on its context.

5. **Learn the tricks of translation.** Fact: certain techniques help you to uncover the meaning of dream objects, people and/or events. Free association: see what that object brings immediately to your mind and so forth. Example: if you dreamt of a cat, the first word that 'cat' might bring to mind is 'dog'; and this might generate 'bone', and so on. Important: keep going until you come to a word that sparks an emotional response, whether positive or negative. Then: go back and see whether this word and what it represents relates to the meaning of the object in your dream. Dream amplification: place the puzzling dream object at the centre of your thoughts. Mindful of the rich cultural symbolism at your disposal – and that of your unconscious mind – consider the various qualities of the object. Example: if you dreamt of a

cat, you might consider the softness of its fur, the watchfulness of its eyes, its aloofness and its patience. Essential: believe that your unconscious has picked the best possible way of symbolising what it means to tell you – and the quality or association that you are looking for should eventually become clear.

(Sources: Michele Simmons and Chris McLaughlin, Dream Interpretation For Beginners, *Julia and Derek Parker,* The Secret World Of Your Dreams, *Strephon Kaplan-Williams,* The Elements Of Dreamwork, *plus additional* PFC *research.)*

EARN MONEY ON THE INTERNET – IT'S A GOLDMINE

Business and the internet are made for each other. Why: businesses have products and/or services to sell and are constantly looking out for new ways to reach their target audiences. The internet boasts a population of millions. Here's how to make money on the net:

1. **Decide what you're going to sell via the internet.** Idea: the value of internet advertising depends largely on what you are selling. Example: if you're publicising a book that condemns the harmful effects of technology, internet users are unlikely to respond favourably. But: if you are selling 'I Love Cyberspace' t-shirts, you might just have a seller on your hands. Best: businesses that trade information are ideally suited to the internet. Why: information is the most valued commodity on earth – more money is made in media and information-related businesses than in anything else. Logical conclusion: a business that trades information has most to gain from cyberspace.

Evidence: for years, people have used mail order as a way of selling valuable information. Example: the late Joe Karbo made a multi-million dollar fortune by self-publishing a 150-page book entitled *The Lazy Man's Way To Riches*, which he advertised extensively in newspapers and magazines. Personal example: perhaps you know how to cook traditional Californian cuisine; you could have 101 of your best and unique recipes printed in booklet form and sell these through small advertisements in the press. Alternative: imagine running your own mail-order company which sells valuable information – but without having to spend money on printing and mailing it to your customers. If a business could sell information whilst dispensing with paper and ink, its overheads would be slashed to the bare minimum and the profit potential increased to the maximum. The Internet offers just this opportunity.

2. **Advertise on the bulletin boards of newsgroups to reach your target audience.** An internet customer can then e-mail their order to you, together with credit card authorisation details; you simply send the purchased information over the internet for downloading to a PC and printing out as hard copy, as required. And: a lucrative business transaction which would have taken days in the world of conventional mail order has taken just minutes on the Internet. Result: less money is spent on paper, ink and mailing; which means bigger profits. Also: less time is consumed by the preparation and despatch of your product; leaving you with more hours per week to enjoy your new-found wealth. Plus: your customer is more than happy at being able to order an information product and receive it directly over the Internet, rather than having to wait days for a reply by mail.

PFC **advice:** you now need to come up with an information product that has the commercial potential to be a huge earner. Celebrity e-mail directories: many celebrities use the Internet regularly. Consider sourcing and selling a directory of celebrity e-mail addresses to other cyberspace users who can then send their fan-mail direct. Winners' guides: if you have the Midas touch when it comes to making money from gambling or competitions, try selling the secrets of your success to other internet users. 'How to' guides: maybe you're a whizz at scrabble, playing the guitar or salesmanship – anything which you can do better than the average person could be the basis of a profitable business. Bottom line: the number of ways that you can make money on the internet is limitless – confined only by your own imagination. And: don't think that you need to charge high prices to make big money – if you can sell an information product for just

£1 to only 0.1% of internet users, you'll create a gross profit of £30,000; and you could be earning that within a two to three-week period!

(Sources: Mark Adamson and Fraser Pearce, Online Services in Europe, The Impact of the Internet on Business Information Services, *plus additional* PFC *research.)*

WHY TENS OF THOUSANDS OF PEOPLE DON'T CLAIM THE SOCIAL SECURITY BENEFITS THEY'RE ENTITLED TO

Fact: it is estimated that an average of 10% of people who are eligible for certain state benefits fail to claim them. Why: some people aren't aware of what they can claim for. Typical: family credit for those families on a low income, housing benefit that reduces council tax payments for those on low incomes. And: other people are too proud and/or embarrassed to claim. Fact: 90% of people claim their social security benefits; they're from all walks of life – and they're simply getting back some of what they've paid out in tax; it's all rightfully theirs. Wise: anyone on a low income and/or who is finding it difficult to make ends meet should visit their local Citizen's Advice Bureau for free, independent and confidential advice on all state benefits, and how to claim them. Citizen's Advice Bureau staff will also help you to apply for benefits; filling out forms etc, on request.

(Sources: The Benefits Agency, consumer groups around the United Kingdom, plus additional PFC *research.)*

FLATTEN YOUR STOMACH IN JUST THREE MONTHS

Having a flat stomach improves your posture, strengthens your back and makes you less susceptible to injury and illness. It will improve your appearance too. And if you look good, you'll feel great. Unfortunately, modern living encourages weak muscles and a sagging stomach. But you can do something about it. Here's how:

Concentrate on the four muscle groups that support your stomach – upper abdominals, lower abdominals, external oblique, internal oblique. Details: the upper and lower abdominals are on the front of the abdomen and form a row of muscles that runs from the ribs to the pubic bone. When they are well developed they are oblong in shape. The top half comprises the upper abdominals, and the bottom half includes the lower abdominals. The external and internal obliques are not as easy to see as the abdominals, but are equally important. They form two bands of muscles that stretch down either side of your body, between your abdomen and waist. They run from the bottom of your ribs to the top of your hips. The internal oblique lies underneath the external oblique.

Basic starting position: lie flat on your back, keeping your knees together and your feet flat on the floor. Bend your knees upwards at an angle of 90 degrees. Press your lower back into the floor. Place your arms flat by your sides. Do: practise getting into this position; and familiarise yourself with it. Before starting any of these exercises, avoid any strain or injury to your muscles by doing this simple warm-up:

Upper body warm-up: Stand up as straight as possible and place your arms above your head. Next: hold this position for five seconds, then lower your arms so they're outstretched by your side. Again: hold this position for five seconds. Then: swing your arms so they're outstretched in front of you - and hold for five seconds. Important: do all three arm movements at least three times each.

Lower body warm-up: Lie down on your left side in a straight line with your right leg resting on the left one. Next: gently lift your upper leg about 12 inches above your lower leg and make a small circular movement with your foot. And: after each circle, lower your leg again and repeat up to five times. Then: turn over, lie on your other side and repeat the exercise with your left leg.

Exercise 1: from the starting position, place your hands flat under your hips, palm side down. Keep your knees bent and your legs together. Brace your abdominal muscles. Bring your legs up until they are at right angles to your body. Use your abdominals to pull your knees towards your chest. Hold this position for two seconds, then repeat.

Exercise 2: from the starting position, keep your knees bent and your legs together. Brace your abdominal muscles. Slowly pull your knees towards your chest. Unfold your legs gradually and point them straight towards the ceiling. Keep your legs and feet pressed together. Rotate your legs slowly in a very small circle, about four inches in each direction. Do half the repetitions clockwise, and the other half anti-clockwise. Bend your knees again before lowering your legs.

Exercise 3: from the starting position, place your hands behind your head. Tuck your chin onto your chest. Press your lower back into the floor. Tighten your abdominal muscles and your buttocks. Breathe in. Breathe out slowly, at the same time raising your head and shoulders until they are a third of the way off the floor. Hold this position for one second, then return gently to the starting position. Remember: never raise your body more than 30 degrees – a third of the way – off the floor. Your abdominal muscles are only capable of lifting you this far and if you raise yourself any higher, your spine will have to do most of the work. This does nothing to help your muscles and could damage your back. Hint: do the exercise slowly and feel your abdominals working. Don't try to raise yourself higher by bouncing, nor by using the momentum you gain from that return movement. Use only your abdominal muscles, and try to 'unroll' yourself off the floor.

Exercise 4: from the starting position, bring your knees towards your chest. Keep your knees bent, and your legs in the air. Your thighs must be vertical; and your lower legs should be horizontal. Place your hands behind your head. Tuck your chin onto your chest. Breathe in. Breathe out slowly, keeping your legs in the same position and raising your head and shoulders a third of the way off the floor. Hold the position momentarily. Lower your head and shoulders, but keep your legs in the same position all the time. Repeat the exercise if you feel good.

Exercise 5: from the starting position, brace your abdominal muscles and your buttocks. Place your hands behind your head. Tuck your chin onto your chest. Breathe in. Breathe out slowly whilst slowly raising your left shoulder and your left hip off the floor. Hold the position for one second then return to the starting position. Repeat the exercise for the other side.

Beginners' routine: warm up; exercise 1 – five repetitions; exercise 3 – five repetitions; exercise 4 – five repetitions; cool down. Continue this for a few sessions until it becomes easy; and then move up to ten repetitions. When you feel comfortable with ten repetitions, move up to 15 repetitions. And: when that becomes easy, go on to do the intermediate routine.

Intermediate routine: warm up; exercise 1 – 20 repetitions; exercise 2 – 20 repetitions; exercise 3 – 20 repetitions; exercise 4 – 20 repetitions; cool down. Continue this for a few days and then move up to 25 repetitions. And: when you are comfortable with 25, go on to the advanced routine.

Advanced routine: warm up; exercise 1 – 30 repetitions; exercise 2 – 30 repetitions; exercise 3 – 30 repetitions; exercise 4 – 30 repetitions; exercise 5 – 30 repetitions; cool down.

This is designed to work the obliques, the lower abdominals, and the upper abdominals. You only need to do the exercises every other day – the abdominals tone up better when you rest them between sessions; but try to do some aerobic exercise every day. Reminder: do consult your doctor before starting an exercise programme if you are overweight, and/or have a back problem, and/or have any special medical needs, and/or don't exercise regularly.

(Sources: Francine St. George, The Muscle Fitness Book, *Gay Search and David Denison,* Getting In Shape – The Scientific Way To Fitness, *Tony Lycholat,* Shape Your Body, Shape Your Life *plus additional* PFC *research.)*

TRIGGER SENTENCES THAT GET YOU UP TO 50% DISCOUNTS ON HOME IMPROVEMENTS

***PFC* tip:** never pay the full price for double glazing, conservatories and other home improvement products – brochure prices are almost always inflated so that salespeople can offer 'personal discounts' and 'special deals' before making a sale – no salesperson expects a canny customer to pay the full price! These are the trigger sentences that you can use to obtain the biggest possible discounts. **1:** 'I understand you've got a special offer on at the moment' – salespeople always have (or are about to have) some sort of discount available; you just need to ask for it. **2:** 'your (named) competitor can beat that by X per cent.' – salespeople hate to be beaten on price by a rival, so they're going to try to match whatever price you state. And they'll do it there and then without checking, because they want to make a sale now. **3:** 'I can't afford that price' – salespeople may then offer various credit packages; look at these carefully unless they're interest-free as you'll almost certainly be able to get a better deal by shopping around. And: if they are 'interest-free' there will be some sort of mark-up built into the price to compensate for the absence of interest – the firm still wants to make a profit on the sale. Advice: see what type of discount they'll offer if you pay in full now. **4:** 'I still can't afford it' – keep saying this and the salesperson will eventually say 'what can you afford?'. State what you want to pay and dare them to match it. Bottom line: you'll be surprised at how many salespeople can be pushed into giving discounts of up to 50% off the brochure price with these tactics.

(Source: PFC *editor Iain Maitland spoke to former and current salespeople in the home improvements industry, and customers too.)*

THE BODY LANGUAGE GIVEAWAYS – KNOW WHAT PEOPLE ARE REALLY THINKING

Only a small part of successful communication involves the words we speak – far more is conveyed by *how* we speak the tone of our voice, intonation and pauses. And even more is expressed by our non-verbal communication, or 'body language'. Experts agree that this provides over 50% of the impact of our message. Why: words tend to convey information, whilst our body is more likely to express our attitudes and feelings. Most people are unaware that they are sending these signals; nor do they know how to read them. When you know what to look out for, you'll be able to interpret people's meanings accurately, and communicate more effectively; in job interviews, workplace discussions and during meetings and presentations. And: you'll be able to spot those unconscious gestures that tell you whether someone's secretly attracted to you!

1. **Posture:** the way that people hold themselves can provide clues about their personality. Good: a firm, upright posture with eyes looking straight ahead is associated with confidence and health. Bad: drooping shoulders and neck suggest dejection, shyness, illness and other negative traits.

2. **Personal space:** we all have a subconscious sense of our own personal space, which consists of four zones – 'intimate', 'personal', 'social' and 'public'. And: our space is so important to us that we become uncomfortable if someone gets too close. But: we also say that people are 'stand-offish' if they position themselves too far away. You can sometimes judge how a person feels about you from how close they place themselves in relation to you.

3. **Pointing:** the way a person feels can be indicated by how they point their body. Positive: people usually turn to face the person they feel most sympathetic to; and vice versa. Also: people point towards things they want. Example: if someone turns away from you towards the

door or another person, it probably indicates where they want to go. Note: if someone is beside you and they turn slightly to face you, they're demonstrating interest. If they continue to face forwards, they are remaining neutral. Turning away means that they wish to be left alone.

4. **Eyes:** these are the most expressive part of a face. Good: when people encounter something they like, their pupils dilate and become larger. Bad: when they feel negative about something, their pupils contract. Bottom line: even though the pupils are small, they can vary in size quite significantly, and this difference can be detected by observant people.

5. **Arms and hands:** someone who folds their arms is often making a protective gesture – it can mean that they feel threatened and/or are in a defensive or negative mood. Practical example: if you are trying to persuade somebody to accept your viewpoint, folded arms suggest that the listener is sceptical. And: if their hands are gripping their upper arms or their fists are clenched, this attitude is being reinforced. Partially folded arms also signal defensiveness. This is usually accompanied by other gestures such as fiddling with cuffs, a ring on a finger, a watch or a handbag. Better: someone who keeps their arms unfolded is signalling that they feel confident and unthreatened. Also: if they are rubbing their hands together, this often signals positive expectations. And: rubbing them together briskly suggests an open attitude to what is being said and anticipated. Plus: rubbing more slowly can mean that the person expects to be the recipient of good news.

6. **Handshakes**: a strong, painful grip suggests the person wants to dominate you. A soft, limp handshake may mean they feel in a weaker position than you; and/or can indicate apathy. Tip: when someone reinforces their handshake by gripping your arm with their free hand, they're trying to indicate sincerity. Note: some politicians use this technique on walkabouts and alienate those people who are familiar with this trick.

7. **Legs:** crossed legs convey the impression of negative feelings

such as shyness, disagreement or even anger. Important: watch out for other negative signals that might be present at the same time. Note: when the upper ankle of one leg rests on the knee of the other leg, the person is betraying a competitive attitude. And: if the upper leg is clamped in place with the hands, a very firm position is being taken by that person. They're not likely to change their mind.

8. **Copying other people's body language:** one of the best ways of recognising whether someone is for or against you is to see whether they mirror your body language. Good: when someone shares feelings or attitudes, they will often adopt a similar body language. Example: when one person crosses their legs, the other will do so too, almost as a sign of agreement. Bad: when they disagree, the body signals start to differ as well. You can copy other people's body language to win their confidence, minimise negative signals and maximise positive ones, to appear more confident.

(Sources: Allan Pease, Body Language, How to Read Other's Thoughts by their Gestures, *plus additional* PFC *research.)*

THE SECRETS OF SUCCESSFUL NETWORKING – BY THE EXECUTIVES WHO'VE MADE IT TO THE TOP

The more people you know, the greater your chances of a successful career. It's not what you know, but who you know. These are the secrets of those executives who have networked their way into top jobs in the United Kingdom. Use them to do the same:

1. **View networking as an ongoing, two-way process.** Why: if you make contact only when you are looking for a job, it will seem as though you're exploiting a friendship. And: that person may not be able to help you at that particular time anyway. Better: make networking part of your day-to-day activities; and attempt to help your contacts too. Benefits: shared knowledge and information, personal satisfaction from assisting

others, and potential advancement in due course – in some firms, an estimated 85% of jobs are obtained through a network contact. Remember: successful people have a good network in place before they need to use it.

2. **Set up a database: names, contact details and useful information such as partner's and children's names, birthday, anniversary and other important dates, hobbies and interests.** And: use this additional information to build warm and strong relationships. Examples: refer to someone's partner in conversations, send personalised birthday and Christmas cards as appropriate. Important: make contact at good and bad times; a redundancy, the death of a loved one. Idea: send a handwritten letter – 'I'm so sorry. Can I do anything for you? If so, please call me.' Result: that person will remember your warmth and support during better times; and when you need help.

3. **Always look to add people to your network of contacts.** Who: anyone can be a potentially useful contact; your next door neighbour, the people you went to school with, that man you say hello to as you're walking the dog. Useful: people who have inside information about a specific company, trade or industry, and/or who appear to be on the fast track to success are definitely worth cultivating. Helpful: join local and professional associations such as a chamber of commerce and your trade body, and read the press, collecting the names of dynamic and successful people around you. Vital: never ignore any contact; you never know when they might come in useful.

4. **Be prepared to network door-to-door on an on-spec basis.** Who: those individuals and/or organisations that can offer a mutual exchange of knowledge and information, assistance and employment prospects. Typical: job seekers come to the reception area, ask if there are any vacancies, are told 'no', and then leave. But: the receptionist doesn't always know about job opportunities – it isn't their job. Best: target the head of a department or the organisation itself. Because: if you can get through to them, they'll be impressed by your ability to achieve and to get what you want. How: make your approach as a top salesperson, not

just another job hunter – you're dealing with an exclusive product here: you. Ask to see their secretary and make an appointment to meet to discuss that product. Tip: 8-9am, 1-2pm and 5-6pm are the times when secretaries may not be around and you can get straight through to the top person for a few brief minutes. Essential: always be polite and friendly to any receptionists and secretaries you meet; they often have closer relationships and greater influence with senior management than line managers do.

5. **Attend all the events you can get invited to.** Target: trade conferences and exhibitions are particularly useful. Sensible: go to events where most of the people will be strangers to you. Your present contacts know all about you already – these strangers don't; so they're the people you want to mingle with. How: start by going one-on-one with other individuals, rather than invading groups who know each other. Tip: avoid staying with only one or two people for the whole of the event; more than ten minutes per person is a waste of valuable networking time. If they are a useful contact, arrange a meeting at a later date. Wiser: keep circulating – aim to walk away with ten new names to add to your network.

6. **Focus on your transferable skills.** Fact: in jobsearch scenarios, most people ask one simple question: 'What do you do?'. Usual response: 'I'm a stock controller for a clothing manufacturer' (or whatever). Problem: unless that person is looking for a 'stock controller for a clothing manufacturer', the conversation is killed. Better: talk about the broad mix of skills, knowledge and experience that you've acquired – and explain how these can be used in a wide variety of circumstances. Better: 'I'm currently working with stock management; introducing a new computer program to simplify and speed up control systems; it can be applied universally to any industry.' Their response: 'How?' – you're now into a valuable conversation.

7. **Talk about what you can do for your contacts.** Truth: too many people concentrate on what they've done, are doing, and would like to do in the future. Important: your contacts are more interested in

themselves than in anyone else – so if you want them to help you, say what is in it for them. Example: 'This computer program could help your particular business in three main ways. First, ...' Bottom line: your contact has one primary concern: 'What's in it for me?' Tell them, and there'll be something in it for you too.

8. **Listen more than you speak; and ask questions.** Note: most of your business contacts will want to talk about their company, their products and their own career. Do: listen to them; it enables you to acquire more knowledge. If you're talking, you're only covering information about yourself – and you know all of that already. Core skill: people like people who listen to them; you'll get them on your side, will learn more – and find out what it is they want to know when it is your turn to speak. Helpful: encourage them to talk by raising questions. Example: 'What do you do that makes you successful in your job?' This generates valuable information; you'll see a pattern of successful attributes emerging, and can develop these in yourself; and promote them in future conversations.

9. **Always follow through on conversations.** Idea: ask a contact for further contacts; people that can help you, and vice-versa. Try for three names and telephone numbers. And: leave people with a reminder of you – but avoid handing out business cards like everyone else; most of these are mislaid by the end of the event. Instead: hand over an information sheet; about that exclusive product and what it can do for them. Essential: send a letter of appreciation after your meeting; it keeps the lines of communication open.

10. **Say 'thank you' to anyone who supports you in any way; offering leads, advice, information; any assistance at all.** Example: one executive got a job because a friend had cut out a feature about a company in an obscure trade magazine and forwarded it to them; they then made an approach to the MD featured in the article, and were subsequently employed on a freelance basis. So they designed a thank you note on their computer, printed it out as a poster, and sent it to that friend.

Key fact: people remember a 'thank you' more than anything else in business.

(Sources: PFC *editor Iain Maitland spoke to managers and directors in different trades and industries across the United Kingdom; all of whom had secured employment through their networking activities. This feature first appeared in* PFC *May 1998, No. 20.)*

THE BEST TIME TO BET ON FOOTBALL MATCHES

***PFC* tip:** last-minute betting is often most advantageous. Why: odds that are set in advance on fixed-odds coupons cannot take account of late changes and developments. Examples: managerial resignations and dismissals, injuries to key players. Outcome: this can give shrewd punters an edge over the bookmakers.

(Source: David Jones, a former bookies' employee from Surrey.)

HOW TO PICK THE MOST SUITABLE EQUIPMENT FOR A SUCCESFUL HOME OFFICE

If you're going to work from home, you'll want to know what equipment to buy for your office – here are your *PFC* top tips:

1. **Buy a computer with sufficient hard disk drive and memory so that programs can be installed and run properly now and during future business expansion.** Installation: a minimum 1Gb hard disk drive is needed. Why: Microsoft's Office 97 Professional software package requires almost 200Mb of hard disk space for complete installation. And: other office packages require similar amounts. Usage: a minimum of 32 megabytes of RAM is advisable, especially if you expect your business to grow.

2. **Choose a monitor screen with the largest viewing area, for comfort and easy reading.** Hint: take a tape measure with you to check screen sizes. Note: there is no industry standard for how monitor screen

sizes are measured. So: some 14" screens have more viewing area than 15" ones. Idea: find a (less expensive) 14"screen with a larger viewing area.

3. **Discover the cost of replacement cartridges before buying a printer.** Reason: some manufacturers sell their printers at a lower than usual profit margin in order to increase sales. Because: this boosts their user base for the replacement printer cartridges – and they can sell these at a huge mark-up as they have a captive market. They cannot lose – you either buy the cartridges or your printer is worthless. Best sources: the cheapest cartridges are available via mail order through magazines such as *Computer Buyer* and *PC Direct*.

4. **Buy a digital rather than an analogue cordless phone if your telephone conversations need to be kept private and confidential.** Why: like mobile phones, cordless phones are susceptible to eavesdropping. Buying a digital one minimises the risk of calls being monitored. Also: choose one that offers a 'scrambling' feature so eavesdroppers will hear only garbled noises. Note: digital phones cost around £100 more than analogue ones – a price worth paying if you want to maintain privacy.

5. **Don't use a 'call waiting' facility on telephone lines used by modem and facsimile machines.** Little-known fact: these devices exchange data using audio tones and the call waiting alert 'beep' can interfere with transmissions.

6. **Photocopy any faxes that need to be filed away in your permanent business records.** Important: faxes printed on thermal paper tend to fade after a period of time, typically within a few months.

7. **Buy a hands-free mobile phone for your car.** Reason: a hand-held mobile is distracting and can lead to accidents. Plus: recent legal cases have shown that you can go to jail if you have a road accident whilst using one. Prediction: expect laws to be passed during this parliament to prohibit their use in cars.

8. **Try to be available all of the time.** Common practice: some

home-based workers use their voicemail whilst working, and access messages later. Bottom line disadvantage: some callers do not like talking to machines and may go elsewhere; others could be offended by your lack of personal attention to their needs.

(Sources: Iain Maitland, PFC *editor, Mark Neely, business books author, plus additional research.)*

A PROVEN HERBAL REMEDY FOR A PERFECT NIGHT'S SLEEP

PFC tip: a very effective over-the-counter herbal remedy for insomnia is 'Passiflora Lehning' drops. Ingredients: avena sativa, passiflora, belladonna, secale and valerian. Proof: recent UK laboratory tests show that the herb valerian alone helped 44% of insomniacs to get 'a perfect night's sleep', whilst a staggering 89% reported 'improved sleep'.

(Source: Agora Lifestyles – call freephone 0500 523 499 for a free copy of the latest issue of any of their newsletters.)

HOW TO DEVELOP YOUR OWN SUPER MEMORY

Your brain is more powerful than any computer, and can store and recall far more material than you could ever use in your entire lifetime. All you have to do to develop an almost photographic memory is to learn how to retain information in a way that makes it easy to recall. Then you'll be able to remember every number, name, date or fascinating fact you ever heard or read. Here's the inside story on key areas and techniques:

Bulk information. Learning is most effective if you study for periods of 20 to 40 minutes interspersed by regular five-minute breaks. Then spend a couple of minutes thinking back over what you have just learned before going on to study the next section. Reviewing is important, and should be done regularly at increasingly long intervals.

First review: this should take place no more than an hour after the learning period. Second review: this should be carried out a day later. Third review: this should take place a week later. Reason: a full and proper review of any new information fixes it into your long-term memory; and makes it easier to recall at a later time.

Memory training. The four essentials are: 'association', 'visualisation', 'imagination' and 'sensation'. Association: stage performers use linking systems which associate the things they need to remember with objects or events. Visualisation: if you visualise what you want to remember, you will remember it far more easily than if you just try to file away a word. It also helps if you visualise something that is personal to you; especially if it is something you own or want to own. Example: don't think 'car', think 'Mercedes'. Imagination: the more imaginative you are, the easier it will be to remember. Make that Mercedes a vintage model, manufactured in the year your father was born. Sensation: as with imagination, the more sensational or bizarre your picture, the easier it will be to remember. Best: a 1930 Mercedes painted in shocking pink with big green blobs all over it.

Mind maps. These are a simple but effective method of note-taking, which show key thoughts in a round form rather than a straighforward list. How: start by putting the subject in the middle of a sheet of paper. Then write the main sub-headings around it in a circle. Draw lines from the centre to each sub-heading before adding more items in circles around the sub-headings. Tip: some people find it helpful to draw bubbles around each item. Next, re-draw your map to re-arrange things in a neater and more logical order – you'll also find that you can make the map more memorable simply by adding little pictures. Example: if your main subject was an apple, draw an apple in the middle of the page and write 'apple' in it. If a sub-heading was apple pie, draw a pie-shape, connect it to the apple with a line and connect your other thoughts ('with blackberries', 'deep-dish', 'cream' and so on) with lines to the pie. Outcome: to recall the whole mind map, think of the apple, and the other contents will come back to you.

The link system. This links items together by fitting them into a story. Example: you are going shopping to buy bread, bananas, eggs, pepper, paper tissues and face cream. Visualise yourself going into a supermarket. The only bread they have is such a big loaf that you can't see where you're going as you're walking along with it – so you don't spot the banana on the floor. You step on it, and go sliding down the aisle. You swerve to avoid hitting a display of eggs, and collide with a box of pepper that bursts open. This makes you sneeze so much that you grab some paper tissues to wipe your nose, but this makes it so sore that you have to find some face cream to soothe it. The more off-beat your story is, the more memorable it will be – exaggerate everything and add colours, sounds, and even smells. These help to make the system work. Movement and attachment are important as well, so make things crash into each other, pile them up, slot them together or make them open a mouth and speak the next word.

The Roman room system. Instead of making up a story around items to remember, associate each item with a feature in the room. Use a room in your own home and go round it in the same way. Example: the shopping list could involve the bread propping the door open, a monkey eating bananas on a chair in the hall, and a fried egg pinned to the kitchen door, which you then open to find that it has been booby-trapped with a jar of pepper. You reach for the paper tissues on top of the refrigerator to wipe your nose, and have to use more to wipe up the mess from a pot of face-cream melting on the cooker.

Numbers. All the systems for remembering numbers with more than seven digits work by breaking the number down into separate chunks and then giving a label to each of them. Best: the 'Number-Shape System' uses a set of images that never changes. You can choose your own images to make them meaningful to you, as long as they are the same shape as the number. For instance: 1 is the shape of a pencil, 2 is the shape of a swan, 4 is a sailing boat; and so on. If the number you want to remember is 214, you visualise a swan using a pencil to write on the side of that boat. Variations on this system are the 'Number-Rhyme

System' where 1 would be a bun, 2 a shoe, and 4 a door, so you visualise a bun in a shoe by a door; and the 'Meaningful Number System', where 1 is a broom because it has one handle, 2 is a pair shoes, 4 is a table because it has four legs; so you visualise a broom and a pair of shoes on a table.

Names. The main reason why someone forgets another person's name is because they weren't paying attention when they were introduced. They've failed to file the information in a memorable enough way to store it in their long-term memory bank. Remedy: when you meet someone new, repeat their name back to them. If you can do it without feeling embarrassed, ask how they spell it. Use the name again as soon as you can. Repeat it once more when you say goodbye to that person. Outcome: that name will be stored permanently in your memory's database.

Your personal items. People lose personal items such as their keys, spectacles or pen because they weren't paying attention when they put them down. Cure: create a special place for the items you misplace regularly. Make it a logical place and visualise it every time you come in to and go out of your home and/or office. Even if you didn't take your keys out with you, check to make sure they are still there.

(Sources: Alan Baddely, Your Memory, A User's Guide, *Tony Buzan,* How to Develop a Super Memory, *Michael W. Eynsenck,* Human Memory, Theory, Research & Individual Differences.)

HOW TO BECOME A FREELANCE CONSULTANT – AND INCREASE YOUR EARNING POWER

If you've always been employed, it is a big step to decide to go it alone as a freelancer. But the jobs market has been changing in recent years and more and more employers are now using freelance consultants to perform specific tasks for short periods rather than employing full-time, permanent staff and paying their wages, NI contributions, health insurance premiums, pensions and so forth. This is where you can make money on a part-time or even a full-time basis as you become more successful. You could even do the same work that you're doing today; but with more money, more freedom – and you'll not have to answer to line managers any more. Here's the inside information:

Finding a USP. To make a good living as a freelance consultant, you need to have what marketing people call a 'USP' or 'Unique Selling Point'. For a consultant, this usually means a rare and/or innovative skill. Example: a good example of a special skill involves the branch of consultancy that has developed in the field of quality control. Fact: there is a British Standard for quality control and it is intended that all of those companies which provide goods or services for the government should earn this BS recognition. Plus: many other large organisations have decided to achieve this as well. The requirements are rather vague, so anyone who understands them and can guide an organisation through them in order to achieve BS recognition is able to charge large fees for their expertise. If you have a similar skill of this rarity and value, then you should be able to succeed as a freelance consultant.

Starting up. You need to begin by setting up your new business in a professional manner. Arrange to pay self-employed NI contributions to the DSS. Inform the Inland Revenue of your new tax status. Register for VAT, if appropriate. Establish an office facility to write letters, send invoices, take messages and do basic accounting. Obtain good quality letterheads, brochures and business cards. Talk to your bank, local authority and small business associations to see if any grants are available for business start-ups in your area.

Promoting yourself. Job search consultants will tell you that the vast majority of white-collar jobs are found by networking – and the same applies to consultancy services. Compile a list of all the people you know in your industry. Write to tell them that you are now a consultant and will telephone them shortly to see how they are getting on. When you telephone, don't ask if there is any work for you – that's too blatant. Instead: wait until they ask what you are doing now, and then tell them.

If they say anything like 'We could do with someone like you here', mention that you'll be available soon, and ask who you should approach. If you're talking to someone you know well, you could ask if they know of any openings, but this is best done face to face. Arrange a lunchtime meeting, when it will be easier to sound them out. If you don't know them well enough for lunch, flatter them by asking for a half-hour meeting to seek their advice and who to approach next; ideally you want them to pave the way for your approach with an introductory phone call. And: they will not only keep you up-to-date with information on potential clients, but also bear you in mind as and when their own company needs help. Key fact: personal recommendations are the best way to build a client base.

Advertising yourself. You won't obtain all of your work through your network. To keep the money rolling in, you'll need to find other ways to get your name in front of people. Best: continuous, targeted mail-shots. Send out a small batch each week, so you start to generate a steady flow of work. Useful: refer to trade directories and professional membership listings, and telephone suitable organisations to check on the correct name and title of the person you want to contact. And: read the financial pages of newspapers and specialist magazines that cover your industry. Wise: look for news of companies moving, developing new products, being taken over; anything that could produce an opening for you. Then start your letter of enquiry by mentioning that you've seen the news and wonder if they need you. Tip: it helps if they know who you are before your letter arrives, so don't be shy about obtaining publicity for yourself. Wise: get into the habit of sending letters for publication to trade newspapers, and telephone the news editor to express your opinion on current events. If you do this regularly they will soon start to telephone you for quotes and describe you as a freelance consultant. Also: get some jobs lecturing or speaking at seminars, write articles on your subject for magazines or write a book. These activities have a three-fold benefit. They raise your profile, enhance your credibility – and allow you to increase your fees to match your status.

Making money. You'll probably want to earn at least as much as you are (or were) getting as an employee. But: bear in mind that you'll have to provide your own office facilities, car, holiday pay, health and pension cover, and other perks; so you'll need to generate more income than an employee just to cover these extras. Guideline: a 50% increase on an employee's annual salary is a good target figure. Tip: having arrived at an annual figure, break it down to a daily rate. Knowing what you want to earn each day helps you to price jobs at a profitable level. Note: you won't get paid for bank holidays, if you have a week off with flu, and you'll not finish one contract on a Friday and start another the following Monday. Calculate the actual number of days in the year when you could be at work, and divide that number into your desired annual income.

Handling contracts. You need to know exactly what you are to do; and achieve. Check where the work is to be carried out – if it is to be done on their premises, you'll need to specify what equipment is provided. If relevant, find out about the hours of work. See if you're expected to perform all of the work yourself or can sub-contract some of it. Essential: discover what information is to remain confidential, and for how long – and who owns the copyright of any written material. Also: see whether you are able to perform similar work for other clients. If not, find out when you can. Important: verify whether you can mention that you've worked for this client when promoting yourself. You'll also want to confirm how much you're being paid, whether this includes any expenses, and when you're being paid. Warning: the value of a service diminishes once it has been completed. You will find that it is always easier to get an initial payment than it is to obtain the final payout – some customers will find fault with what you have done, and raise a whole host of other reasons why they cannot pay. So: get all key terms and conditions confirmed in writing. Note: the agreement doesn't have to involve a formal, legal document. A letter is sufficient – and can be provided by you or your client. Idea: your letter might start with a comment like, 'This is my understanding of what we agreed at our meeting...' and could end with something along the lines of 'Please confirm your agreement.'

Working with your clients. You'll often find your concept of what needs to be done far exceeds what the client actually wants – and you'll have to tread the delicate line between professional integrity and the need to complete the contract and get paid. Typical: you are most likely to encounter a reluctance to spend enough money to do the job properly – in essence, many clients want 'something for nothing'. Wise: simply do the best you can with the time and resources available to you; and express your reservations as diplomatically as possible in your wind-up report. Also: expect to encounter some resentment from the client's permanent staff. Example: if you're setting up a new system and providing training which will benefit them in the future, all should be well. But: otherwise, there will always be some employees who think that you're doing a job they could have done. Unfortunate: what they don't realise is that their knowledge is too narrow, and that your added-value lies in your wider experience and broader perspective. Essential: get the employees on your side. Best: do this by asking for their help. Say that you need their in-depth knowledge; and ask for their ideas too. Flatter them if necessary; just make sure that they take the project on with some enthusiasm. If they feel a part of it, they'll become your best ambassadors.

Bottom line: never take your clients for granted. Tip: you may be convinced that there is a continuous supply of clients in the marketplace, but that doesn't mean you can afford to neglect your existing client base. If you do a good job on one project; you're more likely to be remembered next time they need another job doing. But: they probably won't have you in mind if you don't keep in touch with them on a regular basis. Core skill: add the key people you meet at each job to your network and stay in contact. How: telephone them at regular intervals to swap news of trade and industry developments, ask them for their opinion of any newsworthy events. It is essential that you keep up-to-date with your market; and working your network of contacts is the best way to do it. Example: if you're on friendly terms with people, they might send copies of technical information to you long before these details can be obtained through the conventional channels.

(Sources: Geoffrey Bellman, The Consultant's Calling – Bringing Who You Are to What You Know, *William A. Cohen,* How to Make it Big as a Consultant, *Peter K. Studner,* Super Job Search.*)*

HOW TO GET JUST ABOUT ANYTHING YOU WANT ABSOLUTELY FREE OF CHARGE

You can obtain lots of freebies if you know where to look, and what to do. Here are some of the easiest and best freebies that you can get in and around the United Kingdom:

Free food: people spend a fortune on food from health food shops – but much of it is produced from freely available wild plants. How: a little time spent studying a well-illustrated guide book on wild plants will tell you what you can eat and what to avoid, and will enable you to find plenty of tasty snacks to supplement your diet; and all for free. Examples: wild garlic grows by rivers and streams. The dried leaves of wild blackberries make an excellent tea substitute. If you prefer coffee, it can be made by roasting acorns. Dandelions fried in flour taste like mushrooms. Nettles can be used for spinach. Crab-apples mixed with elderberries make a delicious jam. Roast lamb will taste even more succulent with sauce made from wild mint. Caution: do not forage for food in the countryside without first getting the permission of the landowner.

Free magazines, newsletters and other publications: if you're thinking of subscribing to or advertising in a publication and want to check it out first, telephone the publisher's subscriptions and/or advertising department, and ask for a sample copy or what's known as a 'media pack'. This is a package that is sent out to prospective advertisers; and usually contains an advertising rate card, readership details, a copy of the current issue, and, more often than not, several back issues as well.

Free entertainment: there are many venues that offer entertainment for visitors without charge. Examples: the Sizewell Nuclear Power Station in Suffolk offers guided tours for visitors (01728 653653). The Houses of Parliament in London may be visited too – your local MP can arrange a guided tour, and get tickets for you to watch Prime Minister's Question Time. Details: write to your MP c/o the Houses of Parliament, Westminster, London SW1A 0AA; or look in your telephone directory under 'Members of Parliament' for the address and phone number of the local constituency office. The BBC and independent television companies and radio stations often record shows in front of live audiences. Tickets for these shows are free on application, simply by writing to the 'Ticket Unit' at the appropriate television company or radio station. Tip: ask to be put on the mailing lists for details of forthcoming recordings, request tickets well in advance, and enclose a first class, stamped addressed envelope to encourage a prompt response. Note: many game shows are recorded in blocks; so you may see three or four shows in the same visit – that'll give your whole family an experience to remember.

Free tourist information: when planning a foreign holiday, write to the tourist and cultural departments of the appropriate country's embassy in the United Kingdom. Typical: most of these are based in central London – call 'directory enquiries' for a contact number. You will be sent maps, guidebooks and other documentation free of charge; and these will contain the type of useful information that is normally only contained in expensive guidebooks.

Free buildings: long-term building projects such as office block developments are often managed and supervised from a group of Portakabin buildings located on the site of the works. These buildings are usually hired for the period, but are sometimes purchased outright by the developers, who will then often donate these buildings to local charities once the project has been completed. Idea: phone the property developer and ask if they plan to dispose of any buildings on completion of the work. If so, the chances are that they'll give you free, long-term use of a building; you'll probably have to pay for its collection, which may involve the hiring of a lorry to transport it to a new location – but this will only be a fraction of what the building would normally cost.

Free land: a common method of acquiring land is by 'annexing' it. Example: you may have some wasteland at the bottom of your garden. If you extended your fence to cover it, then you may be entitled to claim it as your own after a 12-year period has elapsed. Why: the almost forgotten Statute of Limitations Act of 1977 forbids any claims to be made against you by the owner of the land after 12 years. But: note that at any time during those 12 years, the owner could reappear with a writ to order you off their land. And: you must try and trace the landowner during the period and be able to show a court that you have done so – but if they cannot be found, you can then apply to a court to have the land registered to you. Best advice: the final stages should be dealt with by a solicitor.

PFC **advice:** even when you have to pay for goods and services, aim to achieve a better price; a discount of 10% or more should be achieved by haggling. In some countries, haggling over the price of goods is considered perfectly normal. And in others, it is common practice to give customers a free gift if they spend above a certain amount. Nowadays, more British shopkeepers are prepared to haggle to win business – particularly if they are surrounded by lots of competitors. But: do be aware that traders who allow haggling will expect you to honour your part of the bargain; and pay up straightaway. So: never start haggling until you are ready to purchase the goods there and then. Best: London's Tottenham Court Road is the top place to haggle for electronic and computer goods; get brand new hi-fis, computers and cameras at substantial discounts.

(Sources: Richard Mabey, Food For Free, Lofty Wiseman, The SAS Survival Handbook, British Rate and Data. *The Free Land article appeared in* PFC *Aug 1997, No. 11.)*

WHY EATING SALAD MAY NOT BE GOOD FOR YOU

***PFC* tip:** we're always being told that eating lots of fruit and vegetables is good for our health – but it's not really that simple! Truth: although fruit and vegetables aren't actually bad for you, some are much better for your health than others. Examples: lettuce and cucumber contain virtually no vitamins or minerals at all – whereas broccoli, carrots and tomatoes are full of them. So: don't make the mistake of thinking that a salad is always a healthy meal – it's not necessarily that good for you at all. And if it's served with cheese and/or covered with mayonnaise or other dressings, it will probably contain far more fat than that lasagne you'd have preferred to have eaten.

(Source: Agora Lifestyles – phone freephone 0500 523 499 for a free copy of the latest issue of any of their newsletters.)

OUTSMART PETTY THIEVES AND STAY SAFE ABROAD

Holidaymakers are often targeted by criminals who know that they'll be carrying money and other valuables around with them. Here's how you can reduce the chances of becoming a victim:

Don't leave your belongings unattended in airports, hotels or restaurants. Carry your own luggage and load it yourself into a taxi. When registering at a hotel, don't put your briefcase or hand luggage on the floor – these are a perfect target for a quick grab. When coming and going fom your hotel room, lock your doors and windows – especially those leading to the balcony. When eating in the hotel restaurant, don't place your key on the table – a thief can note your room number and burgle it whilst you are eating. Never let an unexpected person into your room even if they appear to be hotel staff – check with reception before you open the door. Carry as little cash as possible – put the balance in the hotel safe; and get a receipt. Don't carry your cash, passport and credit cards in the same place. Keep cash in a money belt or deep in your front pockets – pickpockets go for purses and back pockets first as these are the easiest targets. When shopping, don't put your bags down on the ground when reaching for your money – these can be snatched easily and swept away into the crowd. Don't carry your passport unless you need it. Never walk alone and aimlessly in public places – this marks you out as a prime target for a thief.

(Source: International Living *newsletter published by Agora Lifestyles – call freephone 0500 523 499 for a free copy of the latest issue.)*

THE MALE CANCER THAT CAN STRIKE WOMEN

***PFC* alert:** prostate cancer can affect both men; and women. Fact: a tiny minority of women have very rudimentary prostate glands; which is the reason why they may have detectable levels of 'prostate-specific antigen' in their blood. This 'PSA' is a marker for prostate cancer.

(Source: Armed Forces Institute of Pathology, Washington, USA.)

BE A SELF-EMPLOYED INVESTIGATOR – EARN A GOOD LIVING DOING FASCINATING WORK

Private investigators deal mainly with tracing missing persons, accident investigations, checking possible insurance frauds, serving legal papers, matrimonial work, domestic and industrial surveillance, tracing debtors and debt collection, status reports and repossessions. Here are three money-making a private investigator:

Solicitors: most jobs come from solicitors, who are too busy to do outside work themselves. Note: they usually pay a fixed fee for each type of job, such as £35 to serve a set of papers on someone. Process serving: this involves handing court papers or other official documentation to the people named in these documents. Your client will hand you certain papers, and your job is to 'serve' these on the named individual, in person. After serving the papers, you then have to swear an affidavit to say that you have done so. You type out the affidavit yourself, stating that you did, on such and such a day, and in a certain place and at a certain time, serve the named person with the papers. Then you go to a solicitor other than the one who instructed you (or a commissioner for oaths), and sign the affidavit and swear that its contents are true. The solicitor/ commissioner also signs it, and it becomes admissible evidence in a court of law.

Insurance companies: these are another good source of regular work. Insurance enquiries: many people submit inflated and fake insurance claims. Example: someone is claiming a large sum of money for an industrial injury to their leg; and the insurance company suspects that a fraud is being committed. The insurance company would employ you to check this out. You will need to photograph or preferably video the claimant's activities and present this with your report so that the insurance company can consider the claim. You may also be asked to report on accidents. This involves interviewing witnesses at the scene of the accident, preparing scale drawings and/or taking photographs of the site. The information is then used by the insurance companies to apportion liability and decide on the amount to pay out.

Large commercial organisations: any business that has a large base of customers who pay on a deferred basis will have an ongoing problem with debtors trying to delay or avoid payment altogether. The larger the organisation, the more likely they are to use in-house legal staff and they will have many tasks which need doing, similar to those which will be offered to you by high street solicitors. They will have a fixed fee for these jobs. Wise: if you advertise in the *Yellow Pages* and/or in your local papers, you will also receive private instructions, often for matrimonial work or locating missing relatives. You can set your own fees for this work; the normal method is to charge an hourly rate plus expenses, with an 'up-front' retainer. If the job is likely to be prolonged, it is wise to present bills for part-payments at regular intervals.

(Source: PFC *editor Iain Maitland spoke informally to solicitors, private investigators and debt collection agencies across the United Kingdom.)*

OWN A FABULOUS FRENCH PROPERTY FOR AS LITTLE AS £4,500

In France, a Provencal house means Provencal prices, but the PFC team of researchers has found areas that have all of the charm of that fashionable area of southern France; and at a fraction of the price! Where: west of the Rhone Valley lies the plateau of Massif Central. You can find a tumbledown cottage there for as little as Fr40,000 (£4,500). Restored farmhouses start at only Fr230,000 (£25,600). And for a maison de maitre with stables and outbuildings, expect to pay from as little as Fr650,000 (£72,200). Recommended reading: *Your Second Home in Europe* by Cheryl Taylor, published by Agora Lifestyles.

(Sources: International Living *newsletter and* Your Second Home in Europe *published by Agora Lifestyles Limited. Phone 0500 523 499 for a free copy of the latest issue of* International Living *.)*

YOUR COMPREHENSIVE GUIDE TO CONQUERING BACK PAIN

Back pain can come on in a couple of hours, take weeks to subside, and just when you think it is better, it returns, twice as painful as before. Almost as frustrating is the way that some doctors look at your back, prescribe painkillers and tell you, 'there's nothing you can do about back pain'. Fact: this is simply not true. Medical practitioners of various kinds can treat back pain successfully, and by changing your habits, you can do even more than they can to prevent it recurring. Here are the prevention techniques taught by Britain's top private specialists:

Standing: stand tall, but don't be too rigid about it. Important: distribute the weight of your body evenly to each foot. Bend your knees very slightly and pull in the base of your spine. Useful: a good exercise is to hold up a book in front of your face until you feel your head tilting backwards slightly and your eyes gazing slightly downwards.

Walking: aim for a 'military bearing', with your shoulders back, chest forward and stomach in. But: do not lean forward. Helpful: when walking, consciously stretch your back all the way up to your neck. Avoid sudden changes of direction, especially ones that involve twisting your trunk. And: choose suitable footwear – the limp caused by a blister or a corn from an ill-fitting shoe can throw your back out of alignment.

Lifting: never bend over when lifting a heavy object. Avoid using your back; let your legs do the work, because your leg muscles are far stronger than your back muscles. If possible, break down the load into smaller pieces. Get as close to the object as possible. Place your feet either side of it. Bend your knees and squat down, keeping your back straight. Grasp the object firmly and stand up by straightening your knees.

Sitting: choose a well-designed chair – one that is firm, rather than softly-upholstered. Essential: a flat, horizontal seat that meets the back of the chair at a right angle or more. And: the chair should be a height that enables your hips and knees to bend at right angles and your feet to rest on the ground. Typical: for a person of average height, the seat should be 18-19" off the ground. Important: the back should be at least as high as your shoulder-blades, and the arms at least seven inches above the seat. Next: to sit properly, push the base of your spine into the back of the chair. Useful: use a small, sausage-shaped cushion or a rolled-up towel to support your back, if necessary. Don't sit in the same position for too long. When getting up from an easy chair, support as much of your body weight as you can by grasping the arms of the chair. Desk work: your office chair should allow you to sit with your back straight and your forearms resting on the desk. Normal: for a person of average height, the seat should be about 18-19" high, with the desk at about 27-28" from the floor. Tip: if you're going to be typing most of the time, have the desk about two inches lower than this.

Driving: ideally, the seat should be firmly-sprung, with side sections that provide lateral support. It should extend as far forward as the back of your calves (at least 21") and be 11-12" above your heels when they're using the pedals. Key fact: the higher the back of the seat, the better. Helpful: fit a head-rest if you can. And: a lumbar support cushion will improve any car seat too. Idea: if you spend a lot of time driving, it's probably worth buying an orthopaedic seat designed especially for you. Tip: on long journeys, stop the car, get out and walk around at least every two hours.

Sleeping: if you wake up with back pain, your bed is probably too soft. Mattress: if the mattress is sagging in the middle, buy a new, firmer one – ideally, pick an orthopaedic one that is designed specially for your condition. Bed: if the bed is sagging, put boards or even an old door under the mattress; making sure that this support stretches from the head to the foot of the bed. Alternative: try putting the mattress on the floor. Note: your sleeping position is also important – sleep flat on your back without a pillow and take extra care when getting in and out of bed.

(Sources: PFC *editor Iain Maitland spoke off-the-record to bed and back specialists including The British Chiropractice Association, 0118 9505950, The Chartered Society of Physiotherapy, 0171-242 1941, the National Back Pain Association, 0181-977 5474, The National Bed Federation, 0171-589 4888, The Osteopathic Helpline, 01491 875255).*

TOTAL SELF-CONFIDENCE – EASY-TO-FOLLOW TACTICS TO BANISH NERVES

Most people want to conquer their nerves so they can face the world with a new-found confidence. But: deep down, they have a vein of scepticism that holds them back; they feel that any attempts to change are doomed to fail. Great news: it doesn't have to be like this. You can change if you really want to; all you need is the desire to succeed, and some guidance.

1. **Personalise the message.** Scenario: you will have seen books that promise to 'change your life forever'; you may have read and benefited from them. But: many people find that any beneficial effects of such motivational literature are fleeting, and the message is soon forgotten. Why: they do not 'personalise' what they read or hear because they don't really believe that the message was meant for them. Result: they make only a half-hearted effort to act upon it.

2. **Establish desire and belief.** Ask yourself two key questions. A: 'Am I satisfied with things as they are?'. B: 'Do I want to change anything in my life?'. Important: if your answers are 'no' and 'yes' respectively, you have the desire to change. Next: remember that new resolutions don't have to be made only on 1 January; you can take the decision to make a fresh start any time you want. Fact: most people identify personal shortcomings and/or missed opportunities and decide immediately that it's too late to do anything about them. But: these are rash assessments – it's never too late to change; and if you can embrace the belief that you can change, you're on your way to a happier, relaxed life.

3. **Recognise your self-confidence.** Problem: a lack of faith is often triggered off by the competitive world around us; which leads to fears and negative feelings. Examples: a fear of embarrassment, rejection and/or failure, the inability to handle situations, a lack of self-esteem. Truth: self-confidence is not something that people are either born with or without; it's simply a product of your present state of mind. And: self-confidence is available to you if you really want it.

4. **Face up to your fears.** Most fears are irrational. So: if you adopt a rational approach, you'll conquer them. How: list your fears; anything from spiders to public speaking. Next: go through the list, writing out your reasons for each fear. Then: confront your list in a rational manner, and see how irrational these fears really are – now you can begin to eliminate these negative elements.

5. **Exorcise your fears.** How: sit or lie comfortably in a quiet room, close your eyes and visualise your mind as a video recorder. On your

mental video, play a tape showing each of your fears in turn. After playing each section of the tape, rewind and wipe that part clean in your mind. Then play the tape again and – if it hasn't been wiped – repeat the process again, and until the tape is clean.

6. **Learn to relax:** if you relax for a few minutes each day, you'll find that this will help you to combat stress and anxiety. Exercise: beginning with your feet – and then focusing on one part of your body at a time – tense your muscles, hold the tension for several seconds and then release it. As you relax each muscle, visualise the tension flowing out of it. Move up your body, from your toes to your calves, to your thighs and buttocks, to your stomach, shoulders, neck, arms and hands. Complete the exercise by tensing and relaxing the muscles around your mouth and eyes. Helpful: devote a few minutes to this each day – and it will soon be triggered automatically at stressful times.

7. **Define new problems as they arise.** Typical: you'll be aware that you need to take action over some of the things that you're unhappy about. Examples: being less critical of people around you, adopting a healthier lifestyle. But: many self-judgements are subjective; based on perception rather than reality. Example: negative feelings about your personal appearance. These can be eliminated by adopting a more positive approach towards them. Best: change your approach to the world in general; from one that's predominantly reactive to one where you initiate and set things in motion – in essence, take charge of your life.

8. **Take control.** Fact: the human mind can become a strait-jacket for feelings and emotions; and people sometimes feel powerless to do anything about this. However: break free by recognising the natural tendency that everyone has to centre their thoughts on themselves as if they are the focus of everyone else's attention. Truth: we all attach far too much importance to what other people think of us. It's as if we think that everything we do or say is being studied closely; whereas other people are too busy with their own daily lives to be over-concerned about us.

9. Clear your mind. Another by-product of this 'strait-jacket syndrome' is that it allows more into our minds than it lets out. It can cause our brains to become cluttered up with innumerable little problems that we're reluctant to deal with. Analogy: it's like having masses of unanswered mail piling up in an overflowing in-tray. And: the longer we leave things like this, the more reluctant we are to deal with the problem, and the worse we feel about it. Skill: if you can identify this trait in yourself, you'll also know that there is no better time to start tackling it than right now.

(Sources: PFC *health and personal development experts.)*

LITTLE-KNOWN VITAMINS THAT CAN PROTECT YOUR BODY FROM DISEASE

US scientists have discovered the villain that may be responsible for ageing, heart disease, strokes, arthritis, some allergies and a host of other ailments – the villain is oxygen, the very element we need to breathe in order to survive. Details: oxygen becomes harmful when it turns into 'free radicals'. These attack the cells in our body. And the more free radicals our body contains, the more damage they do. Causes: the number of free radicals in our bodies are increased by stress, smoking, pollution, chlorine and even some of the foods that we eat. Good news: it is relatively easy to combat free radicals. We now know that large doses of 'antioxidants' can help to neutralise the damage done. Antioxidants include vitamins A, C, E, beta-carotene and selenium. These vitamins and minerals are found in our food, but not in sufficiently large amounts to work at their full potential. To get the full antioxidant effect, simply take high dosage vitamin and mineral supplement tablets. But: do stick to the dosage recommended on the packet. Very large overdoses of some supplements can be toxic; although you can take almost as much vitamin C as you wish.

(Source: Agora Lifestyles – phone freephone 0500 523 499 for a free copy of the latest issue of any of their newsletters.)

THE SECRETS OF EXAM SUCCESS – GET 'A' GRADES EVERY TIME

If you're sitting academic or professional examinations, you'll want to know how to achieve the best possible results. Here are the secrets of examination specialists around the United Kingdom:

1. **Read through the whole paper from start to finish**. Fact: too many candidates begin work straightaway; and make fundamental errors because of this. Examples: a compulsory question is left unanswered, too few or too many questions are tackled. Better: allow yourself a full five minutes to note the length of the examination, any compulsory questions, the number of questions to be answered and from which sections they are to be taken, and the finishing time. Also: re-check the precise instructions. Note: examination instructions do change, and teachers sometimes fail to pass on this information.

2. **Don't search for expected or favourite questions.** Why: failing to find them may be disheartening, and can put you in a negative mood towards the examination. Wiser: read through the paper not expecting to see the questions you want to appear. And: expect it to be difficult to find enough questions to answer. Reason: this will make you study each question more carefully. And: you're more likely to have your hopes raised than dashed – putting you in a more positive frame of mind towards the entire paper.

3. **Pay close attention to exactly what each question is asking.** Important: many people make an immediate assessment about the meaning of a question – and find themselves providing an inappropriate answer. Typical: a person's anxiety to find a certain topic leads to a particular word or phrase being spotted in a question which is then assumed to be about their favourite topic. Example: someone who has revised 'change management' for a Business Studies examination may see the word 'change' in a question and assume it's the topic they want. Outcome: other, more appropriate questions are ignored because they

don't contain a specific word or phrase. Sensible: underline all the key words in questions. Biology examination question: 'Give an account of the digestion, absorption and use of carbohydrates'. Because: it ensures you read all of the questions properly and note exactly what is being asked. Tip: simply worded questions are not always the easiest to attempt. Those questions that require careful reading can be easier to answer once they have been understood; often they break down into several, easy-to-manage sections.

4. **Schedule your time.** Advisable: divide your time according to the marks allocated per question rather than the number of questions you have to answer. Why: you are here to score as many marks as possible; so adopt a 'marks-orientated' approach in your planning. Useful; jot down the anticipated finishing time for each question; and stick to it. Note: spending an extra ten minutes struggling to provide a clever conclusion to a tricky question is likely to generate fewer marks than completing part of another, new question. Helpful: schedule in some checking time at the end of the examination so you can look back over your answers to see if you have included everything. Ideal: ten minutes should be sufficient for this purpose.

5. **Choose your 'best' question to tackle first; the one that you can answer most fully and obtain the highest marks.** Tip: this acts as a confidence booster to launch you into the examination. Do: study the question again; and decide how you will answer it. Pointer: there are certain key words in every question that tell you the type of question it is and the approach that is required. Examples: 'analyse' means describe, examine and criticise in detail; 'comment on' – offer your opinion; 'demonstrate' – show how and prove with examples; 'discuss' – argue the case for and against; 'explain' – make something clearer; 'outline' means give a brief summary, but without detail.

6. **Plan out your answers before writing them. How: use brief notes to outline an answer to a question.** Include: main ideas, important details, quotes and examples. Example: in that question on

carbohydrates, you might list points under the headings of 'digestion', 'absorption' and 'uses'. Why: this helps to clarify your thoughts into a logical order. When: do it at the start of the examination – you'll be able to record the largest amount of information whilst your mind is still fresh. And: it removes the anxiety that you will forget something if you leave it until later on. Plus: it gives you notes to fall back on if you're under pressure, and can provide a few extra marks if you run out of time and cannot complete all of your answers. Trick: don't let yourself get stuck on a stubborn answer – move on and come back to it later; you'll find your subconscious mind will start providing ideas for you during the examination.

7. **Stick to a standardised essay format; where appropriate.** Beginning: your introduction should set out where your essay is going. Caution: avoid the common mistake of repeating the question and/or providing detailed background explanations; you'll receive no marks for this. Middle: this should comprise the main facts in a sensible order. Be precise and specific, and give examples to back up your comments; these usually score extra marks. Steer clear of generalisations and repetition. End: your conclusion should normally summarise the main points and answer the question in a coherent and logical manner. Tip: don't spend too long worrying about thought-provoking introductions and conclusions – the bulk of the marks are allocated to the middle bit; and those key facts.

8. **Be business-like about multiple-choice questions.** Re-read the instructions and follow them precisely. Why: your paper may be marked by a computer that can read underlined answers but not circled ones. And: check to see if incorrect answers are penalised. If they are, work through the paper and fill in all the 'definites', make informed guesses for the 'maybes' and leave the remaining questions unanswered. If incorrect answers aren't penalised, guess at the 'don't knows' – you've nothing to lose, and everything to gain. Remember: if there are five choices, the law of averages will give you a 20% score, or four marks out of every 20 – which could represent the difference between one grade and a higher one.

9. **Pay more attention to legibility than writing style.** Legibility: your handwriting needs to be clear and readable. Why: you will not be penalised deliberately for illegible writing – but examiners are only human and will be irritated by it; not least because it will take them longer to read and mark your paper. Put them in a favourable mood towards you – it may help; especially if they're unsure whether to give you a '3' or a '4' out of '5' for a particular answer. Tactic: improve legibility by spacing out your writing, avoiding loops that overlap above and below lines and ensuring that no two letters look exactly the same. Style: this is only really a key factor in English Language and Literature examinations. Otherwise: write in short, direct and simple sentences. Reason: you're scoring marks for putting across certain points; not for how you phrase them.

10. **Change tactics for the last half-an-hour; if necessary.** What: if you're running out of time, divide what's left between questions. Fact: it is easier to gain five marks from brief answers to the last few questions than an extra five by adding material to the one question you are currently working on. Common: two, half-answered questions will usually gain more marks than one fully-answered one. And: with ten minutes left, revert to an emergency technique. What: use those brief notes that you made at the beginning of the examination as a skeleton answer to a question – easy-to-read, comprehensible notes will always gain a few marks for you. Why: examining boards lay down criteria for marking brief notes; albeit on a reduced scale. And those few extra marks may make all the difference between a 'B' and an 'A' grade.

(Source: David Acres is a learning support tutor who specialises in study and examination skills. He is the author of How to Pass Exams without Anxiety, *published by How To Books Limited. For more information about the book, phone the publishers on 01865 793806. This feature first appeared in* PFC *May 1998, No.20.)*

HOW TO PROTECT YOUR PARENTS' LIFE SAVINGS FROM EXORBITANT NURSING HOME FEES

Many older people have had to use their life savings to pay for nursing and residential care; and some have even been forced to sell their own homes as well. But such scenarios can be avoided with advance planning. This is what needs to be done:

Problem: more and more elderly people have been going into nursing and/or residential care homes since 1993. Why: legislation shifted the burden of 'care' from the State to local authorities; NHS hospitals then cut down on long-term care beds, and patients occupying these beds were transferred to homes funded by the local authorities. Note: in an NHS hospital, patients are treated free of charge; but when they're moved into a local authority home, that authority is duty-bound to seek to recover the costs of that care from those patients who have assets above certain levels. And: this usually means that any savings in excess of £16,000 (and this can include the value of their own home in some instances) can be taken to help pay for care. Important: local authorities group assets into two categories when assessing how much someone should pay for care. 'Countable assets': all forms of money, stocks and shares, savings and possibly even a house, flat or whatever. These are taken into account. Other assets: personal jewellery, furniture, motor cars etc. These are disregarded.

Solution: convert 'countable' assets into those other forms of assets that are not taken account of in the assessment process. And: consider giving away assets to those relatives and friends who would inherit them in due course. Also: use savings to buy some life assurances to 'compensate' your loved ones on your death; and reduce your savings too! Plus: think about sharing ownership of your home with other family members; or even arrange for it to be given away; and then rent it back. Note: many of these measures will need to be carried out some time before someone goes into care – typically five years – otherwise, the local authority can claim that there was either a 'deliberate deprivation of assets' or 'reckless spending'; and if this can be proved, the assets in question might still be treated as countable assets. Vital: discuss these ideas with a solicitor who will provide appropriate advice on your personal circumstances.

(Source: Bill Habets, How to Protect Your Life Savings against Nursing Home Costs *and* The Government Benefits Handbook. *This feature first appeared in* PFC *November 1996, No. 3.)*

WHY YOUR DENTAL FILLINGS COULD BE MAKING YOU ILL

Evidence is mounting that mercury dental fillings could be a major factor in more than 30 medical conditions. ME, Multiple Sclerosis, Alzheimer's, infertility, headaches, stomach problems and allergies – they've all been linked with those silvery metal fillings. British and American dental societies may tell you that you've no cause for concern – but here are the facts: Dental expert Hal Higgins conducted a study of 2,000 patients with ME-like symptoms of fatigue; and found that 90% of them improved when their mercury fillings were replaced. The improvement figure for MS sufferers was 85%. Alzheimer's patients have discovered that after their fillings were removed, their symptoms decreased or even disappeared. And: autopsies carried out on Alzheimer's sufferers with mercury dental fillings at the University of Kentucky have shown that extremely high levels of mercury existed in their blood streams.

In tests on immunity – the body's natural ability to resist infection and disease – it has been revealed that the number of T-cells that are so vital to successful immunity are increased by up to 300% when amalgam fillings are removed. In a consolidated report of six separate studies of patients who had their amalgam fillings replaced, nearly all of the 1,600 participants reported an improvement in or a cure of 31 types of condition; including Multiple Sclerosis, headaches, migraines, gastrointestinal and urinary tract problems and allergies. And: in other research studies, mercury fillings have also been linked with infertility, Candida, eczema and asthmas.

***PFC* remedy:** if you're worried that your fillings may be causing health problems, you can have a simple test to determine whether or not they are making you ill. If so, you can have them removed. Information: the British Society for Mercury-Free Dentistry, 0171-736 4145.

(Source: What Doctors Don't Tell You, *the newsletter that is dedicated to revealing little-known and hidden medical secrets to the public; including the dangerous side effects of common drugs. Contact: 0171-354 4592. This feature first appeared in* PFC *October 1996, No. 2.)*

ACHIEVE SUPER LEVELS OF CONCENTRATION – A SIMPLE TECHNIQUE TO FOCUS YOUR THOUGHTS

***PFC* tip:** Here's the best way of blocking out distracting thoughts when you're trying to concentrate. Shut your eyes and visualise a 'stop' sign – see the word 'stop' flashing on and off. Say 'stop' over and over again in time with that flashing sign. Clench your hand into a fist and contract your muscles as you say 'stop'. Repeat this process as and when necessary.

(Source: Maureen Reynolds, a PFC *subscriber from Sussex.)*

NINE CRAFTY SECRETS FOR LOOKING LIKE A MILLIONAIRE – ON A SHOESTRING BUDGET

1. **Stick to one colour – and make your clothes work hard for you.** Example: if you choose 'blue', you can go for navy, aquamarine, palest blue – the varieties are almost limitless. And: this way, you know that your clothes will always co-ordinate with each other; and you'll get

more mileage from all of them. Best: certain colours always look more expensive than others, whatever the fabric – black, navy, dark brown and beige. Worst: baby pink, bright pink and turquoise look cheaper than others, whatever their fabric – you'll get everyone's attention, but for all the wrong reasons. Tip: look at photographs of rich and fashionable people, and you'll see that they're nearly always wearing black. Because: it has a slimming effect, and looks classy. Idea: wear a colourful scarf around your neck. Evenings: choose an outfit in black, cream or a subtle neutral colour – you can wear it time and again with different jewellery and scarves, and it won't be recognised.

2. **Go for classic clothes every time – they'll last for more than one season and never look dated.** Good: black polo-necks, white cotton or linen shirts without frills or embroidery, chinos, plain beige raincoats, faded blue jeans, grey flannels, camel coats, navy blazers – all timeless classics that look wonderful whether you're 18 or 80. And: they look more expensive than they are. Avoid: exaggerated shoulderpads, frills, embroidery, three quarter length sleeves and all the latest fashion gimmickry – and you can wear your classics collection in ten years' time and still look good.

3. **Remember quality not quantity is all-important.** Ask any French or Italian woman – they'd rather have one beautiful and expensive garment than three cheap ones. Reason: you're much better off with one dress that looks expensive and makes you feel wonderful, than with three that look cheap, and make you feel that way too.

4. **Learn the key do's and don'ts of buying clothes.** Tip: certain clothes are almost the same whether they're bought at a market stall, Marks & Spencer or a top designer store – jeans, plain cotton or linen shirts and basic knitwear. Just wash market stall buys more carefully. High street cheats: chain store basics look great – if you take ten minutes to revamp them. Idea: cheap-looking buttons are a giveaway – replace them with something unusual. And: re-sew puckered, machine-stitched hems by hand. Also: avoid noticeable patterns – these tell people where

you bought it. Warning: the one thing you mustn't skimp on is accessories. Cheap shoes and handbags always look just that: cheap. Better: bide your time until the sales, and then snap up some top-quality shoes and bags.

5. **Be shop-savvy.** You shouldn't ever pay the full price for anything. Wait until the January and summer sales. Scan through the papers for one-off sample sales and shop clearances. Keep an eye open and check your *Yellow Pages* for nearly new and secondhand designer sale shops in your area. And try charity shops in upmarket areas.

6. **Repair clothes on an 'as necessary' basis.** Fact: you don't want to find that the one thing you need to wear is crumpled or has a button missing. So: instead of hanging up something that's creased or stained and forgetting about it until next time, put it in a 'to repair' bag. Outcome: you'll spend far less time on your clothes than you would if you had to run around at the last moment ironing or scrubbing off grubby marks.

7. **Be realistic when you buy your clothes.** Essential: if you're budgeting carefully, don't choose anything that's labelled 'dry clean only' – you'll either spend a small fortune at the dry cleaners or shrink the clothes when you're trying to handwash them. Important: if you have young children or commute every day on dirty buses and trains, don't choose pastels. And: if you hate ironing, don't go for linen clothes – you'd be better off with wool or cotton knits.

8. **Learn the strategies of successful shopping.** Don't shop in a lunchbreak or at any other time that you're in a hurry – you won't allow enough time to make the right choice. Key skill: however persuasive the salesperson is, don't let them pressurise you into buying anything you're unsure of. You can always ask them to hold something for half an hour, and then go off for a cup of coffee to think it over. And: always ignore that plaintive 'It's the last one in your size' – you'll find that they almost always have one more in the stockroom if you come back later on. Note: too many sales assistants work on commission, and will say you look

wonderful no matter what you're trying on. So: go shopping with a friend who'll tell you what does and – as important – doesn't suit you. Never succumb to sales fever. It doesn't matter if it cost £200 and is now reduced to £20 – if you don't really need it and it's not your style, it's not a bargain.

9. **Plan ahead.** We've all got up late, thrown on the first clothes that are close at hand, walked halfway down the street and realised we look awful – and there's still the rest of the day to get through. Best: on a quiet Sunday afternoon, go through your entire clothes collection, pack up anything you haven't worn for two years and give it to your local charity shop. Alternative: keep it in a box until it becomes fashionable again. Next: try on everything that's left and decide what looks good together, right down to the shoes and the accessories. Then: write it all out so you have at least seven outfits – enough to get you through a week. Bottom line: next time you stumble out of bed, all you have to do is open your notebook, put on the outfit you've listed, and get up and go!

(Sources: PFC *researchers spoke to fashion designers, chain store buyers, retail staff and shoppers around the United Kingdom.)*

HOW TO GET GUARANTEED RETURNS FROM YOUR UNIT TRUSTS

***PFC* tip:** the best unit trusts to choose are 'tracker funds' that follow (or 'track') the FT-SE All Share Index. Why: only a very small minority of fund managers manage to outperform this; which means that almost everyone does considerably worse. Don't take the risk. Instead: go for a tracker fund that buys exactly the same shares as the Index – which has returned 107% over the past 5 years. Best buys: 'Gartmore' and 'Virgin' – no initial charges, 1% annual charges, excellent returns. Bonus: if you wrap up the tracker funds in a ISA, you'll get your growth tax-free.

(Source: PFC *financial expert, Nigel Bolitho, BV Services. Tel: 01954 251521.)*

HARNESS THE POWER OF YOUR MENSTRUAL CYCLE – AND MAKE EVERY DAY THE RIGHT TIME OF THE MONTH

You can improve your love life, career and everything, simply by tuning in to the rhythms of your menstrual cycle; or your partner's. Here's how:

1. **Banish negative associations of the term 'menstrual cycle'.** Test: ask people what it means to most women and men; and you'll inevitably be met with groans and disparaging remarks about 'the curse', 'the wrong time of the month', and so on. Better: compose a mental list of all of the positive aspects that you can think of – going to bed early with a good book during menstruation, for example. Try it – and surprise yourself at the length of that list.

2. **Begin completing a diary charting your personal highs and lows throughout each month.** Markers: your health, powers of concentration, energy levels, sociability, patience levels, creativity, your sexuality, emotional frame of mind, and how much and what you eat. Typical: women often crave chocolate in the days leading up to ovulation. Note: within a couple of months, you'll see a pattern emerging.

3. **Link your personal pattern to the different phases of your menstrual cycle.** Phases: 'pre-ovulation', 'ovulation', 'pre-menstrual' and 'menstrual' – each phase brings different highs and lows. Pre-ovulation: positivity, creativity and mental agility. Ovulation: drive, confidence and increased sexual desire. Pre-menstrual: mood and energy swings, frustration, cravings. Menstruation: a sense of calm, a desire to withdraw.

4. **Understand your hormones; or those of your partner.** Day 1 (of the period): oestrogen levels are at their lowest. Day 5 onwards: oestrogen levels rise and are released into the bloodstream as period comes to an end. Your mood begins to lift; and you feel less stressed. Day 14 (at ovulation): oestrogen levels peak; you feel high and your short-term memory and

mental agility are both excellent. Testosterone levels also peak with ovulation; and sexual drive may become aggressive – it's nature's last chance to get you pregnant this month. Day 22: oestrogen levels fall, progesterone – a natural depressant – begins to rise; and the lining of the uterus begins to thicken. Emotional swings start to occur. Day 25: progesterone peaks and oestrogen falls rapidly; bringing low energy levels. Day 28: oestrogen and progesterone levels reach their lowest levels, the uterus lining is shed, and menstruation is ready to begin over again.

5. **Mark 'Day 14' on your calendar; and work in your important personal, career and business plans around it.** Why: recent UK and US studies have both shown that women peak at their mid-cycle point; they score higher marks in written examinations and achievement tests at that time; and turn in top performances in athletic competitions. And: they experience significant rises in libido, energy, confidence and ambition during the middle of their menstrual cycle.

(Source: Angela Gray is your PFC *relationships expert. The original version of this feature first appeared in* PFC *May 1998, No. 20.)*

BE SUCCESSFUL IN EVERYTHING YOU WANT TO DO

Sit down with a sheet of paper and think about the dreams you have. Write them out, and look at your list. This is how to achieve them:

1. **Create success experiences.** Success depends on several things. First: a clearly defined goal. Second: that goal needs to be broken down into smaller, step-by-step activities. Third: each small step and that big goal have to be realistic and achievable. Example: the initial step towards a richer social life might simply be to go across town to have a drink in a different pub. Do: put yourself in the position where you can meet new people. Don't: go with the idea of talking to the first person you see – you might give yourself a failure experience. Bottom line: being there, having a drink and going home will be an achievable objective – a 'success experience' to set you on your way; the first of many.

2. **Give yourself credit for successes.** Most people lack confidence in at least one area of their lives. Example: many older people are terrified of computers, and are convinced they couldn't master one. But: tutors who run adult education classes in computer skills and literacy will tell you that once they've overcome that initial uncertainty, older people are as fast as younger ones at accumulating skills; and sometimes faster as they have the patience and wisdom to deal calmly with problems and keep learning. Helpful: if you're a little unsure about something, write down all the things that you've achieved in the past – to ride a bike, drive a car, pass exams, all sorts of things. You'll find some of these are linked in some way to the computer skills that you might want to acquire! Examples: before you started driving a car, you might have found that a daunting prospect – after you've been doing it for ten, twenty years or more, you'll wonder what all the fuss was about. It's the same with computers. Remember: if you've been successful before, you'll succeed again and again.

3. **Be a copycat of other people's success.** We're not alone in our dreams – other people have been there before us. And: if they've been there, they can show us the way. Key question: what made them successful? Idea: study them; watch what they do, and how they do it. Talk to them. Example: say you know someone who has got all of his jobs by networking. Watch them – and unlock the secrets of their success. You might find that they never actually ask anyone for a job; instead they just ask for 'advice'. Why: people don't like being asked for something definite like a job – they feel embarrassed and pressured. But: they love being asked for advice and never refuse it – because it acknowledges their expertise and generosity. Outcome: the conversation often leads on to a job offer. So: see what other winners do; and copy them.

4. **Be relaxed.** Successful people are relaxed because they know what they're doing, where they're going, and have confidence in the outcome. Tense people don't succeed. Case study: a man called David Baker was out of work and desperate for money. He became an insurance salesman for a few months – and never sold a single policy. Why: he tried too hard; and it showed. Clients didn't want to buy from

someone who seemed so desperate. They wanted to feel re-assured by the quiet, relaxed confidence that a successful person exudes. Important: you can cultivate that feeling of relaxation from the knowledge and confidence that you're going to be successful. You too know what you have to do, and where you want to go.

5. **Accept problems.** Few goals are achieved without problems arising along the way. But: many people don't seem to acknowledge this basic fact – and give up as soon as they encounter that first difficulty. Motto: anything worth achieving takes time and effort – it probably wouldn't be worth achieving if it didn't. Note: successful people always assume they'll come across problems, identify as many as they can in advance, and are ready to resolve any others they encounter along the way. Essential: acknowledging potential problems gives you the confidence to deal with them. Truth: to the successful person, problems are simply part of the process and are viewed as additional challenges to their competence and commitment.

6. **Talk yourself through difficulties.** Successful people have what's known as 'stickability' – they know success doesn't come easily, and they keep going come what may. Tip: talk yourself through the task in hand – like an air traffic controller talks down a pilot coming in to land in foggy conditions. How: this tactic recognises that the task is a tricky one, requiring concentration and persistence – and it acknowledges that you are capable of achieving it. Result: your confidence will soar sky high.

7. **Make a contract with yourself.** We're all familiar with contracts – once you've signed one, you can't back out; you've got to see it through and fulfil it. Helpful: enter into a self-contract; undertaking to carry out each step towards your goal and in return, giving yourself some rewards for your achievements. Example: if you're seeking a job, you might motivate yourself with a contract to make five on-spec applications a week, in return for a new CD after every twenty applications. Useful: a self-contract helps to create a high level of commitment to your overall goal.

8. **Visualise success.** 'Creative Visualisation' is the most important secret of success. Definition: it simply involves imagining what things

will be like when you have achieved your goal. Example: a boat builder setting up the stem of his boat thinks about the graceful finished craft gliding through the water, sees himself hauling fish over the stern, and feels the wind and spray on his face. Important: never lose sight of your dream – imagine yourself at that executive desk, wheeling and dealing with equally successful people. And: the more detailed your visualisation, the more likely it is that you'll know what you want; and will achieve it. Bottom line: your visualised dream will be a vision to keep you progressing towards your goal.

(Source: John T. Wilson who is the founder of Business Innovations Research, a company at the forefront of the development of business ideas and opportunities. He is the author of How to be an Overnight Success, *published by Information World Limited. Call the publishers on 01736 797061 for more information about this book. This feature first appeared in* PFC *March 1998, No. 18.)*

HOW WRITING CAN MAKE YOU FEEL BETTER

Boost your overall health – simply keep a daily journal of your thoughts and feelings. Study: Recent US research revealed that writing about their chronic asthma or rheumatiod arthritis helped to ease sufferers' pain for up to four months. Details: asthma patients showed an average 19% improvement in lung functions'. And: arthritis patients experienced a 28% improvement in disease severity. PFC advice: feel happier and get healthier – write frankly of your feelings about your most stressful experiences. This will make you feel calmer, and have positive impact on your wellbeing.

(Source: Jurgen Wolf, editor of Brainstorm.*)*

HOW TO BE A REALLY COOL STEP-PARENT – AND ENJOY A HAPPY FAMILY LIFE

Living with your new partner's children may seem daunting, but you can build a unique relationship with them if you follow our step-by-step guide.

1. **Make sure that your relationship with your partner is strong and supportive.** Essential: you need to be in agreement about the big issues: rules, responsibilities and rewards. Important: take time out to be alone together to nourish your relationship – this is crucial for the continuing existence and emotional health of the step-family. Ideas: a lunchtime walk in the park, an evening visit to the pub once a week.

2. **Accept that a step-family is different to the traditional nuclear family:** mum, dad and two children. But: this doesn't mean it can't be as good, if not better. Fact: the key to success is to be aware of the differing values and attitudes of the various family members – in particular, towards discipline, privacy and money. Wise: develop a tolerance towards differences, whilst establishing agreed customs and routines for your new family.

3. **Recognise that becoming a step-parent is never the same as being a parent.** Aim: loving a step-child as your own may not be possible – but to like and respect them is an achievable goal. Best: step-parenting will be more successful if you carve out a different and non-competitive role to their natural mother or father. Discuss how to do this with your partner.

4. **Acknowledge the role and value of your natural counterpart.** Bad: criticising the parent in front of your step-children. Why: this forces step-children to make choices between you, causing distress and tension. Good: encouraging step-children to talk to you about their natural mother or father. Reason: this reduces loyalty conflicts and provides a sense of continuity.

5. **Ensure that any visiting step-children feel at home.** How: give them their own space – a cupboard or shelves for their toys, as examples. And: have things around that are familiar to them: the same type of shampoo and toothpaste that they use at home, as examples. Plus: include them in any chores and projects so they feel part of a family.

6. **Let the relationship develop at its own pace.** Vital: don't rush

it – the desire for an instant, ready-made relationship leads to difficulties and disappointments. Note: it often takes at least two years or more for step-family relationships to settle into place. Core skill: be patient, and give your step-children plenty of time to accept you.

7. **Build your relationship before attempting to discipline your step-children.** Helpful: spend some time getting to know each other. Suggestions: taking up a mutual hobby, going shopping together. But: make sure this isn't forced – pretending to enjoy something that you dislike will eventually cause unnecessary tensions.

8. **Show affection for your step-children equally.** Essential: you and your partner need to put up a united front; particularly over rules and responsibilities. Tip: your partner should give a clear message to your step-children that you both speak with one voice, especially when your partner is absent.

9. Seek help and advice when necessary. Useful contact: The National Stepfamily Association is an excellent source of books and leaflets and has a helpline staffed by qualified counsellors. Address: 3rd Floor, Chapel House, 18 Hatton Place, London EC1N 8RU. Helpline: 0990 168388 (Monday-Friday, 2pm-5pm, 7pm-10pm).

(Source: Angela Gray who is the PFC *relationships expert. The full version of this feature first appeared in* PFC *March 1998, No. 18)*

STRESS RELIEF IN TEN SECONDS FLAT

When you're feeling stressed, take a shower and direct a blast of hot water at your pineal area; that's the little spot at the base of your skull. Why: this triggers the release of histamine, serotonin and other amines into your bloodstream. Result: within seconds, your sinuses will open, your lungs will clear and your back muscles will loosen as if by magic – and you'll feel fully refreshed.

(Source: Agora Lifestyles – phone 0500 523 499 for a free copy of the latest issue of any of their newsletters.)

LEARN TO PHOTO-READ – ABSORB THE KNOWLEDGE YOU NEED IN A FRACTION OF THE TIME

If you change your reading habits, you'll save time, and get more information from newspapers, articles and reports – even dense and complicated documents. Here's how to achieve success:

Daily news: allow yourself no more than ten to 15 minutes each morning to review the press – this forces you to focus. Know your purpose for reading; a strong purpose increases immediately your reading speed and comprehension. Be clear about what you want – then search quickly to find it. Don't read just for the sake of it; unless you are passing leisure time. Look for the most pertinent information that matches your purpose for reading, and disregard redundant information – skip whatever you know already, and go straight to the new information you need.

Articles: read headlines and first paragraphs only to preview articles – reporters present 80% of the key information in the opening paragraph. Then ask yourself what other specific details you want to obtain. Let it go if there aren't any. If there are, skim over the article to spot these details; dipping in as and where necessary to read the relevant paragraphs. Don't read all of the words unless you have the luxury of unlimited time. When you've finished with an article, go straight to the next one – this whole process should not take more than 15 minutes in total.

Reports: in less than 13 minutes, you can obtain 80% of what you need to know from even the most detailed and lengthy reports. How: at the end of your working day, take two minutes to glance through the report's table of contents, layout and conclusion. Decide on three things you need to know from this report. Stop! Do not read any more. Instead: just flip the pages in front of your eyes like a fan, two or three times. Guess where you will find the answers – then leave it alone until tomorrow morning. In the morning, take no more than seven minutes to search for and read the key points you felt you had to know. Double check to see if there are any additional 'life or death' needs associated with this report. If so, spend no more than four more minutes on it now; and up to a maximum of seven minutes the next day.

Complex documents: you'll read dense and difficult documents more easily by approaching them in a positive manner. Before reading a complicated piece of text, close your eyes and relax by taking two or three deep breaths. Say to yourself that you can read with full concentration, recognise key information, and achieve high comprehension quickly to accomplish your needs.

If you believe you can, you will. See detailed material as being just new and different – be relaxed about it. Early confusion can work in your favour – it creates a sense of curiosity that guides you to search and recognise the information you require. It helps your overall comprehension and reading performance.

(Source: Chris Payne who is the managing director of LifeTools Limited, an organisation that runs personal learning courses in photo-reading techniques. This feature first appeared in PFC *August 1997, No. 11.)*

IMPROVE YOUR CONVERSATION SKILLS – INCREASE YOUR CONFIDENCE

Many people are apprehensive about making conversation with groups and individuals they don't know well. Here's what to do:

1. **Relax consciously by breathing slowly, and then simply concentrate on keeping eye contact with whoever is speaking at the moment.** This shows your interest and willingness to participate, which pleases the other person who will feel involved with you as they know that they have your attention.

2. **When you feel comfortable, aim to join in a group**

conversation without becoming the centre of attention straightaway. Do this by making a warm and sympathetic comment, without disagreeing with the speaker. Or ask a general question. People will feel you are part of the group and this will help you to relax.

3. **Be willing to admit at some point that you do not know much about a particular topic and ask for more information.** This involves you in more contact with the speaker.

4. **Make a more positive contribution to the conversation.** Decide to offer a warm compliment: 'I think you handled that situation well.' A positive contribution helps everyone present to relax and open up.

5. **You're now ready to make a contribution of your own** – either one idea, or a short example of how something similar happened to you. Keep it brief at this stage, and uncontroversial. A clearly expressed and relevant idea will always be welcomed. Maintain eye contact as you say it. But don't make any attempt to take the idea any further at this stage. Just enjoy the feeling of success.

6. **As you begin to enjoy conversations again, your goal should be to introduce a new angle on the same topic; or a related one if the conversation seems to be flagging.** Perhaps you can ask someone what they think about a related issue that was raised in this morning's press. You can have planned this topic in advance, and the conversation will then continue on this new topic without necessarily having to involve you again – which leaves you free to relax and enjoy it. Tip: take every opportunity to be with people, rather than cutting yourself off. Also: think about what you intend to achieve each time before entering a conversation, rather than rushing in.

(Sources: Don Gabor, How To Start A Conversation And Make Friends, *Dianne Doubtfire,* Getting Along With People, *Allan Pease,* Talk Language: How To Use Conversation For Profit And Pleasure, *Gael Lindenfield,* Super Confidence.*)*

UPGRADE YOUR AIR TRAVEL – WITH THREE LITTLE WORDS

***PFC* tip:** the words 'a courtesy upgrade' can get you a first or business class seat for the price of the economy fare. How: as you hand your tickets over at the check-in, just ask the clerk if it is possible to obtain a courtesy upgrade to first class or business class – this simple tactic has been found to work successfully in more than 50% of cases. Helpful: if you've used this airline on previous occasions, mention that you're a regular customer. And: dress smartly, so that you won't look out of place in a more expensive section. Plus: if you own shares in the airline, mention this at the checkout – it will almost certainly get you an upgrade.

(Source: International Living *newsletter published by Agora Lifestyles – call 0500 523 499 for a free copy of the latest issue.)*

HOW YOU CAN CHOOSE YOUR BABY'S SEX

Many parents want to pick the sex of their child, and pay a fortune to clinics to do it. But you can choose their sex naturally; and it won't cost you a penny. Here's how:

The basics: natural sex selection depends primarily upon two components; one from each partner. First: the woman must arrange the correct timing of intercourse in her menstrual cycle. Second: the man should adjust his sperm count to the required level. Outcome: when these two essential conditions are met, intercourse usually leads to the conception of a child of the chosen sex.

The timing of intercourse: to conceive a boy, intercourse must take place at ovulation; for a girl, intercourse should occur before ovulation. Explanation: there are two types of sperm: the male-bearing androsperm and the female-bearing gynesperm – androsperm are fast-moving but die easily, gynesperm are slow-moving but hardy. Also: conception can only occur at or after ovulation, when the egg leaves the ovaries and enters the fallopian tube. At ovulation: the vagina is bathed in alkaline mucus in which both sorts of sperm are viable. But the faster-swimming androsperm are more likely to win the race to the egg after intercourse on the day of ovulation; hence a boy. At other times: the vagina is usually acidic, and most androsperm cannot live long in an acidic environment, whereas the gynesperm can survive for up to five or six days. So they will still be there to fertilise the egg if intercourse takes place some days before ovulation; thus a girl.

Sperm count: for a boy, sperm count must be high; to conceive a girl, sperm count should be low. Reason: male-bearing androsperm may be fast swimmers, but they do not cope well with the hazards of the vagina. So many die off when they are ejaculated into the women's body that a higher number of them are needed to provide a greater statistical chance of one of them surviving to fertilise the egg. Hence, a high sperm count is required for boys. And: because female-bearing gynesperm are tougher and live longer, their numbers do not diminish so drastically and many will survive even in a low sperm count. Thus, a low sperm count favours girls.

Identifying ovulation: to increase your chances of success, the day of ovulation has to be pinpointed. Usual: ovulation normally occurs 14 days before the menstrual cycle is due. Example: for a 28-day cycle, ovulation should take place on day 14. Note: even with varying cycles, ovulation will still usually occur 14 days before the next one begins. But: if cycles fluctuate significantly – perhaps between 30 and 34 days – the day of ovulation could be on day 16, 17, 18, 19 or 20. Solution: monitor your daily temperature. When: take your temperature each morning before you get out of bed, and record it. Ovulation occurs when there is a mid-month drop in temperature followed by a sharp rise to a higher level where it stays roughly the same for the rest of that cycle. Tip: the temperature should normally go up on the day after ovulation. Other pointers: increased libido, slippery vaginal mucus, pain in the lower abdomen.

Changing sperm count: to boost your prospects of having a child of a particular sex, you may want to amend the sperm count. Fact: sperm count is very variable, and much affected by environmental conditions.

Key factor: the temperature level in the scrotum. Hot: increasing the temperature will lower sperm count – this is best for a girl. How: tight-fitting pants and trousers, hot showers. Also: more frequent sex lowers sperm count too. Cold: reducing the temperature will raise your sperm count – and is best for a boy. How: loose pants and baggy trousers, cold showering, cold sponging of the genitals. Plus: giving up smoking will soon improve sperm count.

For a boy: if you want to conceive a boy, the man should keep his genitals cool in boxer shorts and loose trousers, allowing cool air to circulate around his testicles. To keep the sperm count at a high level in the month that you want to conceive, abstain from intercourse for one week, but no longer. Note: abstaining for any longer than that and sperm will become old, slower moving and weaker. Wait for the slippery, ovulatory vaginal mucus, and make love once while the sperm count is high. Important: once, only. The woman should try to have an orgasm, and before the man. Why: on orgasm, a woman releases some alkaline fluid that favours the androsperm.

For a girl: if you want your next child to be a girl, the man should keep his genitals warm in close-knit Y-fronts and tighter trousers. To lower the sperm count, have unprotected sex every other night from as soon as the period finishes until five days before ovulation. Then stop, or use a barrier method of contraception for the remainder of that cycle. Note: if conception does not occur after three months of trying, gradually creep up one day a month nearer to ovulation. But: don't get too near or you will have another boy. Warning: do not make love if there is any sign of the slippery ovulatory mucus. Ideally, as much time as possible should elapse between intercourse and ovulation to allow plenty of opportunity for the male-bearing androsperm to die off before the egg appears at ovulation.

(Source: Hazel Chesterman-Phillips is the mother of two girls and one boy, conceived with her simple and accessible sex selection method. She is the author of Choose the Sex of Your Baby, *published by Bloomsbury. Call the publishers on (0171-494 2111) for more information about this book. A longer version of this article first appeared in* PFC, *April 1998, No.19.)*

DANGER! YOUR MICROWAVE COULD BE POISONING YOU

Microwaving food can make you ill if you don't do it properly. Why: waves are produced and absorbed in irregular ways by the food within the oven. And: this leads to 'cold spots'; parts that are not cooked fully and can be dangerous if they contain harmful bacteria. You can avoid this if you take some simple precautions:

1. **Be wary of cooking instructions in the microwave booklet.** Sensible: use these as a guide only; slightly more or less time might be needed. Example: food taken from your refrigerator will be colder than room temperature; and will probably need to be microwaved for longer than is stated in the instruction manual.

2. **Always cover the food.** Essential: arrange the food evenly on the dish, add some water, and put on the cover. Check: the dish and the cover are safe to use in the microwave. Note: steam building up under the cover helps to kill off dangerous bacteria. Important: the cover should allow some of the steam that's generated to escape – this ensures the pressure inside the dish is kept at a safe level.

3. **Take out any bones before cooking meat.** Reason: if you leave them in, they'll act as a shield against the microwaves; and prevent the surrounding meat from being cooked fully. Also: never microwave large pieces of food – cut them into smaller bits. Because: it makes it easier for the microwaves to enter completely and cook the food fully.

4. **Keep the food moving.** How: do this by rotating and stirring it regularly; perhaps halfway through its defrosting, cooking or reheating time. Fact: nearly all microwave ovens have some areas where the waves aren't as strong as others – regardless of what the manufacturers tell you. So: moving the food around ensures that every part of it receives equal amounts of heat.

5. **Don't remove the food immediately.** Better: when its cooking

time has finished, leave the food in the oven for two more minutes. Reason: even though the microwaves will have stopped bombarding it, the food will continue to cook from its own heat; consequently distributing the heat more evenly within it.

6. **Cook leftovers at a high setting.** Wise: reheat at a temperature of at least 70°C; and for a minimum of two minutes. Warning: just warming food so that it is hot enough to eat may not be sufficient to kill any bacteria that may have developed overnight.

***PFC* top tips:** check your microwave oven's door hinges, latches and seals once a month – if they are warped or damaged in any way, have the oven examined by qualified service personnel. Microwave radiation leaks can be extremely hazardous. Also: don't stand too close to a microwave oven whilst it is operating – if radiation is leaking out, you want to be as far away from it as possible. Plus: check regularly to see that the mechanism that switches off the oven when the door is opened is working properly – again, seek professional advice if it is not.

(Sources: the US Department of Agriculture, Meat and Poultry Advice, plus additional PFC *research. The original version of this feature first appeared in* PFC *April 1997, No. 7.)*

HOW TO ELIMINATE CAR ACCIDENT DISPUTES IN A FLASH

***PFC* tip:** carry a loaded camera or disposable camera in the glove compartment of your car – and take photographs if you're involved in an accident. This minimises disputes about what did and/or didn't happen. Note: even if the camera isn't loaded, pretend to take photographs; the other driver won't know the camera is empty and is far less likely to lie if they think you've got the photographic evidence needed to disprove their statements.

(Source: PFC *legal experts.)*

YOUR OWN HOME COMPUTER FOR JUST £15 – AND OTHER UNBELIEVABLE BARGAINS

If you know where to look and what to do, you can pick up a whole host of unbelievable bargains – an exercise bicycle for £2, a fax machine for £5, a television for £10; even a home computer for only £15. Here's how:

Where: auction sales specialising in repossessed goods and where most of the vendors are organisations such as the Inland Revenue, Customs & Excise and/or finance companies – those that have repossessed items from the original owners or seized them to meet unsettled debts. Fact: private individuals who are selling goods at auction want to obtain the best price and will often set a high 'reserve' price – below which the goods will not be sold. But: organisations that are selling by auction are more interested in a speedy, trouble-free disposal of the goods than in getting the best possible price for them. They may wish to sell the goods at any price – and might even be obliged by law to do so. They'll seldom place a reserve price on anything. And: if there isn't a reserve price, then the highest bid – however low that may be – is successful. Bottom line: if an easy sale produces a low – or even a ridiculous price – so be it. Bonus: most auctions are attended mainly by dealers who intend to resell what they buy at a profit later on. So: everything will go at rock-bottom prices – you'll be paying far less than the retail or even wholesale prices.

How: to identify the right type of auction, look at the auctioneer's catalogue. Sensible: check the lots' on offer for phrases such as 'The Inland Revenue', 'On behalf of HM Customs & Excise', 'By order of the County Court Bailiffs' and 'By order of the Liquidators'. Note: when you see these types of organisation listed as vendors, you can be pretty certain there won't be any reserves on these lots; or that they'll be very low. Hint: you can also telephone HM Customs & Excise, finance companies, bailiffs, liquidators, local authorities, and repossession firms in your area – and ask them which auctioneers they use. Also: call the Department of Trade and Industry's 'Insolvency Service' on 0121-698 4000 and ask them for the contact details of the Official Receiver in your region. Then get in touch to discover which auctioneers are used in that locality.

What to do: view lots carefully before bidding – a bid is almost always legally binding. Tip: if there are several similar lots, don't try to get the first one – you'll find the later ones go for lower prices. Important: decide on the top price you're prepared to pay, and stick to this – it's very easy to get carried away in the excitement of the bidding, and to bid more than you intended to do. Note: in addition to your bid price, you'll have to pay a buyer's premium of around 10% and VAT on the bid price and that premium. Wisest: attend at least two auctions as a spectator to get a feel for how it all works.

(Source: John McCaughey, The Repossession Auction Handbook *and* The Computer Auction Handbook. *The full version of this feature first appeared in* PFC *December 1996, No. 4.)*

THE TWO BEST WAYS TO LOWER YOUR BLOOD PRESSURE

1. **Eat more fruit** – in a recent US study, those people who ate the least fruit were more than 50% more likely to develop high blood pressure than those who ate the most fruit.

2. **Lose some weight** – in the same study, those people who weighed the most were 450% more likely to have high blood pressure than those who weighed the least.

(Source: Harvard School of Public Health, Boston, USA.)

SIXTEEN COLLECTIVE INVESTMENTS YOU MUST NOT BUY IF YOU WANT TO MAKE MONEY

It's very easy to be dazzled by the success story of collective investments. Because: we're constantly being told that they offer the same high profits as shares but have a broader spread that protects us from risk. But: that's not a good enough reason to sign up for the first offer that comes your way. Important: you need to be selective or you'll find yourself with a fund that simply doesn't come up to standard. Helpful: we've analysed the performance and potential profitability of all funds; and identified 16 poor performers to avoid at all costs. Europe: Britannia European Growth, Lincoln European, Old Mutual European, S&P European Growth. North America: Govett American Strategy, NPI North American Rtl, Stewart Ivory American. UK All Companies: Abbey General, ABN AMRO Growth & Income, Solus UK Growth. UK Equity Income: Baillie Gifford Income A, Henderson UK Equity Income, M&G Dividend. UK General Bonds: Govett Corporate Bond, Lloyds TSB Premier Income, Sovereign Controlled Performance.

(Source: Bruce McWilliams, PFC*'s fund expert who appears weekly on Bloomberg TV's Fund Focus, and writes a funds column for the* London Evening Standard.*)*

YOGA FOR BEGINNERS – A STEP-BY-STEP GUIDE TO A STRESS-FREE LIFE

'Yoga' means 'union' – and involves the linking of our physical, emotional, intellectual and spiritual powers into a single holistic approach. Details: yoga is designed to free and develop the whole person in us and is achieved through three basic techniques – developing the body through physical exercise or postures (asana), controlling the will and emotions through correct breathing (pranayama), and freeing the mind through meditation techniques (dharana). Here's how it can work and make you a more complete person:

Neck and shoulder exercises: 1. Sit up straight on a hard-backed chair. Look to the front and breathe in through the nose. Slowly turn your head to the right; at the same time breathe out. Breathe in, moving your head back to the front. Breathe out, moving your head to the left this time; and so on. Repeat the exercise several times. 2. Repeat the first exercise; this time moving your head down on the out-breath so your chin rests on your chest; and dropping your head back for the second part of the exercise. 3. Breathe in, at the same time holding your arms straight up above your head whilst throwing back your head. Breathe out, swinging your arms and head down to the front, with your head ending up between your knees. Repeat six or seven times. Wise: always breathe through your nose rather than your mouth.

Stretch and twist exercises: these loosen up the rest of your muscles. 1. Stand straight with your feet close together; and join your hands in a prayer position on your chest. Retain this position for two minutes. Then: lift your arms – still in the prayer position – above your head and straighten them; at the same time breathing in. Breathe out, dropping your arms. Repeat this arm-lifting exercise five or six times. 2. Lift your arms again; but this time hold your hands apart above your head. Stretch them forward towards your toes, breathing out. Breathe in, straighten your back, and stretch your arms straight back above your head. Repeat the exercise several times. 3. Repeat the second exercise; but this time stretch your arms to the left, and then to the right. Keep your torso to the front. 4. Lower your arms and gently swing them left to right – one arm at the front, one behind – whilst twisting your body.

Spine and back exercises: a correctly aligned spine and supple back are important features of yoga practice. 1. Sit up straight on the floor. Keep your legs straight out in front and lift your arms straight up above your head, whilst breathing in. Breathe out and try to touch your feet or calves; whilst keeping your arms and legs as straight as possible. Breathing in and out, hold this position for 30 seconds. 2. Lie face down on the floor with your hands by your sides. Breathe in and lift your head, bringing your arms straight out to the front to support you. Hold this position for 30 seconds whilst breathing in and out; and coming back down on an out-breath. Important: yoga postures are balanced. If you stretch one way, always stretch the other way to compensate.

Health: yoga doesn't just tone you up and keep you fit. Better: these exercises have therapeutic effects on all parts of your body. Best: it can alleviate or even remedy such problems as arthritis, asthma, back pain, constipation, headaches, heart, kidney and liver complaints, hypertension, insomnia, psoriasis and varicose veins. Example: the shoulder stand – 'sarvangasana' – is good for poor blood circulation, nervous disorders, stomach, abdominal and urinary complaints, throat and nasal ailments. Useful: a balanced diet will also enhance the health benefits of yoga. Crucial: if you have any problems that affect your health in any way, always check with your doctor before starting a yoga course.

Stress: yoga offers many exercises that reduce body tension and help to alleviate stress. 1. On hearing bad news, sit quietly with a straight back and place your hands on your chest. Try to slow your breathing, feeling the breath expanding and deflating your lungs in the process. 2. If you feel worried, place your fingertips on your forehead, and consciously slow down your breathing, making it as quiet as possible. 3. If you're feeling irritable, place your hands on your chest in a prayer position. Close your eyes and breath calmly and slowly.

Deep seated stress: a regular series of postures controlled by nasal breathing may be necessary. 1. Lie on your back with your legs arched up and separated, and with the feet just below the buttocks. Spread your arms out to either side of your body so that you form a 'T' shape. Breathe in and out slowly, letting your weight sink into the floor as you exhale. Do this for five minutes. 2. Staying on your back, fold your legs up and wrap your arms around the back of your thighs. Hold this position for two minutes. 3. Sit back on your heels. Tuck your head between your knees, letting your arms hang loosely behind you alongside of your legs. Breathe in and out; slowly and easily. 4. Stand up straight with your arms by your side and your feet hip-distance apart.

Perform that third neck and shoulder exercise. 5. Adopt the shoulder stand, followed by the corpse posture. Best: practise this sequence of five exercises twice a day in addition to your normal yoga practice.

Relaxation: yoga is a flexible form of discipline, and can be practised in small or large ways; at home or at work, for a minute or for an hour. Typical: stress in the office – a consequence of being hunched over a computer all morning – can be relieved by a few simple stretching exercises. 1. Sit up straight and link your fingers together at the back of your head. Take a deep breath and breathe out, bringing the chin down to the top of your chest and drawing the elbows closer together. Hold the position, breathe in again and then release. Repeat this four or five times. 2. Sit up straight and breathe in. Then stretch your arms above your head; linking your fingers together so that the palms of your hands are facing the ceiling. Hold this position before breathing out and bringing your arms down slowly. Repeat the exercise four or five times.

(Sources: Swami Vishnu-devananda, Learn Yoga in a Weekend, *Howard Kent,* The Complete Yoga Course, *Vanda Scaravelli,* The Awakening of the Spine, *plus additional information from the Yoga for Health Foundation, 01767 627271.)*

SENT FREE TO YOUR HOME; AN ENDLESS SUPPLY OF FOOD AND TOILETRIES

***PFC* tip:** Here's a great way of sampling goods for free. Watch out for any new foods, toiletries and other items coming onto the market – glossy monthly magazines are the best source of information. Next: write to the manufacturer expressing interest, and asking for a free sample – even if one isn't advertised. Then: you'll find that if a trial-sized sample isn't available, they'll send you a full-sized one instead. Bonus: you don't even need to send stamps to cover postage – they'll send it free of charge!

(Source: Sonia Smith, a PFC *subscriber from the Midlands.)*

SELLING YOUR HOME? HOW YOU CAN SAVE AN EXTRA £4,000

Ninety-five per cent of prospective home sellers go to an estate agent to market and sell their properties, and are charged an average of between 1.5-4% of the selling price; that's as much as £4,000 on a £100,000 property – you could save almost all of that simply by selling your home yourself. Fact; estate agents don't do anything that you can't do, and you'll often be able to do it much quicker and cheaper. Also, you'll learn organisational and marketing skills by selling your own home. And you may just do it better than an estate agent too. Here's your step-by-step guide to DIY selling:

1. **Value your property.** How: estate agents value properties by comparison – by simply comparing your property with similar ones on the market, knowing what they sold for, and pricing yours accordingly. There's no magic formula; and nothing to stop you doing exactly the same. First: view other properties for sale that are comparable to your own, ask people what their properties sold for, and establish the price of your own property. Next: quantify your figure by asking three estate agents for no-obligation valuations; most people are too involved emotionally with their own homes to be truly objective about its value to possible buyers.

2. **Market your home effectively.** Typical: an estate agent will put a 'For Sale' board outside your property, place a photograph and brief details of it in their window and in the press, and send particulars to anyone on their records who might be interested in such a property. You can do this too; and more. First: erect your own 'For Sale' sign – try red lettering on a yellow background for maximum visibility, and use both sides of the board so it can be seen more easily by passers-by. Important: keep it simple and easy to read; emphasising the telephone number so that people phone you initially instead of calling in person which is often more inconvenient. Tip: have an answering machine installed to take messages when you are out and to minimise interruptions at inconvenient times. Ask callers to leave their address – so you can send out information about

the property before arranging visits with those who are genuinely interested.

3. **Provide detailed information about your home in your own property particulars** – as many details as possible on printed A4 sheets. Attach a photograph of your home rather than a photocopy. Check all information carefully for accuracy to ensure it does not mislead nor misrepresent the facts. Tip: protect yourself by adding 'We accept no responsibility as to the accuracy of these particulars; they are provided only as a guide. Prospective purchasers should satisfy themselves as to their accuracy by inspection or otherwise. These particulars do not constitute any offer of a contract or part of a contract.' Plus: put advertisements in specialist publications such as *Exchange & Mart* and *Loot*, the national newspaper for DIY property sellers and buyers.

4. **Get rid of time-wasters.** Sensible: give precise and extensive details of your property in advertisements and information sheets so that potential buyers can identify if it is suitable for them or not. The more detailed the information, the easier it is for people to screen the property; saving their time and yours. Also: ask people about their situation when they call – most will exaggerate their interest and how fast they're able to proceed. Key questions: 'What is the telephone number of your solicitor?' should reveal their true circumstances and level of interest.

5. **Show potential buyers around your property.** Wise: never redecorate extensively before putting your property up for sale – it arouses suspicions, making people think that you're covering up serious flaws. In summer, open all of the windows before a visit to freshen the atmosphere. In winter, turn on the heating in every room to make certain the whole house is warm and welcoming. The smell of coffee, bread and/or cakes can be enticing – save time and effort by putting a coffee bean or a vanilla pod under the grill just before visitors arrive. Cut flowers and plants placed around the home can make it seem clean and inviting. Tidy up your garden; and have window boxes, hanging baskets

and pots dotted around. Give visitors a room-by-room guided tour and have bills for any household expenditure, improvements and repairs close to hand for easy reference. Important: make it clear what is and what isn't included in the price – carpets, curtains and garden furniture are common sources of disputes. Follow the tour by allowing visitors a few minutes alone so they can talk in private – going off to make a tea or coffee gives them this opportunity. Don't be too enthusiastic as this is offputting; it can make you seem desperate and will encourage people to make a lower offer.

6. **Appoint a solicitor to handle procedures from acceptance of an offer through to completion.** And: ask your buyers to contact their solicitor at the earliest opportunity – and to get in touch with yours. Caution: keep control of the sale through to completion. Too many sellers leave the matter to their solicitors – the sale will then proceed at their pace, rather than yours. Best: agree a completion date with your buyers at the outset and make certain that the solicitors are aware of this – it creates a sense of purpose. Speak to your solicitor and buyers at regular intervals – make a note to call them once a week for progress reports, and to keep everything moving along. Seek to exchange contracts as soon as possible – your buyers are then committed to go on and purchase the property. Keep your 'For Sale' board up until the exchange takes place – it acts as an incentive.

(Source: Alison Rollé is the PFC *property expert. She is a founder member of* Loot, *the property newspaper that offers marketing services to DIY property sellers. The full version of this feature first appeared in* PFC *August 1997, No. 11.)*

THE SECRET TAX SAVING STRATEGIES OF THE TOP TAX ACCOUNTANTS

You could pay anything up to £1,000 per hour to obtain the advice of a top tax accountant in the City of London. But we've done it for you; here's the tax-avoidance strategies they recommend to their clients:

Tax free savings: various investments provide a tax-exempt return – with no tax deducted or to pay at a later date. National Savings: savings certificates pay a fixed rate of compound interest over a five-year period – proceeds are tax-free. Index-linked certificates accumulate in line with the retail price index. Hold your certificates for the full five years, and you'll get a bonus. Using the National Savings Bank allows you to receive the first £70 of interest paid tax-free.

'Age allowance trap': although older people benefit from an increased age allowance, this may be reduced if your income exceeds a certain figure, resulting in a lowering of the tax code. Tip: if the excess income is from interest or dividends, you can avoid the reduction in personal allowance by transferring your capital to an alternative form of investment – thus retaining your full, enhanced allowance.

'Personal Pension tax havens': subject to certain, age-related limits set by the Inland Revenue, all the money that you contribute to an approved pension scheme of any kind will attract income tax relief at your highest rate. Your money will be free of capital gains tax and you'll be able to take a tax-free lump sum at retirement age. As a tax-efficient investment, this method of providing money for the future has few equals – it is a way of having your own tax haven for your exclusive benefit. But, and it a big but, low interest rates mean smaller pensions. Today you need twice as big a pension pot to get the same pension as in 1990.

Unclaimed millions: pensioners and other people on low incomes who believe that too much tax has been deducted from any interest received from bank and building society accounts or other interest-bearing securities should contact their local Inland Revenue office for advice. It is estimated that millions of pounds are waiting to be claimed. But note that from 6 April 1999 you can't reclaim tax on UK dividends even if you are a non-taxpayer.

Capital gains tax (CGT): gains or profit resulting from the sale of most assets are potentially subject to capital gains tax. Important:

planning and timing are the key factors to consider when seeking to reduce your CGT liability. How: make use of both spouses' annual exemption – this is the amount of gain you can make in a tax year before CGT is payable. Both husband and wife have an annual exemption. Take gains to avoid wasting the annual exemption – unused annual exemptions cannot be carried forward for the future. Make certain that you carry forward capital losses if they are not used to mitigate CGT this year.

Inheritance tax (IHT): this is both a gift tax and a death duty. Details: it is levied on what you give away in your lifetime and what passes to your estate on your death; these are collectively known as chargeable transfers. And: there is a 'nil rate band' available to everyone. This is similar to the personal allowance for income tax; and represents the amount that you can give away tax free during your lifetime and on your death. Note: the total transfers made within seven years of death in excess of the nil rate band and the amount passed to your estate on death in excess of the nil rate band are subject to inheritance tax.

Reducing the IHT bill: find out the current nil rate band – if your total assets do not exceed this band, you don't have a problem. But: remember to include the value of your home when adding up your assets. If you do have a potential IHT liability, there are various ways of reducing it – or even eliminating it altogether. Drastic: give away everything you have now and live for a further seven years – the transfer will then be tax-free. But: this is impractical and undesirable for most people. Better: transfers between husband and wife are exempt from IHT; so if you leave everything to your spouse in your will there will be no IHT liability on your death. Note: the IHT problem may recur when your spouse dies. Also: equalise your estates; as both husband and wife have their own nil rate band you could share your assets, and (if you can afford to) write your wills so that on the first death an amount equal to the nil rate band passes to your children and the balance to your partner. When the surviving partner dies the nil rate band applies again. So: this option places an amount equal to the nil rate band outside the reach of the Inland Revenue. Plus: you and your spouse can each give away an amount up to the 'annual exemption' limit and can also hand over as many small cash gifts to as many people as you like. Children and grandchildren can be given sizeable gifts as and when they marry. Gifts to charities and for national purposes are exempt from IHT, as are gifts to main political parties.

Warning: remember that your estate will be taxed at the prevailing rates at the time of your death; which may not necessarily be the same as the current arrangements. Any plans you make must be flexible enough to allow for future changes. Note: the gift of an asset must be a genuine and outright gift – if you attach conditions to a gift, it may fall outside of current legislation and a tax liability might be created. And: artificial gifts – such as selling an asset for far less than it is actually worth – could also cause problems with the Inland Revenue.

***PFC* alternative:** instead of preserving your assets for your children, a radical alternative is to spend them in your lifetime; and leave little or nothing on your death. Why: if you are insurable you can take out a suitable life assurance policy which is placed 'in trust' for your children or other beneficiaries and will pay an amount equal to what you would like to leave on your death. Outcome: the proceeds of such a policy will be free of inheritance tax; and you will have the benefit of the use of your own money now. The premiums for the policy can be taken from today's income or assets. Tip 1: if you already have life policies, these can be converted easily to 'in trust' status. Tip 2: Marry before you die. That delays IHT and your partner might be entitled to a widow(er) pension from your works pension scheme if it has one.

(Source: PFC *financial expert, Nigel Bolitho 01954 251521)*

BURN OFF AN EXTRA 150 CALORIES WITHOUT MOVING A MUSCLE

***PFC* tip:** recent US research has shown that people who eat a lot of fibre – via fruits and vegetables – use up 150 more calories a day than those adhering to a diet of the same caloric content but without that extra fibre. So: to lose weight, eat at least five servings of fruits and vegetables a day.

(Source: Agora Lifestyles – phone 0500 523 499 for a free copy of the latest issue of any of their newsletters.)

WHY DRINKING COFFEE CAN BE GOOD FOR YOU

Coffee has had a bad press in recent years, and is subject to many myths. Examples: 'it's unhealthy', 'it damages your heart'. But: the reality is that the latest worldwide research has shown that there is little or no evidence that drinking coffee in moderation is likely to create any health hazards for most people. In fact, coffee can bring some very definite health benefits, according to recent medical studies. Let's look at the myths and reality:

Myth: the plain and simple fact is that many of the ill effects commonly associated with coffee are just not true. In particular:

'Drinking coffee harms your heart'. Fact: researchers involved in a massive study in America concluded that 'any suggestion of a positive association between heart disease and coffee is eliminated'. Source: *Journal of the American Medical Association*.

'Coffee causes palpitations', those uncomfortable flutters that occur now and again in even the healthiest people. The new research is categorical in its findings: GPs should not tell patients suffering from palpitations to cut down on coffee. Source: consultants at the Royal Infirmary, Edinburgh, Scotland, following a study to establish whether or not there was any link between coffee and palpitations.

'Drinking coffee affects adversely your blood pressure and heartbeat'. Truth: reports on caffeines releasing natural body chemicals that affect blood pressure and heartbeat show that these effects are found only when caffeine is taken in sizeable amounts by people who normally never consume it. The effects are not found in those who drink coffee on a regular basis. Source: *Heart,* the specialist medical journal.

Reality: telling someone to stop drinking coffee is just taking away one of the pleasures of life for no sound reason. There are numerous benefits:

Coffee boosts the brain. How: it helps you to think more quickly, have a better memory and improved reasoning powers. Bonus: this increase in mental performance is more marked in older people than in younger ones. Source: *Psychopharmacology.*

It increases energy and endurance. Details: strong coffee helps people work longer and harder and stave off exhaustion; the caffeine stimulates the body's energy reserves. Sources: *International Journal of Sports Medicine, Canadian Journal of Applied Physiology.* Also: drinking two cups of coffee before a night shift can be as helpful for staving off sleepiness as having a nap before starting work. Sources: *Sleep, Neuropsychobiology.*

Coffee can minimise cold symptoms. Note: the after-effects of a cold can affect your moods, hand-eye co-ordination and reaction times, but a cup of coffee can produce a 'feel-good' factor that gives you a lift and reduces some of these sluggish symptoms. Source: *University of Bristol Newsletter.*

It can limit feelings of depression: those feelings that, left unchecked, can even lead to an increased risk of suicide. Data: a ten-year survey of 86,000 nurses found that those who drank coffee were less likely to commit suicide than those who did not. Source: *Archives of Internal Medicine.* And: this finding supports a ten-year follow-up of 128,000 in a medical care programme which discovered that the chance of death by suicide dropped as people drank more coffee. Source: *Annals of Epidemiology.*

Coffee can cut road accidents; a coffee break could make the difference between life and death for drivers. Why: one in five of all road accidents in Britain is caused by drivers falling asleep at the wheel. Researchers say that caffeine helps to keep people alert and vigilant while on the road. Source: *British Medical Journal.*

Coffee may have a protective effect. Basis: a study of 10,000 people in Scotland found that those who did not drink coffee at all had a significantly higher rate of heart diseases than coffee drinkers. Source: 'Journal of Epidemiology and Community Health.'

Bottom line: this exhaustive research shows that coffee presents no great risk to health, providing it is drunk in moderation. Definition: an intake of 500-600mg of caffeine per day; about six cups of strong coffee. But: different coffees contain varying amounts of caffeine – 80-90mg in a standard (150ml) cup of ground coffee; 60mg in a standard cup of instant coffee; and just 3mg in a standard cup of decaffeinated coffee. Wise: work out your own intake of caffeine based on the type of coffee you drink. Note: researchers also agree that people who drink coffee – and other caffeine-containing drinks – do not become dependent or addicted to it.

(Sources: the Coffee Science Information Centre, a UK-based organisation that assesses worldwide medical research on coffee and caffeine.)

WHY YOU SHOULD ALWAYS USE A CREDIT CARD TO PAY FOR AN AIRLINE TICKET

1. It is easier – you can make all of the arrangements over the telephone. **2.** It speeds up the process if you require a refund – airlines provide refunds within seven days for tickets purchased by credit card; it takes longer if the tickets have been paid for by cash or by cheque. **3.** You can get credit for the ticket if the airline goes bankrupt. **4.** The ticket number of your flight will be printed on your credit card bill – if you lose your ticket, this makes it much easier to have it replaced. **5.** If your ticket is stolen, the thief cannot cash it in – the refund can be credited only to your credit card account. **6.** You get automatic insurance cover – check with your credit card company for details of the coverage available to you. **7.** Programmes allow you to build up frequent flier miles every time you use a credit card to pay for travel.

(Source: International Living *newsletter published by Agora Lifestyles – call freephone 0500 523 499 for a free copy of the latest issue.)*

A CLEVER WAY OF PROTECTING YOURSELF AGAINST INTEREST RATE RISES

***PFC* tip:** you can protect yourself against your bank's interest rate rises by 'capping' them; it's your own personal insurance policy. How: you pay a premium to buy a 'Base Rate Cap' contract from your bank. And, at the end of each quarter, you'll be compensated by your bank for the difference between the strike rate and the base rate on your contract – if the rate rises over the strike rate during that period. Bottom line: employ this little-known tactic during stormy economic trading times, and freeze your borrowing fees.

(Sources: PFC *financial and investment specialists.)*

A LITTLE TROUSER TRICK

Get the sharpest crease in your trousers – run a line of paper glue all along the inside of the crease, press and allow to dry. But remember, do it on the inside not the outside!

(Source: Edna Gayther, a PFC *subscriber.)*

AN EFFORTLESS WAY TO REGULATE YOUR APPETITE

***PFC* tip:** stick to a weight-loss programme simply by avoiding cornflakes, white bread and artificial sweeteners – these all increase your appetite for up to three hours, and encourage you to eat more and put on weight. Remove them and you'll soon free yourself from bouts of depression, enjoy a renewed enthusiasm for life and improve your mental alertness too.

(Source: Agora Lifestyles Limited – phone freephone 0500 523 499 for a free copy of the latest issue of any of their newsletters.)

UNDERSTAND THE CRIMINAL MIND AND BURGLAR-PROOF YOUR HOME

Crime statistics categorise house-breaking in three ways: **1.** Professional thieves who know what they want, work quickly and efficiently, and usually create minimal damage. **2.** Casual thieves who strike when they spot an easy opportunity; they may cause some damage to property and belongings. **3.** Thieves who steal and enjoy vandalising and defiling their victims' properties. There are various measures you can take to make your home less vulnerable – almost all thieves are thwarted by sensible, easy-to-employ precautions.

Doors: all external doors should be secured with a five-lever mortise lock and a cylinder rim lock. Ensure products are kitemarked to BS3621 standard. Reason: these locks cannot be opened with skeleton keys, and it shouldn't be possible to pick them. Note: wooden doors should have two or more bolts. Also: metal plates fitted at the lock and hinges make doors harder to force. If there are plate glass panels in or around the door, replace these with laminated glass. Do fit a security chain that enables you to open the door just far enough to check on visitors. Also, consider fitting an interior door viewer. Many insurance companies refuse to meet burglary claims if your locks do not meet specified requirements; check that yours comply with the terms and conditions of your insurance policy.

Windows: key-operated locks should be fitted to all windows. Even professional burglars admit these are a deterrent. Warning: be careful not to leave the keys in window locks. Better: keep them in a safe but readily accessible place; remember that you might need those keys in a hurry if there's a fire. Important: don't think that small windows cannot be entered; unscrupulous thieves use their children to enter the smallest of spaces. Helpful: it is worth fitting shutters or security grilles to vulnerable windows, but ensure you still have adequate means of escape in the event of fire. Also: don't leave small valuables by an open window, even when you're in the house. These can be snatched in a second. Skylights and similar windows should be protected with mortise security bolts.

Patio/french doors: a five-lever mortise lock is advisable, plus extra mortise bolts for wooden french doors. Crucial: to prevent patio doors from being levered off their hinges, an additional base-mounted patio door lock is a good buy. Note: as patio and french doors are manufactured in various materials, check with the supplier to ensure you purchase the appropriate security devices. Porches: have your letterbox mounted on your main entrance door, so you won't have post lying on your porch floor when you're out.

Exterior lighting: an exterior light which operates by an infra-red sensor and switches itself on when anything enters its range is a powerful deterrent to night-time burglars. Easy: you may be able to buy a sensor to convert an existing outdoor light. Alternative: an all-night light using a low-energy light bulb. Exterior pipes: drainpipes can be treated with a special paint so burglars are unable to climb them.

Sheds and garages: these are popular targets for opportunist thieves, as they normally contain items that can be snatched quickly. Any petrol mower is easy to sell on at a good price. Similarly at risk are garden furniture and tools and barbecues. Worry: integral or adjoining garages can offer an undisturbed route into your home; a really determined professional burglar will remove house-bricks to gain entry. Locksmiths will advise on specialised locking systems for your garage.

Other common-sense measures: when leaving your home unattended, remember to close all windows – an open window tempts the opportunist thief. Make sure ladders and tools that could aid entry are locked away out of sight. Don't leave valuables on view inside your home. Closing the curtains, leaving on a downstairs light and even switching on a radio can deter that opportunist thief. Tip: timer switches set to turn lights on and off make an empty house seem occupied. Never leave bicycles unattended at the side of your house – these are popular targets for casual thieves. If you're going away for a few days, cancel milk and papers and ask someone to close your curtains in the evening and open them in the morning. If you're covered by a Neighbourhood

Watch scheme, tell your co-ordinator when your house will be unoccupied. When going on holiday, ensure your luggage is labelled properly. Idea: use labels that are not viewed easily – gangs are known to operate at airports noting down addresses from the luggage of departing holidaymakers.

Also: a dog that barks is an excellent security measure – few burglars will tackle a dog when there are other properties in the area. Or: a doorbell that plays the sound of a barking dog is a worthwhile alternative. Alarms: there is a vast array of equipment available, from DIY to professionally installed systems. Note: many DIY kits are supplied in a basic form and may require additional detectors and equipment to provide adequate protection. Professionally installed systems are more expensive, but the extra cost has to be weighed against the time and effort to fit your own DIY system. Marking possessions: marking your house number and postcode on bicycles, cameras and electrical equipment improves your chances of getting them back if they're stolen. How: marking can be done inexpensively with an ultra-violet pen. And: a 'Coded For Keeps' sticker displayed in a prominent position might deter a would-be burglar too. UV pens and stickers may be available from your local police station. Useful: having photographs or video recordings of your more valuable goods is helpful if you need to make an insurance claim on them. Important: make a written record of your marked property and keep it in a secure place.

Plus: Neighbourhood Watch schemes perform a valuable role in assisting police in the fight against household crime. If there isn't a local scheme in operation, consider starting one – your nearest police station will offer guidance. Advisable: be a 'nosey parker' if you see anything suspicious: ring the police immediately if in doubt. If we were all as vigilant as we might be, it is estimated that burglaries could be halved.

Warning: don't let unidentified and/or unofficial people into your home, especially if you are elderly or on your own. Wise: check through a door-viewer or a window before answering the door. Keep the doorchain on when opening the door. Ask for official identification – representatives of all government bodies, local councils, utility services and bona-fide organisations carry identification. Double check by noting down details and telephoning their office for verification. If you're still unsure, ask them to call back; and arrange for someone you know to be with you at that time.

(Sources: Vivian Capel, Home Security plus additional PFC *research.)*

THE VERY LATEST, HOTTEST SHARE TIPS – DIRECT FROM A CITY INSIDER

***PFC* tip:** phone 0171-447 4018 and ask for your free copy of the Sharecall Directory – your key to a wealth of investment information. Contents: the share price access system – which enables you to telephone for an up-to-the-minute share price check on any share that you own.

(Sources: Fleet Street Letter *newsletter and* Finance Confidential *newsletter published by Fleet Street Publications – call 0500 823873 for a free copy of the latest issue of either newsletter.)*

IMPOTENT? MOTHER NATURE'S HELPING HAND

Impotence is a very common problem experienced by nearly all men at one time or another. Most men want to remedy the situation without taking drugs, which too often cause unpleasant side-effects. Here's how you can restore your potency the natural way:

1. Ask your local health food shop for yohimbine; or yohimb as it's sometimes known. This is a herbal remedy derived from the bark of a West African tree. Fact: a drug produced from yohimbine has proved to be incredibly successful in a massive study in Canada where it restored potency in up to 62% of cases. Note: the herbal version is safer but less potent than the drug, so this prescription-free course will need to be followed for a longer period of time. Also: other natural substances that are available from most health food shops and are credited with the ability to stimulate and prolong sexual activity include: the herb ginseng, containing pharmaceutically active ingredients that influence erectile function; nutmeg, credited with delaying ejaculation; ginger, which is supposed to help overcome impotence; guarana, now being used in some coffee substitutes and shown to have a 'wake-up' effect on male genitalia.

2. Adopt a health-promoting lifestyle. Truth: a man's ability to obtain and maintain an erection depends almost wholly upon what might be termed 'the hydraulics'; having a sufficient supply of blood to the penis in order to erect it. And: the secret of good circulation is a sensible, healthy lifestyle. Key findings: researchers have discovered that men with erectile problems often have low levels of one or more of vitamins A, C, E, B_{12} and the nutrient zinc. Wise: increase your intake of these. And: avoid a diet that is rich in saturated fats. These can contribute to temporary and/or chronic impotence, and may even be a direct cause of it. Expert: Dr Padma-Nathan of the University of California believes that more than 50% of all cases of impaired erectile function are the result of the tiny arteries leading to the penis becoming obstructed because of an excessive intake of high fat foods. Also: don't drink alcohol excessively. This deadens your senses and interferes with the erectile mechanism, leading to temporary or even long-term failure. Research: excessive chronic drinking eventually leads to less testosterone being produced, which in turn diminishes libido and sexual prowess.

(Sources: Agora Lifestyles Ltd plus additional US and UK research. Call freephone 0500 523499 for a free copy of the latest issue of any of their newsletters.)

BECOME AN INSTANT WINE BUFF

Many people are nervous about buying and drinking wine; they're not sure what to ask for, and don't know how to taste it. Here's your step-by-step guide to becoming a ready-made expert:

1. **Dry, acidic white wines are excellent with fried fish and sea food.** 'Chablis' used to be popular until it became so expensive (at £9-£12 a bottle); 'Muscadet' (£5-£6) now fits the bill. Also: 'Verdiccio di Castelli' (£5-£6) from north-eastern Italy and 'Sauvignon Blanc' (£5-£6) from New Zealand are good choices. Best: for excellent value, try an 'Alsace Riesling' (£6-£8) – the king of Alsacien wines; piercing acidity with clean, pure fruit flavour and a bone dry finish.

2. **Full-bodied white wines go well with white meats; especially spicy stews, stir-fried dishes and strongly-flavoured vegetable dishes.** 'White Burgundy' from Beaune in the Cote D'Or is superb; but can be expensive (£10-£50). Alternatives: 'Macon Blanc' (£5-£6) from the Cote Maconnais and 'Gewurztraminer' (£5-£10) from Alsace, Chile and South Africa are a perfect match for spicy foods. Outstanding: 'Tokay-Pinot Gris' (£6-£10) from Alsace – the 'dark horse' of Alsacien wines, and ideal with food, especially duck dishes. It has a rich, buttery texture, high alcohol, and concentrated and powerful flavours with a touch of spice.

3. **Light and fruity red wines are best drunk with very light food, or on their own.** Slightly more acidic than average reds, from cooler climates like Beajolais, Saumur and Chinon, are terrific with sausages and other meats with a high fat content such as pork pie or paté – the acid cuts through the grease and brings out the flavour. Heavier, full-bodied, tannic red wines made from Cabernet Sauvignon, Tempranillo or Syrah-Shiraz in Australia are best served with heavy foods; red meats, cheeses and robust spicy dishes. Favourites: mature red wine is appealing, but for economy seek out Bulgarian vintages which can be found at incredibly low prices in some supermarkets. Try 'Lovico Suhindol', 'Cabernet Sauvignon', 'Cellar Reserve 1992' (all at around £4). Good French red wine can be expensive, particularly with a well-known name

like 'Chateauneuf du Pape' (£12-£18) – instead pick a wine from one of the nearby Cote du Rhone villages such as 'Lirac'; bursting with character and excellent value at about half the price (£6-£7).

4. **Be prepared to pay a little extra for your bottle of wine.** Why: the more you pay, the higher the proportion of your money is spent on the actual wine. Note: the price of a bottle of wine always includes certain fixed costs such as shipping, storage, insurance and delivery; which can add up to £2 a bottle. And: for less expensive wines, you're paying more for these costs than for the wine itself. Pointer: the average price of a bottle of good quality wine is £4 to £6. Better: try paying £8 to £11 for an above-average – and sometimes superb quality – wine. Tip: avoid paying over £12 for a bottle unless you're sure of what you're buying. This applies particularly to famous wines such as Champagne, Chablis, Burgundy and Claret. You can often double the price you pay; and get only a 10%-15% increase in quality – you're paying for the name. Obscure wines at a lower price are a better bet for good value; especially if they have an unpronounceable name. Reason: a name that can't be pronounced is harder to remember, and doesn't sell as well. Tip: try 'Vergelesses-Bataillere 1994', an excellent Premier Cru Red Burgundy (£13).

5. **Decode the language of the label.** Fact: the name of the wine may be just about anything; a grape variety, a brand, a town, a district – even a fantasy name. 'New World' – North and South American, South African, Australian and New Zealand – labels are easy to understand as they provide detailed information, often with the help of a second or 'back' label. But: Italian, German and French labels can be cryptic, and provide few details. Helpful: look for these indications of quality and style: 'A.O.C' (Appellation d'Origine Controlée), 'D.O.C' (Denominazione di Origine Controllata), 'D.O.C.G' (Denominazione di Origine Controllata Guaratita). Wise: pick a wine from a single estate that is grown, made and bottled by the one producer; you should find their name is as large and as prominent as the name of the wine. This indicates pride in the product; and you'll not be disappointed. Hint: try 'Chateau Beauregard Saumur Blanc' from the Gourdon Family, Loire: a superb light white wine (£4.50).

6. **Vary your purchasing methods.** Look beyond local supermarkets and high street off licences: to increase your choice, and taste wines that high turnover stores won't stock because they're only available in small quantities. Try mail-order wine specialists. Popular: The Wine Society, Stevenage, (01438 741177); Waitrose Direct, Bracknell (0800 188881); Tanners, Shrewsbury (01743 234455). And: look for wine merchants when travelling around. Recommendations: Valvona and Crolla, Edinburgh (0131 5566066) have the best selection of Italian wines in the UK. D. Byrne & Co., Clitheroe (01200 423152), offer a brilliant worldwide selection.

7. **Learn to 'taste' wines.** How: always use clean wine glasses that taper inwards – these trap the aroma of the wine. Important: never fill the glass more than two-thirds full – more than this and you'll force the aroma out of the glass. Train yourself to look at the wine and note the colour before you sniff it – you're seeking a first impression of its scent, or 'bouquet'. Crucial: spend some time smelling before you taste – this allows you to gain that all-important first impression. 50% of the pleasure comes from the smell, or 'nose'. Your tastebuds can really only identify four tastes – 'saltiness', 'sweetness', 'acidity' and 'bitterness'. Technique: when tasting, let a few drops of the wine fall behind your front lower teeth whilst sucking in air so that the wine is oxygenated as it passes over your tongue. More of the vapour is sent from the back of the mouth into the upper nasal cavities and comes into contact with the olfactory nerve – this gives a heightened sensory perception, or 'three-dimensional' impression.

8. **Start storing wine at home.** So: you can build up a collection of favourite wines and will always have a choice. How: store table wines and sparkling wines horizontally so the wine is in contact with the cork – this keeps the cork moist and stops it shrinking so the air cannot enter the bottle and spoil the wine. Where: an even temperature is important, so a cool cellar at 8-11°C is best – or use the cupboard under the stairs. Avoid: the kitchen and out-houses where temperatures can vary considerably and spoil the wine. Also: wine is affected adversely by

transportation. Tip: allow wine to rest for at least two weeks before serving – this restores its equilibrium, and you'll enjoy it at its best.

9. **Serve wines at the right temperature.** Ideal: red wines should be served at 12-14°C, a few degrees lower than the temperature at which they'll be drunk – they will then warm up in the glass, and produce the best taste. Dry white wines should be served at 8-10°C; and sparkling and sweet wines at 5-8°C – these are more palatable at cooler temperatures. Hint: if you have an inexpensive and very acidic white wine that you don't want to throw away, save it for a hot day. Then chill it down to 3-4°C and drink it outside in the sunshine as an aperitif. Accompany this with canapes of smoked salmon or sardines on toast – perfect! The very cold temperature and the oily food will mask the excess acidity; and a degree of acidity is refreshing and appreciated on a hot day.

(Source: Peter Edwards who is your PFC *wine expert. He is a member of the Association of Wine Educators, and runs wine tastings for trade and consumer groups and vineyard exploration holidays in Europe. The original version of this feature first appeared in* PFC *June 1998, No. 21.)*

ARE YOU LOSING £278 EVERY YEAR UNNECESSARILY?

Britain's householders waste around £6.5 billion each year by failing to buy energy-saving appliances and not installing energy-efficient measures around their homes – this works out at £278 per year for every household. Fact: the biggest drain on household budgets comes from a lack of roof, loft and cavity wall insulation, draught proofing, heating controls, high efficiency boilers and energy saving refrigeration, washing machines and tumble dryers. Myth: energy efficient products are often more expensive than their conventional alternatives. Reality: many products – such as cavity wall insulation – cost far less than consumers think and produce big savings, year after year. And: most investments in energy efficiency measures can be recouped in full within three to five years. Bonus: 'cashback' offers and grants for people on social security benefits and/or who are over 60 years may also be available to help finance many of these measures. Examples: £200 cashback on a condensing boiler, plus grants towards the cost of loft and cavity wall insulation.

(Sources: Energy Efficiency Advice Line plus additional PFC *research.)*

REVEALED – 13 MAGIC WORDS THAT WILL SELL ANYTHING

***PFC* tip:** use at least three of the little-known 'power words' in any advertising and sales material, and you'll boost your chances of making a sale. Words: free, easy, discover, guarantee, new, proven, safety, results, save, you, love, money, health. Reason: these words act as the trigger that makes people want to buy goods and services. And: the more power words you use, the more likely you are to become a successful seller.

(Sources: PFC *business and marketing specialists.)*

WANT TO LOSE WEIGHT? TAKE TOP US DOCTORS' ADVICE

If you find it hard to stick to a diet, you should learn those simple, easy-to-follow tactics that enable you to lose weight; permanently!

1. **Start at the right time.** Essential: women should begin a weight-reducing diet during the first two weeks of their menstrual cycle. Quote: 'The level of the oestrogen hormone – which acts as an appetite suppressant – is higher then. This means it is less stressful to cope with a reduced intake of food; thus increasing your chances of maintaining the diet'; Dr Phillippa Wall, University of Sydney, Australia.

2. **Eat breakfast.** Quote: 'People who don't eat breakfast usually have a metabolic rate 4-5% lower than normal. Because of this, their bodies don't burn fat as efficiently and they can expect to gain weight – even if their overall daily calorie intake remains constant'; Dr Wayne Calloway, George Washington University, US.

3. **Maximise the power of your mind.** Quote: 'Anyone can easily psyche themselves into appetite control and eating satisfaction'; Dr Barbara DeBetz, New York psychiatrist. Ideas: always put food on individual plates – having serving dishes on the table will tempt you into having larger portions and second helpings. Serve food on smaller plates – this will deceive your brain into thinking you're having a larger meal. Have low-calorie foods that take up lots of room on your plate – this will make you feel you're eating more. Eat with a cocktail stick – you'll eat more slowly, and the slower you eat, the fuller you'll feel. Throw away leftovers – keeping them in your refrigerator is often a subconscious attempt to provide yourself with night-time snacks. Know when you are likely to be tempted to eat between meals – and arrange activities that make it impossible for you to snack during those times.

(Sources: Dr Phillippa Wall, Dr Wayne Calloway, Dr Barbara DeBetz. The full version of this feature first appeared in PFC *May 1997, No. 8.)*

CLICK, CLUNK, SQUEAL – LISTEN TO YOUR CAR AND SAVE A FORTUNE

Ears are the best tools that a car mechanic can have. Why: by listening closely, they can detect slight changes in the sounds of a car – and these can indicate whether something is wrong with it. Too many people switch off their hearing when they're driving and ignore their cars' cries for help. Better: if you listen, you'll save yourself an absolute fortune in repair bills. Here are some of those funny sounds that a car can make – and what they're trying to tell you:

1. **'Tweet, tweet, tweet'** – as if a bird is trapped in your engine. Likely cause: a frayed and/or slipping fan belt. Acid test: does the sound become more distinctive when you're accelerating? Fact: fan belts stretch through usage, and can eventually become so loose that they no longer turn the alternator effectively. Then: the battery isn't charged fully, and it goes flat. Additional warning sign: a scream from the engine when starting the car from cold. What to do: check the fan belt for wear –

replace if worn. If loose, tighten by slackening the bolt holding the alternator, levering the alternator with a large screwdriver or piece of wood until the belt is tight, and tightening the belt again. Tip: check the fan belt is tight enough by pressing down on it with your thumb – you should be able to displace it by no more than its own width.

2. **'Click, click, click'** – similar to the sound of someone typing inside your engine. Possible reasons: low oil level, worn valves or tappets. Question: is the sound most noticeable when the engine is idling? First: top up with oil to the required level indicated on the dipstick. Useful: don't rely on your oil warning light to tell you when your car is low on oil – by the time the light flashes, some damage may already have been done. Note: if the noise continues, take your car to a garage for repair. Other warning signs: the car burns oil and/or emits a blue cloud of smoke.

3. **'Clunk, clunk, clunk'** – heavy thumping noises from beneath the car. Problem: worn universal joints in the drive shaft of front-engine, rear-wheel drive cars. Definition: universal joints allow for some movement between the engine and the rear wheels, but this movement eventually leads to those joints wearing out. And: if you continue to drive, the drive shaft may fall apart whilst you're driving, causing an accident. Bottom line: if you have an older car, you may be able to replace just the universal joints, but for newer cars, the whole drive shaft will probably need to be replaced.

4. **'Squeal, squeal, squeal'** – coming from your tyres. Probable causes: fast cornering, under-inflated tyres. Vital: check your tyres are inflated to the correct pressures as specified in your car's handbook. Advisable: check the pressure of your spare tyre at the same time; inflate, as required. Tip: test pressures again a few days later to see if you have a slow leak in one of the tyres. Important: under-inflated tyres, over-inflated tyres and tyres of differing pressures will all affect the car's steering and the lifespan of those tyres.

5. **'Tick, tick, tick'** – from the direction of the tyres. Likeliest reason: a stone or nail in one of your tyres. Query: is it most apparent when you're driving at low speeds? Fact: a stone is rarely serious, and is

easy to remove. But: a nail or piece of metal can work its way into the tyre and puncture it. Remove carefully – take the car to a garage if metal is embedded in the wall of the tyre.

6. **'Thump, thump, thump'** – coming from your tyres. Possible causes: the tyre wall is bulging or that economical retread tyre is now shedding its tread. Key question: have you bumped a kerb recently? This can cause the tyre to bulge. Best: replace the tyre before it flattens – or bursts on a motorway. Hint: avoid driving at more than 45mph for at least four hours after fitting a new tyre. Driving too fast before the tyre has settled can throw it out of balance, causing the car to shake and judder.

7. **'Clatter, grind, clatter, grind'** – from the direction of your wheels. Problem: wheel bearings may be starting to break up and need replacing. Pointer: is it at its loudest when you're driving around corners? And: does the sound change to a whining noise when you're driving at speed? Unfortunate: bearings on most newer cars are sealed for life, and require replacements. Use a garage which will have the specialist equipment needed for the job. Warning: continuing to drive with worn bearings may lead to them breaking up, which will cause serious damage, and even an accident.

8. **'Screech, screech, screech'** – coming from your brakes when you're stopping the car. Typical: newly fitted brake pads make this noise whilst they're bedding in. Alternative: your old brake pads have worn away and their metal studs are rubbing on the disks or drums. Acid test: when did you last replace your brake pads? Note: if a new set is not put on, braking will become dangerously inefficient. Plus: the studs will cut a groove into the disks or drums. Result: brake pads will still need to be changed – and the disks or drums will have to be skimmed as well. Helpful: replace brake fluid at least once a year – it attracts moisture and condensation which can corrode master and wheel cylinders.

9. **'Pop, pop, pop'** – motor racing sounds from your engine. Probable source: a hole in the exhaust system. Question: does the noise become louder as you're accelerating and decelerating? Confirmation: start the car, and let it tick over. Open the bonnet and look back from

the exhaust manifold until you identify a hole by sound or by touch – you may be able to feel gases coming through a join in the exhaust pipe or from the silencer. Essential: this problem needs to be remedied immediately – gases can leak into the car, causing carbon monoxide poisoning. Warning signs: runny nose, sneezing. What to do: small holes in the exhaust and cracks on pipe joins can often be repaired easily with a repair kit from a motor accessories shop. Hopeful: this should extend the exhaust's life by several thousand miles. Larger holes and split pipes mean that part or all of the exhaust need replacing. Shop around for the best deal.

(Source: John Mustoe is the joint-editor of The Penny Pincher Paper, *a newsletter for people who hate waste and want to save money. For further information about the newsletter, call* The Penny Pincher Paper *on 01234 771173. This feature first appeared in* PFC *March 1998, No. 18.)*

PURCHASE A LATEST MODEL COMPUTER – FOR HALF PRICE

***PFC* tip:** buy a second-hand computer if you want a value-for-money deal. Why: brand-new computers lose up to 50% of their value within the first month; and a further 10%-20% in the first year. And: most computer faults occur within the first four to six weeks of initial purchase, and will be resolved by the original owner. So: buying a year-old computer offers the best, most reliable deal. Recommended buys: Compaq for desk-tops, Toshiba for laptops. Tactic: if you're buying from a dealer, ask for a three-month guarantee; just in case.

(Source: Computer guru, Jon Godfrey.)

OUTSMART INHERITANCE TAX WITH THIS SIMPLE GUIDE

Inheritance tax is charged on any transfer over £231,000. Given the price of the average house, this puts many UK property owners at risk. Yet relatively few people have made provisions to protect their families and loved ones against this tax. Tip: you can give away up to £3,000 a year free of tax and can carry this relief forward a year; which means that a married couple can give away £6,000 per annum without any inheritance tax liability. You can also make any number of small gifts of up to £250 free of tax; but not more than £250 to one person. Better: the Finance Act 1992 created a class of property which is exempt from Inheritance Tax, conditional only on requirements of a minimum ownership period. 100% relief applies to interests in unincorporated businesses, owner-occupied farmlands and farm tenancies. Meaning: you can avoid inheritance tax entirely if you convert your estate into business or agricultural property qualifying for 100% relief. Attractive: a business, an interest in a business.

(Source: PFC *financial experts.)*

MAKE YOUR DEODORANT WORK HARDER

***PFC* tip:** if your antiperspirant and/or deodorant runs out just when you need it most, simply hold the canister's nozzle under hot running water. This will rejuvenate it; and give you an extra few squirts – enough to see you through the day.

(Source: Marie Hollis, a PFC *subscriber from London.)*

FOOTBALL CRAZY? HOW YOU CAN MARRY IN YOUR FAVOURITE STADIUM

The 1994 Marriage Act enabled local authorities to license a wide range of premises to hold non-religious wedding ceremonies. And: since then, more than 2,000 properties have been approved – including stately homes, caves, ships and even football grounds. You can choose your ideal venue by asking these key questions:

1. **Where exactly will the ceremony be conducted?** Don't assume automatically that it will take place in the most attractive area; it could be carried out in a side room.

2. **Which days and times are available?** Note: the venue's primary function usually takes precedence over wedding ceremonies – if you want to marry on your favourite football pitch, you may have to do it on a weekday.

3. **Do members of the public have access to the venue?** Tip: don't think about getting married at a tourist attraction if you'd prefer a quiet, private ceremony. Weddings attract crowds.

4. **Who will be in charge of arrangements on the big day?** Essential: make sure you meet this person well in advance and be certain that you have confidence in their organisational abilities. Also: see if you like them personally and want them to play a special part in your wedding day.

5. **How many parking spaces are available?** Fact: many city venues are desperately short of parking space; larger weddings may be better suited to out-of-town and country venues.

6. **Are any other events being staged at the venue at the same time?** Important: do select a time when nothing else is taking place so you'll have the staff's full attention, and you won't have your ceremony disturbed.

7. **Where can photographs/video recordings be taken?** Note: many venues will restrict photographs to certain areas and may ban video recordings altogether.

8. **Who is liable for any damage?** Wise: arrange insurance cover if you are liable – particularly if you're marrying in a stately home full of valuable antiques.

9. **How many weddings have you staged to date?** Tip: always take up references – but not from those hand-picked couples recommended by the venue's staff. Better: ask for a list; then select your own at random.

(Sources: Midge Gillies, The Wedding Book – A Complete Guide to Getting Married *plus additional* PFC *research.)*

GET THE LATEST BEST-SELLERS – FOR LESS THAN HALF-PRICE

We're all familiar with those book clubs that offer you an initial pack of books at a terrific discount but then insist that you purchase so many more for the next year or two; and all at not-so-great discounts. What we wanted to know was this: 'Is there an organisation that offers you a similar range of books with big discounts and no strings attached?' Findings: *Wallace and Gromit: The Lost Slipper* (£9.99 to £4.99), *AA Illustrated Guide to Britain* (£25.00 to £7.99), *Bridget Jones's Diary* (£12.99 to £4.99) – these and many more cut-price hardback and softback books are available from The Book People Limited. Call (01942 724444) for more information and their latest catalogue.

(Source: PFC *researchers.)*

BEWARE! LIFE INSURANCE POLICIES THAT DON'T PAY

***PFC* tip:** beware of 'whole of life' insurance policies that offer a huge amount of life cover for a small initial monthly premium. Why: check to see if that premium has to grow – perhaps by 10% a year – to maintain the life cover. If so, your monthly premium is set to double every seven years for life. Question: can you afford this? Typical: too many people take out this type of policy, then find that their circumstances change – and they're forced to stop the premiums. Result: they have very little left in terms of a paid-up or surrender value – they've lost most or even all of their money. Best: avoid these schemes, opting instead for the traditional type of policy. Bottom line: these won't offer so much cover initially, but the regular premium should be fixed; which means that you won't be stung by rising premiums in the future.

(Source: PFC financial and legal experts, plus additional research.)

HOW TO FIND LOVE LATER IN LIFE

It's not always easy to discover love in your 40s, 50s and beyond – we all lead such busy and hectic lives that it's hard to find time; and even then we don't know how to go about it, it's been so long. Here's how to succeed:

1. **Look on it as a project.** Be businesslike about romance; set about finding it in a professional way. First: get out and about more – socialise with colleagues at lunchtimes, after work and in the evenings. And: go to different places with them – pubs, restaurants and clubs. Also: mix with neighbours, existing friends and family more often. Widen your circle of contacts as far as possible – the vast majority of new relationships are made with friends of friends. Plus: join an adult education course, an amateur dramatics group, a creative writing course, the local bird watching society – anything that brings you into regular contact with lots of people.

2. **Join a reputable introduction agency.** Fact: thousands of people join introduction agencies each year, and the majority form lasting relationships. Reason: people use agencies because they are wary of meeting strangers in clubs and bars. And: they know that people who belong to agencies are sincere – they've paid a membership fee of between £50 and £1,500. Where: obtain details of agencies in local and national newspapers. Tip: apply to agencies advertising in papers that you personally like – you're far more likely to meet someone with similar interests and outlooks.

3. **Advertise in the 'romance' pages of your local newspaper.** Truth: people from all over the United Kingdom advertise for friendship, companionship and love in the classified advertisements of newspapers and magazines. Why: it works – the average advertisement generates between 20 and 50 responses. Tip: the simplest, most straightforward advertisements produce the largest postbags. Avoid: humour – something that seems funny to you now may be misunderstood by someone who reads it later on in a different mood and other circumstances. Safety warning: always communicate via a box number so that your name, address and phone number are not given out to anyone until you feel happy to provide this information.

4. **Don't be idealistic about your prospective partner.** Everyone has a dream of what their 'perfect' partner should look like, but seeking physical perfection inevitably leads to failure and disappointment. Reason: your perfect partner may exist, but they almost certainly don't look as you'd expect them to do. Acid test: think of past relationships – you've probably had partners who have been short and tall, blonde and dark-haired, and so on. Don't: establish requirements that focus solely on physical appearance if you want to find someone that you can be happy with, and can make happy.

5. **Concentrate on personality rather than looks.** Make a list of the main qualities you'd like to find in a partner. Helpful: thinking about a previous love can be useful here. Also: draw up a list of your qualities too. Typical: you'll be surprised at how similar your two lists are. Look for someone with those features that you have in common. But: don't set too many requirements as this reduces your chances of meeting someone suitable. Essential: cast your net as wide as possible – that way you've a better chance of finding the right person for you.

6. **Be realistic about yourself.** It's important to be sensible about what you have to offer. If you're an average 50-year-old man, you're not going to be chased by lots of beautiful 20-year-old girls. But: you will probably find that special person if you mix with people of a similar age,

nature and status. Opinion: many matchmakers believe that most people are looking for a mirror image of themselves. Idea: this does ensure you have something in common to build upon.

7. **Focus on what you can offer a potential partner.** Note: too many people looking for love via introduction agencies and classified advertisements concentrate on describing who they wish to meet and what they want from a partner. Problem: this discourages interest as other people want to know all about you. Better: describe yourself – you'll receive more replies that way. Basics: sex, age, general location, personality, likes. Avoid: dislikes – people are much more responsive to positive, upbeat descriptions. Key words: these words appeal to the broadest spectrum of potential partners – 'reliable', 'loyal', 'genuine', 'thoughtful', 'positive', 'honest'. Use: at least three of these words in a description in order to maximise responses.

8. **Take pride in your appearance.** It's easy to let yourself go when there isn't anyone special in your life. Examples: clothes are worn for another day to reduce washing and ironing, and junk food is eaten more often because it is convenient. Outcome: you'll look and feel less attractive, and lose confidence in yourself and what you have to offer. Better: pay extra attention to your needs. Buy something for yourself each week if you can afford to, even if it's just a colourful tie or a pair of jazzy socks. Have a haircut, a massage; anything that makes you feel good.

9. **Keep smiling.** Why: a happy, smiling face is the most attractive feature of all. Problem: it's easy to get out of the habit of smiling when you're on your own – smiling is a social device. Learn to do it in private when nobody else is there. How: read a funny book, watch your favourite comedy programme – just try to see the funny side of life. Best: make a deal with yourself to smile at least three times an hour from now on. Result: get into the habit of smiling regularly, and it will come naturally when meeting potential partners.

10. **Keep trying.** Don't expect instant success. Fact: some people are lucky enough to find their ideal partner within a few weeks of starting their

search. Typical: expect it to take longer – up to a year or more. Helpful: measuring your progress every couple of months can be a morale-booster – how many more places have you visited, hobbies have you tried, and friends have you made? Don't: just focus on meeting one special person; that will come in time. Important: enjoy your search – have fun meeting new people and pursuing different activities. Bonus: you'll widen your circle of friends, and they'll have friends who may be just right for you.

(Sources: Pat Jones, the PFC *relationships expert. Who, is the founder of Local Links, the fastest growing introduction agency in the South East of England. You can find out more about 'Local Links' by calling 0800 515104. The original version of this feature first appeared in* PFC *October 1997, No. 13.)*

SLOGANS THAT WIN PRIZES

Most people don't enter competitions because they're not sure what to write in the part which says: 'Complete the following sentence in no more than X words.' This tie-breaker section is all-important – it's the 'win or lose' part of most contests, and inevitably determines the winner. But: consistent winning is all about technique – once you've learned the various styles which win prizes, it's simply a matter of deciding which you are most comfortable with and practising. Choose from the following styles:

Play on words: this is a useful technique for a humourous tie-breaker. One winner said that a bicycle shop offered 'wheelie great deals'. The more of a 'groaner' it is, the better. They are always very popular with competition judges. You might win a trip to the Louvre with a line like 'With more taste for less Monet, what have I got Toulouse?'.

Homonyms: use words that sound or are spelled alike, but which have two or more different meanings. For example, a bride won a dream wedding by completing the sentence 'After the wedding...' with 'Aisle Alter Hymn!'.

Adaptions: this involves adjusting the titles of well known films, songs or books to fit the slogan requirements. As an example, 'A Dish called Wonder' won a prize from a manufacturer of cook-in sauces soon after the film *A Fish called Wanda* was released.

Alliteration: put together several words which all start with the same sound. For example, 'It's better with a bit of butter!'. It's not necessary to make every word start with the same sound – in some cases it can make it sound too contrived: 'Clever colour creates cosy attention', for instance. But used carefully, alliteration always attracts attention.

Contrasts: use two words of opposite meaning to produce an eye catching effect: 'High quality goods at a low price' and 'You get friendly hellos and lots of good buys'. Most thesauruses list antonyms – words which mean the opposite – so browse through their pages for inspiration.

Spoonerisms: this technique involves transposing the initial letters of words to create something humourous. As an example, 'mint of history' instead of 'hint of mystery'.

Malapropisms: the 'unintentional' misuse of a word by confusing it with one of similar sound can often produce amusing results. The most mundane of slogans can take on a new look with a malapropism. For example, the slogan for household paint declares: 'They're a pigment of my imagination'. Don't forget to jot down any ones you may hear on a day-to-day basis, as they could come in handy one day.

Rhyming couplets: when in doubt, send in a two-line rhyme. Armed with a good rhyming dictionary, this technique is easy to learn. The trick is to get the rhyme and scansion – the metrical rhythm of the verse – exactly right. Read it aloud, counting the number of syllables in the first line. The number of syllables in the second line must match exactly without being forced. Be careful that your regional accent – whatever it may be – doesn't influence your choice of rhyming words.

Triple rhymes: you can make your rhymes stand out even more by using three rhyming words rather than just two: 'For beauty care and shining hair, Boots is the store that's always there'. Look for more unusual rhymes, rather than the overworked 'test/best', 'savour/flavour', treasure/pleasure/leisure' and 'delights/excites/invites' combinations.

Alternatives: other tie-breaker tasks fall into two categories. 1: writing an ending for a limerick involves being given the first line or two and having to make up the rest yourself. To complete it successfully, remember there should be a rhyming 'punchline' in the last line, so it often pays to begin here. Make long list of words that rhyme – as your punchline must end with one of these, you're getting the most difficult part over with. It's then fairly easy to work backwards, filling in the central couplet. 2: naming a logo character. What you're looking for here is something that's particularly apt to the product. For example, what would be a suitable name for a character who is a regular saver with a bank which pays terrific interest rates? Ivor Lottabrass, perhaps. Flicking through a joke book will give you lots of ideas; the cornier, the better!

***PFC* tips:** study the instructions for clues. Typically, you will be asked to provide an 'apt', 'original' and/or 'amusing' slogan. 'Apt' means appropriate to the goods being promoted, the prize on offer, or the theme of the competition. A good tie-breaker mixes together two or more of these three factors. 'Original': your first thoughts are likely to be similar to those of countless other entrants. Discard them. If two or more entries are similar, they are considered unoriginal, and are scrapped. 'Amusing': there is a thin dividing line between funny and rude. By and large, daring slogans don't win. Picture your judging panel as elderly spinsters and you won't go far wrong. Identify the product's positive features and include these in your slogan. Keep the slogan simple and sincere. Don't go overboard with accolades – they make your entry sound phoney and reduce your chances. Make your slogan unique to the product – if it isn't mentioned in the introductory wording, refer to it by name. Avoid vague statements like 'You've tried the rest, now try the best' which apply to anything. The closer you get to a personalised entry, the better your chances. Don't knock rival products – there's no such thing as bad publicity. As far as you're concerned, they don't exist. Don't ask for a prize. Phrases such as 'I'd like to win a Bermuda holiday because... I've been unemployed for three years and need a break' comprise 25% of entries and never win. Judges are looking for something positive and upbeat.

(Sources: Kathy Kantpowicz, editor of Winner's Friend. *Kathy is the author of* The Essential Guide to Comping *and* Tackle That Tie breaker *published by Agora Lifestyles Limited. Call freephone 0500 523499 for a free copy of the latest issue of* Winner's Friend. *The original version of this feature first appeared in* PFC *July 1997, No. 10.)*

HOW TO BE THE WORLD'S GREATEST GRANDPARENT

Being a gran or granddad isn't always easy. But if you follow our step-by-step guide, you'll soon become a number one grandparent:

1. **Treat all grandchildren equally.** Why: children have very strong feelings of fair play and what's right and wrong. Guidelines: make sure your grandchildren receive the same amounts of presents, attention and cuddles. And: take the same interest in all of their hobbies, exams and jobs. Essential: never compare – for example, do not comment if one grandchild obtains a higher grade in an exam or has a better job than the others. Also: avoid taking sides in family arguments.

2. **Speak about the past with your grandchildren.** Fact: these conversations will become part of their memories. As a grandparent, you can bring a sense of continuity to children, whatever their age. Tip: the past often fascinates young children, especially those things that they have only read about or seen on television. Examples: your schooldays, the clothes you wore, what your childhood home was like to grow up in.

3. **Talk about the present too** – you need to be a vital, active part of the family. Idea: keep abreast of the topics that interest your grandchildren and they like to talk about. Example: watch the daytime television programmes that fascinate your pre-school grandchildren. Important: do be aware of children's changing interests, and grow with them. Grandparents sometimes forget that something that interested a

child at five may embarrass them at ten. Examples: Sooty, Thomas the Tank Engine, Postman Pat.

4. **Be ready to listen to your grandchildren – this isn't always as easy as it sounds.** Typical: you may feel that your grandchild's problem is insignificant. Remember: it is not a minor problem to the child – otherwise they would not want to discuss it. Example: the death of a small pet such as a goldfish or a hamster. Better: listen to what they have to say, and talk them through it. Wise: talk about your own experiences of grief, and how you came to terms with it.

5. **Keep a confidence – you should never divulge anything that a grandchild says to you in secret.** Problem: you may feel you should tell the parents what you know. But: this will lead to a loss of trust between you and your grandchild. Suggestion: explain how you feel to your grandchild, and ask if you can speak about what is concerning you to their parents. Alternative: persuade your grandchild to speak to their parents themselves. Bottom line: maintain that trust.

6. **Share experiences with your grandchildren**. Example: a grandfather could try a teenage grandson's hair gel; and then discuss the differences between hair creams and gels. Tip: it is these little snippets of conversation that strengthen a relationship. Do: always comment in a sincere way. Don't laugh at a teenager's clothes, hairstyle, or the way that they look. Remember: the fashions when you were young, and your parents' reactions.

7. **Open up the lines of communication.** Difficulty: you may live some distance away from your grandchildren. Good: keep a conversation going with letters, tapes and photographs – you could even go on-line on the internet. Note: you may not always get a prompt reply (or any response at all) but you will be talking to them – and they will remember. And: keep in touch by remembering their birthdays, sending a small gift or money as an occasional treat, and writing a postcard for them when you are away on holiday. Result: your grandchildren will be relaxed in your company when you meet again.

(Source: Doris Corti is a grandmother who has written a book based on her experiences. Successful Grandparenting *is published by How To Books Limited. You can obtain further information about the book by calling the publishers on 01865 793806. The original version of this feature appeared in* PFC *April 1998, No.19)*

INSIDER TIPS ON HOW TO BEAT THE BOOKIES – TIME AND AGAIN

It's true – you really can make money from betting on horse racing. But to succeed, you must think like a professional gambler. Professional gamblers are on a constant quest for 'value' – horses that stand a better chance of winning than the odds suggest. The pros don't expect to win every time, but if their calculations are correct, they'll come out on top often enough to make a good profit. Look at it this way: if you back horses at 2-1 or better and 40% of them win, you'll be a steady winner – even though more than half of your selections lost! How do you find 'value' bets? Here's the inside information the bookies really don't want you to know about:

Look for horses from in-form stables in fields with less than nine runners. Following a winning stable is usually a profitable strategy. Avoid betting on races with more than 12 runners – inevitably, these are something of a lottery. Don't back horses which are odds-on – they'll almost certainly represent poor value for money. And: steer clear of multi-horse accumulators and heavily advertised 'fun bets' such as Union Jack, Lucky 7 and Pontoon – overall, the returns from these combination bets are much lower than those from betting on single horses. Place single bets to win. Exception: in races with a heavily backed favourite and an obvious 'second best', back this second horse each-way if the odds are 4-1 or better. If your selection is placed, you'll get a quarter (a fifth in large fields) of the odds on the each-way half of the bet. Why: you'll recover at least your stake money. Bonus: on the odd occasion that the horse wins, you'll pocket a tidy sum. Bet in the morning. Reason: odds are often shortened later, close to the start of the race. And: ask if an 'early price' is available – these tend to be offered on the bigger races of the day. Tip: make sure the quoted odds are written on your slip – it prevents disputes later on. Avoid paying tax by betting on course whenever possible. If not, it's worth shopping around for the best deal. Why: most high street bookies charge nine percent tax, but some phone-based services offer eight percent. Do: pay tax on your bets, rather than opting to pay it on any winnings. Reason: if you decide to pay later, you're effectively backing yourself to lose.

Use a money management system to maximise returns from your betting. Set aside a starting bank of betting money – £100, £200 or £500, as examples. Important: make sure that you can afford to lose this money if the worst happens. Stake 5% on your first selection, whether from your own judgement, a racing advisory service, or a newspaper tipster. If your horse wins, add the winnings to your betting bank, and place 5% of the new, larger bank on your next selection. If it loses, increase your stake on the next selection so that the winnings (based on the forecast odds) will be sufficient to recover your losses on the first horse and give you the profits a 5% stake would have produced. If this horse loses too, increase the stake again so that the winnings will recover all the losses on the first two horses and provide the profit that a 5% stake would have given. After a three-horse losing run, reduce your next bet to 5% of the bank. If your selection wins, the next bet should be 5% of the new bank; if not, you should increase your stake again, as described. Given a reasonable success rate, this method should ensure that at least half of your losing selections are 'cancelled out' by winners. With this enhanced success rate, you should be able to withstand the occasional, longer losing run. And by staking a percentage of your bank, your winnings should grow at an increasing rate.

(Source: Nick Daws is your PFC *gambling guru. He is also the editor of* British Gambling News, *Britain's leading gambling newsletter, published by Maple Marketing (UK) Limited, 11 Knowsley Avenue, Southall, Middlesex UB1 3AX. The full version of this feature first appeared in* PFC *October 1997, No. 13.)*

ARE YOUR SUNGLASSES DAMAGING YOUR EYESIGHT?

***PFC* warning:** ordinary, dark sunglasses can be harmful to your eyes. Why: they cause the pupils of your eyes to dilate, which allows damaging ultraviolet light to penetrate into your eyes. Best: choose glasses with lenses that screen out at least 95% of ultraviolet rays; buy these from opticians rather than over the counter in your local supermarket.

(Sources: PFC *health specialists.)*

GETTING MORE MONEY FROM YOUR INSURANCE CLAIM

Insurance companies view most claims as being inflated and fraudulent, don't want to pay out, and employ a whole range of dubious tactics to avoid doing so. Example: let's say you take out a new insurance policy and forget to mention that you had a similar policy cancelled a few years ago – perhaps you'd arranged a cheaper policy elsewhere when it came up for renewal, stopped making the payments on the original one and the insurers subsequently cancelled it. That's no big deal – until you come to make a claim on that new policy and the insurance company turns around and says 'Sorry, you withheld a material fact; we're not paying you'. It happens. So how do you improve your chances of getting your insurance claim paid in full, and without any hassle? Here's what you need to know:

1. **Complete all parts of the proposal form fully and accurately.** Note: some people are tempted to omit any facts that they think might lead to a higher premium, or an outright refusal. Examples: earlier claims on household policies, minor traffic offences, previous insurance cancellations or rejections. Wiser: include anything and everything that might be considered a material fact. The chances are that they'll not lead to a higher premium at all, or at worst, only a modest one. But: omitting a material fact can lead to a rejected claim later on, and the loss of hundreds or thousands of pounds.

2. **Fill in each and every section of a claim form in detail.** Motto: if in doubt, include it. Why: this document sets the tone for the settlement of your claim and any investigation. Incorrect or omitted statements will be held against you – and may invalidate the claim. Always: quantify your claim and be able to support it. Example: if you are claiming the cost of a clock, you need to be able to state the value and back this up with a receipt or some other form of verification. Tip: a claim that is in excess of an insurer's in-house limits will normally be queried. Unfortunate: in-house limits can vary quite considerably from one company to another, and are hard to predict. Example: an insurance company might investigate a £300 claim for a camera, but pay out £5,000 for roof repairs without query.

3. **Employ a loss assessor on more complex claims, especially those that might exceed in-house limits.** Who: a loss assessor is someone who will appraise the value of your claim, and pursue payment from the insurance company on your behalf. Important: don't confuse a loss assessor with a loss adjuster. Difference: a loss adjuster is appointed by the insurer when a claim exceeds their in-house limits. The insurance company will tell you that this person is independent, and will protect your interests too. This is wholly untrue. Why: the clue is in the name 'loss adjuster'; they're here to adjust the claim – in a downward direction.

4. **Bring in your loss assessor at the earliest possible stage.** When: find a loss assessor before you complete that all-important claim form, and ask them to help you to do it. They will enable you to complete it to your best advantage. Where: ideally, appoint someone who has been personally recommended to you – your insurance broker may be able to help here. Don't ask your insurance company – they're not here to help you at all. They would prefer you to be unrepresented as this makes it easier for them to reduce or eliminate the pay-off. Essential: negotiate a fee with the loss assessor before you begin. Guidelines: on modest claims of around £500 to £1,000, most assessors will probably not want to get involved – but they'll almost certainly give you some useful advice during your discussions, and it will be free of charge. On larger claims,

negotiate a flat fee if it will be cheaper than one based on a percentage of the eventual payout. Do your sums in advance.

5. **When progressing an insurance claim, ignore any indifferent or off-hand treatment that you receive from the insurer.** Typical: bland, standardised responses to your questions can be especially infuriating when you are attempting to discover what is happening; so too are phone messages that go unreturned. Note: the expertise of the person dealing with your case is often minimal, from a junior clerk up to the head of a very small section at best. And: they are expected to follow procedures without showing any initiative at all. Outcome: your case progresses extremely slowly, to the point where you feel the company is being deliberately obstructive. Too many claimants give up and go away or accept a lower payout when this happens – and that's exactly what those procedures were aiming to achieve.

6. **Speed up your claim by presenting yourself in person at the office, if possible.** This can have an electrifying effect on the staff handling the paperwork, and ensure that the matter receives immediate attention. Tip: a polite but insistent approach is sensible: 'I'm very happy to stand here until this matter is resolved satisfactorily'. Alternative: if you cannot go to the insurance company's office, try contacting someone at a much higher level as this can produce prompt results. But: don't just refer the problem to the next person up the line; the section manager, or even the department manager – they won't have the authority to make a speedy decision. Best: approach the managing director and request assistance, again in a pleasant but persistent manner. Tactic: faxes and e-mails appear more immediate and urgent and tend to have greater impact than letters. Or: go in and ask to see them now. Response: you'll often find that the attitude of senior personnel is: 'Why the hell are we wasting our time with this – pay them off.'

7. **Treat the loss adjuster with caution.** Remember: they are not your friend, nor are they there to help you or offer advice. They are

employed by the insurance company, work for them and have one aim – to reduce the payout as far as possible. Never ask for their opinion on a valuation, as this implies that you are uncertain of it and may be open to negotiation. And don't request their assistance in any other way; the fact that the loss adjuster lives in the same town as you and the insurance company is based a long distance away doesn't mean that the loss adjuster will side with you at all. They are being paid by the insurers, and are therefore loyal to them. Never utter anything but the truth but don't volunteer the truth unless it is asked for; especially if it won't be in your favour. Let the loss adjuster work things out for himself. Similarly, treat your loss assessor with respect. Always: be open and honest in your dealings with them. Do not say or do anything that might compromise your position or his own.

8. **Consider litigation, if all else fails.** How: it is easy and inexpensive to issue a county court summons for up to £5,000; you can represent yourself, and the hearing is very informal and relaxed. Good news: the vast majority of insurance companies will pay out after receiving a county court summons. Because: it is not worth their while attending court to defend the action, and most of them will realise that they are going to lose anyway. Bottom line: claim for any insurance payout due, the costs of employing a loss assessor, plus court costs too.

(Source: Peter L. d'Ambrumenil who is the managing director of Dispute Resolution Services Limited, a company that specialises in resolving disputes outside of the traditional court system. This feature first appeared in PFC *April 1998, No. 19.)*

A COMPLETE GUIDE TO HOME-BUYING ABROAD

You can buy a quality flat or house abroad for as little as £15,000 – you've then got a ready-made holiday home, and a useful source of extra income. You can rent it out for as much as £5,000 a year. Here are our top tips for success:

1. **Identify your individual requirements.** Key question: is this a holiday home, an investment, or both? For a holiday home, criteria might include: sunshine levels, leisure and social activities, and the proximity to airports, mountains and/or the sea. For an investment, your criteria may incorporate: possible rental incomes and anticipated increases in property values. Fact: if you're buying a property to rent out when you're not using it, the three most important factors to consider are position, position and position. To re-sell, a property in reasonable condition is likely to be a better investment than an exceptional property in a less attractive location – that exceptional property is constrained by the values of surrounding properties. And: if you are buying for investment purposes, be aware that in most countries property values increase at around 4%-5% a year; so always do the sums for your individual circumstances.

2. **Set your budget.** Question: what can you afford to spend? Note: the cost of homes in many southern European and Mediterranean countries is low; but the associated purchase costs can be as much as 20% of the purchase price. So: if you are buying for investment purposes, you are going to need to own the property for three years or more just to recoup your buying costs – don't expect to make a quick killing from buying and selling properties. And: remember to allow for repairs, maintenance and upkeep costs in your calculations as well as a letting agent's fees of about 10-30% of any rental income.

3. **Find out about the laws and purchase procedures in your favoured country; and do it before proceeding.** Problem: most people buying a property abroad assume the process will be similar to the one in the United Kingdom; but they are often very different. Example: in Spain, anyone with financial dealings must have a fiscal number – an 'NIE' – which has to be used in all dealings with the Spanish tax authorities. Without that NIE, you cannot register the title deed of a property, open a bank account or take out an insurance policy. Essential: always check the facts with an official and reliable source – but note that these may not necessarily be one and the same. Remember: estate agents

and property dealers are there for one reason only – to take your money. Wise: employ an English-speaking local professional such as an accountant to handle your affairs; find one by personal recommendation.

4. **Shop around.** Statistic: more than 60% of people who buy properties overseas regret their choice. Why: they did not do enough research in advance. Better: subscribe to newsletters such as *International Living*, (0500 523499), read books such as *Buying a Home Abroad*, Survival Books (01937 843523), and attend exhibitions such as 'World of Property', Outbound Publishers (01323 726040). Also: use directory enquiries to contact the appropriate embassy or high commission of that country – it will almost certainly be based in central London. This is a useful source of advice. And: too many buyers set unrealistic deadlines for themselves. Example: they try to find and buy a property within a long weekend, or a week's holiday. Main question: would you purchase a UK property in the same way – 'No'. Best: take your time. Don't buy the first half-decent property you see. And: visit the property when you're not in a holiday mood; and go out of season. If you still like it when the weather is cold and wet, the chances are you'll like it all year round.

5. **Consider the practicalities.** Important: never assume that electricity, water and sewerage services are laid on. Many older properties lack even the most basic facilities; such as a clean water supply and sanitation, let alone reliable electricity and/or gas supplies. Also: don't take on a property that requires any renovation work – it's even harder to get good builders abroad than it is at home. Guidance: a property in need of total restoration will cost at least as much to restore as it does to buy; and can add up to two or three times the purchase price. And: the costs are rarely recovered when you sell. It is hard to re-sell a renovated older property at more than the average market price for older properties in that area. Wiser: new or recently built flats and properties. Warning: don't rely too much on a builder's warranty – the value of this depends on the reliability of the builder, who may go out of business next month. Ask about other homes they have built, then go to see them and speak to the occupants. If you're getting a ten-year warranty, view the builder's

ten-year old properties; talk to the residents, learn about the problems that have arisen and how these have been dealt with by that builder.

6. **Discover the tax implications of buying a particular property.** Fact: taxes levied on non-resident property owners can be substantial – and may include property taxes (rates), residential tax, capital gains tax, wealth tax, and inheritance tax. Tip: before buying a property, check that there are no outstanding property taxes from previous years – in some countries, the new owner assumes responsibility for all unpaid property taxes and related debts. And: find out the 'fiscal value' of the property. Reason: property taxes are usually based on the fiscal value – or 'notional letting value' – of the property, not its purchase price. Fiscal value is normally 50-60% of the purchase price. If it is higher than this, you will need to appeal – in some countries, many other taxes such as income tax, wealth tax, transfer tax on property sales and inheritance tax are also linked to this value. Note: if you're planning to retire abroad at some stage, do remember to check on the income tax rates, social security and other taxes incurred by residents of that country.

7. **Be ready to negotiate.** Myth: dual pricing – where one price is quoted for locals, and a higher one is given to foreigners – is rare. But: it is true that many locals are astonished at the prices paid by foreigners for nondescript properties in uninspiring areas – so be prepared to negotiate even if you think you're getting a bargain. You can get an even better one. Note: in popular areas, asking prices are often unrealistically high to snare unsuspecting and uninformed foreigners. Expect: a 10% reduction at least; but ask for 20% – especially if you are able to pay cash. Guideline: check property prices advertised in local newspapers, magazines and property journals. And: before making an offer, check to see exactly what is included – in some countries, it is common for sellers to strip a house, removing everything except the structure.

8. **Take expert, independent legal advice before you sign anything, or hand over any money.** Best: obtain legal advice in a language in which you're fluent; and from an experienced lawyer.

Warning: don't rely solely on the advice of those who have a financial interest in the property you are buying. Alert: many expatriate professionals practise abroad – don't assume that a fellow national will offer you a better deal or do a better job than a local national. Reason: most frauds are perpetrated by foreigners on their fellow countrymen. Also: have a survey done, and a valuation. Helpful: local town halls may have a foreigners' department where staff speak English. Residents' associations, property owners' organisations, associations of foreign business owners, English-speaking clubs and expatriate organisations are other useful sources of advice and recommendations. Bottom line: consulates provide their nationals with local and practical information and assistance; including details of lawyers, translators and other organisations and individuals.

(Source: Mark Hempshell is a PFC *expert; he writes extensively about living and working overseas. This feature first appeared in* PFC *May 1998, No. 20.)*

SPREAD BETTING SECRETS THAT IMPROVE YOUR ODDS

If you're looking for a betting opportunity that allows you to use your skill and judgement and win serious amounts of cash, consider spread betting. Why: because you can back an individual or team to do well or badly, you can bet on the result and/or the margin of victory, and you can close and re-open your bet at any time during the event. What's more, there's no tax to pay – with spread betting, the tax is paid by the bookmakers.

How: instead of placing a bet at odds of 6/4 or whatever, you simply stake a fixed amount per unit on an outcome, whether runs made in a cricket game, or goals scored in a football match. The bookmaker then quotes a spread between two figures. If you think the result will be lower than the bottom figure, you can place a 'sell' bet; if you expect it to be higher than the top figure, you can put on a 'buy' bet. Example: you want to bet on an England-Australia Test Match. Your spread-betting bookmaker quotes a spread of 220-240 for England's first innings. You think England will score less than 220, so you place a 'sell' bet at £5 a run. The Australian fast bowlers work their magic, and England are out for 120. Outcome: you win your stake unit of £5 multiplied by the difference between the bookie's lower figure of 220 and the actual score of 120. Multiplying £5 by 100 produces a cheque for £500.

But what if the result goes against you? Say an English hero gets a century and England are eventually all out for 300. Outcome: you deduct the bookie's lower figure of 220 from the actual score of 300 and multiply this by the unit stake of £5. So, £300 minus £220 multiplied by £5 means your losses would be £400. Important: a 'buy' bet works exactly the same way. If you 'buy' England for £5 a run at 240 and they eventually score 300, your winnings are 300 minus 240 multiplied by £5; producing £300. If they score only 190, you lose 240 minus 190 multiplied by £5, equalling £250. But don't worry – you can minimise the risk of losing big money with a *PFC* trick of the trade.

Best advice: place bets whilst the event is actually taking place. This is known as 'in running', and it enables you to take your profits when your bet is doing well, and to cut your losses if events move against you. How: you can close a bet at any time by placing an equal bet in the opposite direction. Let's look at some examples:

Profit-taking: at the start of a Test Match, you 'buy' England at 240 for £5 a point. By lunch, they are going well at 110 for two, and the quoted spread has increased to 270-290. However, you suspect a mid-innings collapse may be imminent, and decide to take your profits now. So, you 'sell' England for £5 a point at 270. This means you can take a profit of 270 minus 240 multiplied by £5 which produces £150 – whatever England's final score may be! Benefit: if your predictions were correct and England collapsed at 190 all out, you'd still collect £150 winnings. But if you'd allowed the original bet to run, you'd make a loss of 50 multiplied by £5, a total of £250.

Loss-cutting: you can bet 'in running' to cut your losses too. Imagine you initially 'sold' England for £5 a run at 220. By lunch, they've reached 110 for two and the spread has increased to 270-290. By taking out an equal and opposite 'buy' bet now, you can accept a loss of 290 minus 220 multiplied by £5, which equals £350. Alternative: if you let that bet run and England go on to make 500, you'd be looking at a loss of 500 minus 220 multiplied by £5 – a whopping £1,400.

Other advice: here are our top tips for spread betting success:

Bet against popular sentiment. Reason: bookies' spreads have to reflect the actual bets being placed, and people are naturally more optimistic when betting on their own teams. Betting against well-supported teams such as Manchester United and England can often represent the best value for money.

Be aware of the potential downside of any bet – and bear in mind that some markets are inherently riskier than others. Note: cricket innings scores can vary so widely that potential winnings can be substantial. But losses can be equally significant as well. Always bet 'in running' on these events.

Concentrate on long-term markets such as the number of Premiership points gained by a football team during a season. Because: the facility for betting 'in running' maximises your chances of making profits and cutting losses.

Decide in advance what you can afford to lose, and act immediately if events move against you. Essential: if your potential losses reach this figure, automatically close the bet and accept the losses. Never hang on, hoping to recoup these losses; they're more likely to worsen. Closing the bet may feel like an admission of failure, but in the long run this policy is the only way to make money consistently from spread betting.

Open accounts with more than one spread betting bookmaker. Why: by comparing the spreads between firms, you can reduce and in some cases eliminate the bookies' advantage completely. How: quoted spreads differ, and you can place a bet with the bookie who offers the lowest spread if you are buying or the highest spread if you are selling – this reduces the bookmakers' advantage. Bonus: when there is no overlap between spreads, you can occasionally place a bet which is bound to win. Example: say one bookie is quoting a spread of 210-230 for a cricket innings whilst another is offering 240-260. By placing a 'buy' bet for £20 a run with the first bookie and an equal 'sell' bet with the second one, any result will guarantee you a net profit of £200. You've eliminated their advantage completely.

Be inventive with your betting – by betting on those markets that you understand really well, you'll increase your chances of beating the bookies. Note: spread betting bookmakers will always try to accommodate you. Examples: the total points scored in a rugby match, the total winning distances at a horse-racing meeting, the total of goal scorers' shirt numbers in a football match.

Try 'index bets' – our personal favourites. Here, points are allocated to individuals or teams taking part in a tournament or competition such as the FA Cup or Wimbledon. Typical: the winner is allotted 100 points, the runner-up 70, semi-finalists 50, quarter-finalists 33, and so on. A spread is quoted for each participant and you can 'buy' or 'sell' as before. Example: if you think Tim Henman's the best bet to win Wimbledon next time around and he is quoted at a spread of 41-45, you can 'buy' him for £5 a point at 45. If he wins you get 100 minus 45 multiplied by £5; a total of £75. If he goes out in the quarter finals, you'd lose 45 minus 33 multiplied by £5, which totals £60.

(Source: PFC *gambling expert, Nick Daws. The full version of this feature first appeared in* PFC *February 1998, No.17.)*

SEND YOUR CONFIDENCE SKY-HIGH WITH OUR EASY-TO-FOLLOW TIPS

We all experience moments when our self-confidence falters; perhaps as a relationship ends, or during a period of unemployment. But we can learn from these times, and come back stronger and better than ever.

Here's how:

1. **Start by doing things you're good at.** Ideas: having a friendly conversation with a neighbour, playing a computer game, tidying up the household accounts. Focus on the things you can do well, and congratulate yourself along the way. Examples: 'I really cheered up George with that chat', 'I've zapped another alien – that's brilliant!', 'I've balanced those accounts quickly – and we've some money left over for a treat'.

2. **Try plenty of new things – be different, do something you've never done before.** Suggestions: surf the internet, take up rollerskating or play bowls, sign up for an adult education course. Important: view the results as a learning experience, not as a 'win or lose' situation. Best: take risks. Why: people with high self-esteem take lots of risks – they expand their 'comfort zone' and accept they'll make mistakes. And: they treat these as part of their learning curve. So: the more mistakes you make, the better – they're a sign of growth.

3. **Congratulate yourself when you make mistakes.** Because: these show that you're getting better. Useful: have a list of treats ready, anything from buying flowers or having a bubble bath to going on a day trip. Message: you're telling yourself you're worth it – the more you believe this, the better you'll treat yourself, the more confident you'll feel, the more you'll do.

4. **Use 'affirmations'.** Definition: these are positive statements you say to yourself. Example: 'I am Anna and I am loving, capable and joyous!' Note: these should be pertinent to you and your present situation, be in the present tense, and include qualities you want to develop. Outcome: these will work into your subconscious mind and produce great results – a loving, capable and joyous person, for example.

5. **Watch what you say to yourself.** Fact: we all talk to ourselves, whether consciously or subconsciously. Danger: talking negatively can damage your self-confidence. Example: 'Damn it, I'm so disorganised.' Guideline: would you talk to a friend like this? Better: say out loud (or

under your breath) 'Cancel'; and replace it with something gentler. Alternative: 'I'm usually well organised but occasionally I slip up'.

6. **Act 'as if'.** Meaning: until we've regained the confidence we'd like to have, we should act 'as if' we have it. Key questions: how would a confident person look? What would they be doing? And what would they be saying? Consequence: in the process of acting 'as if', you'll discover you have become that confident person. And: find your self-image – this is the image you have of who you think you 'should' be. Essential: make sure this is realistic, and you will achieve it.

(Source: Theresa Cripps in the co-ordinator of the National Depression Campaign. The full version of this feature first appeared in PFC *April 1998, No. 19.)*

HOW TO PROFIT FROM YOUR PRINCIPLES

You can invest ethically and still make terrific profits from your investments. This is how you do it:

1. **Decide on the key ethical criteria that are of most concern to people.** Fact: a recent NOP survey revealed the three main concerns are 'environmental damage and pollution', 'unnecessary exploitation of animals' and 'exploitation of Third World countries'. So: avoid investing in companies involved in these activities. Better: look for companies that try to benefit society in some way. Examples: 'environmental improvements and pollution control', 'products of long-term community benefit' and 'training and education' are major concerns, according to NOP findings.

2. **Choose an adviser who can highlight those ethical funds which meet these criteria.** Important: ensure that you pick an independent financial adviser who can make the best possible match between these ethics and the packaged ethics available from product providers. Avoid: company agents or direct salespeople who don't offer genuinely independent advice. Contact: EIRIS, which has a database detailing 1,000-plus companies and their areas of corporate activities.

They can also provide you with a list of IFAs who offer advice on ethical investment, (call 0171-840 5700) for information.

3. **Consider the company offering the products.** Note: often, the so-called ethical products are on offer from companies that pursue activities that people do not wish to finance. Example: Eagle Star operates a successful environmental fund. But Eagle Star is owned by British and American Tobacco, and public opinion has turned against smoking. Tip: as a general rule, avoid funds with the word 'environmental' in the title. Why: it is often little more than a marketing ploy.

4. **Make your choice from the remaining funds,** applying your usual investment selection criteria to find the best performing or best value contract. Best buy: Friends Provident Stewardship, tel: 01722 413366. Also: Henderson Ethical, (tel: 0345 832832), Jupiter Ecology, (tel: 0171-412 0703), NPI Global Care, (tel: 0171-623 4200) and Scottish Equitable Ethical (tel: 0800 454422) are all good, solid performers which are a match for most non-ethical funds.

(Sources: PFC *financial and investment experts around the United Kingdom.)*

ELIMINATE HEARTBURN PERMANENTLY

Most people experience heartburn from time to time, particularly after a heavy meal such as a Christmas dinner. Identification: a 'burning' pain behind the breast bone and/or at the same level in the middle of your back. Cause: stomach acid rises up into the gullet, which becomes inflamed and painful. Note: heartburn has nothing to do with the heart – it is a digestive problem usually associated with eating and posture. Here's how to beat it:

1. **Improve your eating habits.** Add: more fruit, vegetables and high fibre. Limit: spicy and fatty foods, hot drinks, acidic fruit drinks and spirits. Reason: these cause pain as they pass over any inflamed area. Best: eat little and often, chewing slowly and well before swallowing. Key point: do not overfill your stomach.

2. **Sit up during and after meals.** Don't: eat food slumped in front of the television – this enables stomach acid to rise up into the gullet. Also: avoid smoking after meals – smoking on a full stomach can increase the likelihood of suffering from heartburn. Because: it relaxes the muscle at the end of the gullet which then enables acid to rise up. And: avoid stooping and bending at the waist – gravity encourages acid to move from the stomach to the gullet.

3. **Allow enough time for your evening meal to be digested before going to bed.** Ideal: 60 minutes. And: try raising the head of the bed by six inches – gravity helps to keep acids in the stomach. Tip: some people find symptoms are reduced by sleeping on their left side.

(Source: PFC *health experts.)*

FIVE SIMPLE STEPS TO BOOST YOUR BRAIN POWER

You can improve your work performance with a 'brain train' workout – a daily programme of mental skillbuilders that enables managers and their teams to concentrate better, make faster decisions, solve problems quicker and be more creative. Here's what to do:

1. **Thought master.** This exercise allows you to build your powers of concentration whilst making you aware of intrusive thoughts. How to: concentrate on the second hand of your watch for one minute, silently repeating the number 'one' as you do this. If a distracting thought comes into your head, maintain your concentration but move to 'two'. If another distracting thought occurs to you, keep concentrating but go on to 'three'. Record your score of intruding thoughts. Benefit: with daily practice, you will reduce the number of intrusive thoughts – and improve your concentration.

2. **Brain buddies.** Your brain comprises a left and right cortex. Important: think of these as two buddies working together to better your performance. What to do: each day, write out two sentences with

your non-dominant hand – the one you don't normally write with. Note the time it takes to do this. The next day, do the same again – and every day after that. Outcome: this workout strengthens the buddy who's been lacking exercise.

3. **Working tools vocabulary.** Words are the working tools of your brain – you need a strong vocabulary to develop your mind. Tactic: find a new word to add to your vocabulary each day. Write the word and its definition in your diary and start using it straightaway. Gain: you will improve your communication abilities.

4. **Whole brain pictures.** Think of a different word every day – and create a 'whole brain picture' from it. Example: 'ocean' is an evocative word. In your mind, see yourself walking on a beach and hear those crashing waves. Smell the ocean breeze as you taste the salty spray hitting your face. Touch the sand between your toes. Result: this will develop your five senses.

5. **Breathing space brain** (BSB). Your brain needs to rest occasionally – to relax effectively, you need to develop your 'breathing space brain'. Technique: sit or lie on your back, relax your body and close your eyes. Begin breathing easily, and listen to its sound. If your attention drifts from your breath, bring it back. Continue for several minutes. Next: repeat the exercise but concentrate instead on a favourite word. Examples: 'calm', 'peace', 'wealth'. Say the word silently to yourself each time you exhale. Do this for several minutes. Benefit: you can use BSB whenever you feel stressed out or want to boost your performance.

(Source: Tony Buzan, originator of the world-famous 'Mind Mapping Techniques', and Richard Israel, one of America's leading sales trainers. Together, they are the authors of Superself, *an innovative book on harnessing the power of the brain to boost sales performance, published by Gower Publishing Group. Call the publishers on 01252 331551 for details of the book.)*

HOW TO TRACE YOUR FAMILY TREE

Most people want to know more about their ancestors – not least to see if they're related to someone rich or famous. This is your step-by-step guide to success:

1. **Before you start, obtain as much information as possible from family members.** Tip: when writing to elderly relatives, raise specific questions rather than open-ended requests such as 'What can you remember about your grandparents?' Better: 'What were your grandparents' names and where did they live?' This focuses their attention and produces more informative answers. Note: be prepared for inaccuracies – family histories may have been embroidered to make them sound more exciting. Wise: when seeking information, ask for names, dates and places – these enable you to cross-reference more easily, and to double-check facts.

2. **If you're going to do the research yourself, find out about genealogy before setting off for the record office.** Good idea: join a family history society – this provides you with a support system. Your nearest library will have details of a local one. Helpful: buy a good genealogical handbook – one that can offer possible solutions to problems you may encounter on the way. Recommended reading: *The Oxford Companion to Local and Family History* by David Hey (OUP 1996). Also: buy the monthly publication, *Family Tree Magazine* from your newsagents.

3. **Don't restrict your searches to births, deaths and marriages at local record offices, the Public Record Office and the Family Records Centre in London,** (call 0181-392 5300). Wiser: use other records such as census returns, wills, service and occupational records. These not only help in the search but provide additional social and historical information about your relations. Warning: some registers have indexes that are helpful for quick referencing – but they're not always accurate and complete. Best: check the original records, wherever possible.

4. **Don't believe everything you read.** Fact: names were often written down as they were heard, not necessarily how they were spelt. Example: 'Dakin' has appeared in records as 'Daykin', 'Deakin' and even 'Dickens'. Important: you need to cross-reference all possible spellings of a name with dates and places. Also: never assume that the ages stated in records are correct. Reason: our ancestors were not as conscious of ages and dates as we are in the twentieth century.

5. **Never make assumptions.** Example: many people assume their family belonged to the established church – but this is not always the case. Find out what other churches were in the area, and see what records survive from them. And don't jump to conclusions. Example: if you find what appears to be an ancestor's baptism, check the burial register to make sure that child didn't die in infancy. It may have been a person of a similar name and age.

6. **Read up on the social history of the time and place you're researching; and think yourself into your ancestors' lives.** Essential: try to discover their occupations so you can understand their movements. Fact: before the railway age, ordinary people rarely moved far – although some needed to move further afield to find work. Consider: social mobility too – Granny might swear that her grandfather always spoke like a gentleman but he may have started life as a blacksmith.

(Source: Dr Susan Morris, Director of Research at Debrett Ancestry Research Limited. The original version of this feature first appeared in PFC *February 1998, No. 17.)*

UPGRADE YOUR AEROPLANE SEAT EVERY TIME

If you're booking a flight in the coming weeks or months, you'll be thinking about the possibility of getting an upgrade. Here's how you can do it:

1. **Make sure you're a member of the airline's frequent flyer or**

mileage programmes on the routes you are likely to travel. Why: an airline's first loyalty will be to those passengers who are loyal to them, so its members are most likely to be picked for an upgrade before anyone else. How: ensure your membership details are recorded in your passenger name record (PNR) before leaving for the airport. Note: frequent flyer and mileage programmes are free to join – contact the relevant airlines for details. Bonus: some are linked with hotel programmes too, for even greater benefits, such as cut-price rooms.

2. **Dress the part of a first-class or business class traveller.** Reason: airlines seek to fill remaining seats with those passengers who will not look out of place in a higher class. In: smart casual clothing. Out: T-shirts, jeans, leggings, shell suits.

3. **Don't pre-book a special meal of any kind.** Why: airlines allocate meals to seats well before take-off and staff don't want to spend the flight hunting around a full plane to get your meal to you – they'll simply keep you in your booked seat instead of upgrading you. That way, they'll know where you are.

4. **Travel alone or as a couple because seats tend to be available in singles or pairs** – staff are not going to try to upgrade and re-seat a group who will often want to sit close together. Note: full fare economy passengers will normally be chosen to upgrade ahead of those passengers with discount tickets.

(Sources: Mark Hempshell, PFC *expert.)*

ASSERT YOURSELF THROUGH POSITIVE SPEECH

Most of us have had the experience of coming away from an encounter thinking 'I wish I'd said so-and-so', or 'I wish I'd thought of that earlier'. But assertiveness skills are not instinctive; they have to be learned. It takes time and practice to be spontaneous. What matters most are the words and phrases that you use on the spot – you need to be able to respond there and then, not have to think about it for a few minutes, or refer to a book or manual. Here's what you should be doing:

1. **Say 'no' with a smile.** Saying 'no' to a request is acceptable, so respond with 'I'd be pleased to help, but I'm unable to on this occasion'. Resist the urge to make a long and detailed excuse – you don't have to make excuses or justify yourself. The more you say, the less credible you become.

2. **Don't use self-deprecating language.** It's easy to fall into the habit of beginning a conversation with 'I know I'm not very good at this, but...', 'I realise I'm being a bit thick, but...', or something along these lines. This implies you believe you are inferior in some way. Rather than re-phrase these 'self put-downs', drop them altogether. Say 'I'm going to convert this disk myself', 'I want to be certain I understand this before I start', or whatever.

3. **Never start a conversation with an apology.** Do you hear yourself saying 'I'm sorry if I'm taking up your valuable time, but...', or something similar when approaching someone? This is a gentle way of starting a conversation, but can make you sound nervous. Use 'Excuse me...' instead. Even better, don't rephrase, just omit it altogether – by doing so, you've already begun to assume a more assertive manner.

4. **Don't use approval-seeking language.** Another form of 'self put-down' is the approval-seeking behaviour indicated by the regular use of 'Can I...', 'May I...' and 'If I can just...'. Here, you're intimating that your request is of low priority or importance by suggesting that permission is in some way required for you to do something.

5. **Be prepared to state your beliefs.** An assertive and self confident person uses 'I' statements in their conversation. As examples, 'I'd like to hear that again' and 'I'm borrowing this for a few minutes'. Adding non-verbal gestures such as a smile can reinforce this approach.

(Source: Tim Field, the founder of The UK Workplace Bullying Advice Line, and author of Bully in Sight – How to Predict, Resist, Challenge and Combat Workplace Bullying *published by Success Unlimited. Call the advice line on 01235*

212286 for information about the book. The original version of this feature first appeared in PFC *July 1997, No. 10.)*

MAXIMISE RETURNS FROM LOW-RISK UNIT TRUSTS

***PFC* tip:** BRUT – 'buying the right unit trust' – is a simple evaluation procedure used by the professionals to pick winners in the UK unit trust market. This is how it works:

Buy *Money Management* or *What Investment?*, or any other magazine which lists unit trust performance by investment category. These magazines portray the value today of £1,000 invested one year ago, two years ago, three years ago, and five years ago. Rankings within each sector are also reported. If a fund performed in the top quartile during the period, it will be bold-faced to highlight its good performance.

The BRUT technique to isolate winners is: 1. In the five-year category, circle the bold-faced top quartile funds. 2. Circle the bold-faced top quartile funds in the three-year category, but only if you circled them in the five-year category. 3. Choose the top quartile two-year funds; again only the top quartile performers in the three- and five-year categories. 4. In the one-year category, choose the top quartile funds that were also top quartile funds in the two-, three-, and five-year categories. Ignore: the ten-year category – the manager and fund philosophy might have changed over such a long time. And: the one-month and six-month categories may depend upon short-term success; they're not necessarily representative of the longer-term performance. Disregard them. Also: ignore top performers who haven't been around for five years. With so many funds with proven track records, why look to a fresh fund without any experience? Warning: a fund's super performance in the most recent year could mask weaknesses in the earlier four years. Eliminate those funds where the latest year was great but the other years were sub-standard. Outcome: from this shortlist of consistent, high-performing funds, choose the one with the cheapest charges – this way, you'll maximise returns for minimal risks.

(Source: Bruce McWilliams unit trust expert & author.)

HOW TO CLAIM HASSLE-FREE ACCIDENT COMPENSATION

Thousands of pounds are paid out every week to people who have suffered injuries of some kind. Road accident claims are the most common; others are made for workplace injuries, typically resulting from contact with machinery. Medical negligence claims can be made when treatment goes wrong. Note: many personal injuries do not lead to claims, because they were caused by a friend or relative; but if you've been injured, you should claim as it is the insurance company which pays out, not the person who was responsible. Here are the key facts:

How to claim: to have a strong case, you must have suffered some pain and/or emotional distress and will probably have needed hospital treatment at some stage. And: the accident should at least be partly someone else's fault. Example: if you stumble over an unrepaired, cracked pavement or a pathway damaged by cable installation, you may be eligible for compensation. But: if you drove into a bollard and injured yourself and were driving the only car on the road at the time, your chances of a payout are slim to nil.

What to claim: to establish how much could be received for a particular injury, ask your solicitor to look at similar cases which have been settled in the past, and make an appropriate claim. Tip: allow for inflation in your calculations. In addition to receiving a sum for pain and suffering, it is possible to gain compensation for mental injury such as nervous shock. You can also claim for loss of earnings, medical treatment, travel costs, property damage such as ruined clothing, and home nursing and help from relatives. Always: claim for everything; you will not be offered anything unless you ask for it.

Legal costs: many people do not claim accident compensation because they are worried about the legal costs involved in any action. Success: if your case is successful, the legal fees will almost certainly be paid in full by the other party's insurers. Failure: you can protect yourself against the possibility of losing the case and being liable for costs by asking your solicitor to work on a 'no win – no legal fee' basis. You pay an insurance premium – £95.68 for road-related accidents and £161.20 for others – which covers this prospect. Note: the solicitor will normally ask for a higher fee for taking such a gamble.

***PFC* recommendation:** choose a solicitor with relevant experience – not necessarily the same one who drew up your will. Take out insurance cover if the outcome is unpredictable. Make sure your claim commences within the three-year time limit. Note: most insurers reject initial claims (however valid) but agree an out-of-court settlement immediately prior to attending court. Be persistent.

(Source: Julie Wilson, a legal expert involved in personal injury claims. The original version of this feature first appeared in PFC *November 1997, No. 14.)*

SHAPE UP WITH MINIMAL EFFORT

Most of us are brilliant procrastinators when it comes to losing weight. So how can we bypass that inertia and get into shape? Here's how:

1. **Pick a date.** Mark out a starting time for your health and fitness regime. Regard that date as a formal appointment; it's as important as a crucial job interview, or even your wedding. Why: the anticipation can help you to prepare psychologically for the coming regime. Don't: let anything but a major life change make you miss that date.

2. **Set your target.** Focus on a special event that you'd like to be in better shape for. Examples: an anniversary celebration or a summer holiday. Reason: short-term goals stimulate your motivation, and make you more likely to succeed. Tip: build specific targets in right through your programme to maintain that motivation.

3. **Increase your exercise.** Exercise is safe if you build slowly up to

it. Beginning: do no more than ten minutes of gentle exercise a day. Later: add an extra five minutes per day from the end of the first week, then another five a week later, and so on. Always: warm up and cool down with some gentle stretching exercises.

4. **Design phase one of your programme.** Plan an intensive phase into your diary, comprising 30 minutes of swimming or walking each day, to be followed by a weight loss eating programme. Judge honestly what you can realistically manage. Important: check with your GP before undertaking any significant exercise. Duration: Phase One should last up to about six weeks.

5. **Don't diet immediately.** If you feel you want to lose weight too, avoid dieting until at least ten days into Phase One. Why: this allows your body to start burning off excess fat. Note: dieting without exercise forces your body to attempt to eliminate muscle – leaving you feeling tired, and even less fit.

6. **Lose weight slowly.** Never crash-diet. It doesn't work – you'll just put the weight back on later. And: severe dieting creates a shortage of vitamins and nutrients in your body which can have adverse effects on your health. Remember: you didn't become unfit overnight – so allow time to get yourself back in shape. Better: aim to shed one or two pounds per week – at most. Best: a slow and steady diet is far less stressful, and more permanent. Note: by this stage, active exercise will have speeded up your metabolism to which aids your weight-loss.

7. **Drink plenty of water.** Water should play a key role in your health and fitness programme. Vital: drink a minimum of eight tumblers daily to help flush out the toxins released when your body eliminates excess fat. Also: if you drink alcohol in the evening, drink two full, tall glasses of water before going to bed. Why: this prevents lactic acid build-up and late night cramps.

8. **Plan your maintenance programme.** Now plan Phase Two. This

could simply be a three- or four-times-a-week version of Phase One. Plus: Re-introduce the intensive phase when you really need to, and try to keep at Phase Two in-between. This will keep you toned, shapely and happy too.

(Source: Kristin Centofanti, an expert in the use and application of electronic muscle stimulation for health and fitness purposes. The full version of this feature first appeared in PFC *October 1997, No.13.))*

KEY QUESTIONS TO IDENTIFY A TOP-NOTCH TAX ADVISER

You can pick a tax adviser who is qualified and experienced enough to help you with your tax affairs by asking certain questions. These are the questions, and the answers you want to hear:

1. **Do you belong to a professional body?** Fact: the tax industry is unregulated – there is nothing to stop anyone from calling themselves a 'tax adviser' and offering advice for a fee. Essential: make sure the firm you use includes people who are members of a professional body with a code of practice and a formal complaints procedure. Best: The Chartered Institute of Taxation, (0171-235 9381) and the Association of Taxation Technicians, (0171-235 2544). Vital: do check that the person you're talking to is actually registered with the body before dealing with them.

2. **What tax qualifications do you have?** Check to see that they have relevant tax advisory qualifications. Look for: the initials ATII and/or FTII after their name. Again: it is advisable to double-check this with their professional body. Professional con-artists lie.

3. **What are your main areas of expertise?** All tax advisers have specialist areas – individual taxation and corporate taxation, as examples. Pick a firm with cross-category expertise, or an individual with specific knowledge of your trade or industry. Why: it saves time and unnecessary explanation of your background circumstances.

4. **Do you have professional indemnity insurance?** By law, all independent financial advisers must have this cover, to protect themselves and their clients against human error. This is not the case with tax advisers – yet the consequences of their mistakes can be horrendous. Example: a tax investigation could take up over 100 hours of your time, and cost more than £5,000 in accountancy fees. Always: check this cover exists, by asking to see the policy. This is especially important with small, owner-manager operations.

5. **What personalised services can you offer to me?** Don't: select a tax adviser simply to fill in your tax return. Why: you can do this as well as they can – the form is relatively straightforward, and you know your financial affairs better than anyone else. Wise: choose someone who will conduct a review of your tax circumstances to ensure that all possible ways of reducing the tax bill are explored. And: make sure all details and anomalies are revealed to the Inland Revenue. This helps to minimise the risk of investigation.

(Source: Gerry Hart, former national president of the Chartered Institute of Taxation.)

TRANSFORM YOUR CAREER WITH A SHOWCASE SPEECH

Speaking to an audience is a golden opportunity to supercharge your career. These are the best ways to wow that audience:

1. **Use a colourtext system** – you'll never lose your place. Write the speech out in full on 7" by 9" paper. Important: use heavy paper that is easy to separate as you're reading. Block capital text is best; it's easier to read. Essential: use felt-tip pens in varying colours, one paragraph in blue, the next in green. Underline key words in red for emphasis.

2. **Get in close, speak from the table or within the crowd for a special, intimate relationship.** Avoid: a stage – it is a barrier between you and the audience. It creates an 'us and them' feeling and you won't get the results you deserve.

3. **Use a mike, if necessary** – and make sure it's a free-standing one so you can still use both hands when speaking. Don't: test the mike by blowing on it or saying 'one two, one two' – it looks unprofessional and clichéd. Better: just tap it gently to make sure it's working.

4. **Have a glass of water handy** – without it, your mouth will dry up. Also: use the glass of water as a prop, a punctuation device to control your audience. Example: take a drink while they're laughing at a joke; you'll soon train them to keep laughing until you've stopped drinking.

5. **Start with a couple of announcements** – they'll ensure people are unaware you'll be reading your speech word for word. After all, it's natural to read these. You can then go straight into your speech, and they won't even notice you're reading. Advisable: bring your head up and look around regularly to convey a natural impression. Make eye-contact to build a rapport.

6. **Offer soundbites** – a speech can only ever be an exercise in superficiality. Give it too much substance and it becomes a lecture. And: remember that the average audience has a very short attention span, so you need to keep moving on. Tip: to be memorable, it needs bullet points, catchy words and humour. Try some one-liners – you can pinch these from joke books and personalise them to suit your situation. Do make them topical if you can. Helpful: laugh at your own jokes occasionally – it bonds you with your audience.

(Source: Mitch Murray, Britain's top funny speechwriter, and author of One-liners for Weddings *and* One-liners for Business Speeches. *The full-length version of this feature first appeared in* PFC *September 1997, No. 12.)*

IMPROVE YOUR CHANCES OF WINNING THE LOTTERY

Pick the six winning numbers and you'll make millions from the National Lottery. And you can increase your chances of getting that winning line if you use a technique called 'wheeling'.

This is how it works:

Principle: with the pools, a full eight-from-ten perm (requiring 45 entries) guarantees a jackpot-winning line if your ten choices include eight score draws. You can do exactly the same with the lottery. Example: to cover seven numbers – so that if any six are drawn, you'll win the jackpot – you can use a 'full system wheel' (FSW) of seven lines.

Entry one: 1 2 3 4 5 6.

Entry two: 2 3 4 5 6 7.

Entry three: 1 3 4 5 6 7.

Entry four: 1 2 4 5 6 7.

Entry five: 1 2 3 5 6 7.

Entry six: 1 2 3 4 6 7.

Entry seven: 1 2 3 4 5 7.

Note: numbers 1 to 7 have been used for simplicity – but you can use any combination between 1 and 49. Plus: as well as winning the jackpot with six correct numbers, this system enables you to win six more five-correct or five-plus-the-bonus prizes! Minus: the main drawback of FSWs is that the number of entries required increases rapidly with the number of selections you wish to cover. An FSW covering eight numbers needs 28 entries, for ten you'll need 210 and by the time you reach twelve, it's a staggering 924.

Alternative: to cover a good spread of numbers without breaking the bank, choose a 'short system wheel' (SSW) – this will not cover every possible winning combination, but still improves your chances of multiple wins. Example: an effective SSW involves starting with a full system wheel and picking one or more key numbers. These are 'bankers' that must come up if your entry is to win. From your chosen FSW, delete all lines that do not include those key numbers. Note: covering any combination of eight numbers usually requires 28 lines – but with one key number this reduces to 21, with two it comes down to 15 and with three, to a mere ten.

Tip: when picking numbers for these systems, include at least two which are over 31. Fewer people pick high numbers – most go for birthday and anniversary dates – so if you do win the jackpot, you won't have to share it with as many people! Also: avoid the most popular 'lucky' numbers of 3, 4, 7 and 9 – at least one or more of these feature in most people's selections. Again, if you don't want to share your winnings with too many others, go for the unpopular numbers every time: to boost automatically your chances of a bigger win.

***PFC* recommendation:** perhaps you'd prefer a system which guarantees at least a small prize – and maybe multiple prizes or the jackpot – if you can find winning numbers from a total of 16 (almost one-third of the numbers available). If so, this SSW is for you. It requires only five £1 entries.

Entry one: 1 2 3 4 5 6.

Entry two: 7 8 9 10 11 12.

Entry three: 1 2 13 14 15 16.

Entry four: 3 4 13 14 15 16.

Entry five: 5 6 13 14 15 16.

(Source: Nick Daws, PFC *gambling guru. The original version of this feature first appeared in* PFC *September 1997, No. 12.)*

THE SIMPLE SELLOTAPE SOLUTION

Find the edge of the Sellotape first time – simply affix a small button underneath it. But don't forget to put it back again afterwards!

(Source: Edith O'Brien, a PFC *subscriber.)*

USE STRESS TO MAKE YOU MORE SUCCESSFUL

There is a widespread belief that stress is bad for you. But if you are to perform to your maximum ability, certain levels of pressure and challenge must exist. If you can balance these, then stress will work for you, and help you to succeed:

1. **Plan your day.** Whatever goals have been set for you by other people, it is important that you have realistic self-goals. Helpful: look for various 'small satisfactions' during the course of a job, rather than just a large one at the end. Example: dealing each day with a set number of letters, faxes and phone calls which help towards the completion of a major project should be a source of satisfaction in itself. Important: accept that yesterday has gone – it can't be repeated nor improved. As for tomorrow, what you do now will shape its course. Concentrate on today.

2. **Be true to yourself.** The best way of managing stress and turning it to your advantage is to accept the way you are. Acknowledge you're less than perfect – we all are. Idea: look at someone you admire, and identify their weaknesses – everyone has them. Then concentrate instead on what you can do well, and your successes.

3. **Identify with others.** It's easy to become over-pressured by your interpretation of another person's attitude. Seeing both sides allows you to regain balance. Practise the key skill of listening – with your ears for the words, and your eyes for the body movements supporting them. Accept that everyone will approach life differently. Example: if you consider yourself a perfectionist, others may view you as a 'pain in the neck'. Don't judge people by your own viewpoints – they may approach situations in a different way, but it doesn't mean they're wrong.

4. **Learn to relax.** Discover whatever it is that works for you – whether listening to music, gardening or walking in the countryside. Important: budget 'breathing spaces' into your working day so that you can relax regularly – these can be as simple as getting out into the fresh

air at tea and lunch breaks. Also: when feeling stressed, stop! Train yourself to take deep breaths, look out of the window, have a glass of water or walk around for a few minutes. If you want some peace, put on a pair of personal stereo headphones; even if you're listening to silence, it helps. Then return to what you were doing

5. **Eat and exercise effectively.** Eating five small meals a day provides better support for your body than the occasional large one. Drink two litres of water per day to flush through your body's systems. Best: white meat, dairy products, fresh fruits and vegetables, whole grain foods (cereals, bread, pasta). Avoid: red meat, salt, sugar, white flour, fats and 'junk' food. Surprise: be careful of 'diet' foods – they may have less calories, but are often high in saturated fats. Also: regular exercise improves the condition of your heart, reduces blood pressure and cholesterol levels, and increases your sense of well-being. Must: take 20 minutes for a brisk walk three times a week to maintain good health.

6. **Learn to fall asleep.** Sleep is essential if you're to balance pressures and challenges. Use this breathing process to help you to sleep restfully. Exhale for twice as long as you inhale – count in your head as you breathe in and out. Choose a count you feel comfortable with – but always in a 2:1 proportion. Examples: 6:3 seconds or 8:4 seconds. Keep it all effortless – breathing must be smooth and continuous, without stops or shakiness. Don't pause between exhaling and inhaling, and avoid emptying your lungs. Follow this pattern: eight breaths on your back, 16 breaths on your right side, 32 breaths on your left side. Tests have shown that very few people make it to the end of this routine because it works so well.

7. **Use time efficiently.** Good time management is one of the essential features of making stress work for you. In particular: make 'to do' lists, and prioritise tasks into their order of importance. Allocate realistic deadlines for each task – underestimating the time involved in doing work is a major cause of self-inflicted stress. Do the important tasks at your most active periods of the day, leaving more routine matters

to other times. Complete each task before going on to the next one. Don't think about other tasks until you have finished the first one. Avoid juggling paperwork – read it once then act on it, and file it or bin it, as relevant. Once a decision has been made, forget about it and move on. Don't create unnecessary stress by worrying whether it was right or not. Put any uncompleted tasks to the top of your list for the next day.

8. **Keep a stress diary.** Compile a record of stress-related incidents over the next month. How: divide each day's page into four sections – 'event', 'people involved', 'response', 'ideal response' – and complete as and when you feel stressed. Example: event: having to deal with too many phone calls. People involved: sales reps. Response: incomplete work, sharp replies, headaches. Ideal response: measured discussions with reps. Why: this diary should enable you to identify problem areas. And: you can then plan how to deal with the particular problems. Example: turn on answering machine, and return all calls at one convenient time.

(Sources: Harald Øyen, a UK-based expert in human performance enhancement, and Associate Advisor of the Industrial Society, Gordon Veniard, PFC *self-development expert.)*

HOW TO GET ON YOUR FAVOURITE GAME SHOW

Do you sit at home answering all the questions on a game show? Cash in by becoming a contestant and win those prizes. These are an insider's secrets:

1. **Go for the simple games.** Why: the value of prizes is often disproportionate to the difficulty of the contests. Examples: general knowledge and luck-based games tend to offer large sums of cash, cars and exotic holidays. More demanding contests can involve many gruelling weeks of research for a relatively modest prize.

2. **Apply for shows that don't feature people like you.** Reason: some

groups are under-represented amongst applicants – the over 50s, ethnic minorities and the disabled for popular shows, female contestants for serious and intellectual shows. And: producers are always looking for a good mix, representing a cross-section of the population.

3. **Get hold of an application form, rather than writing an on-spec letter** – most game shows will tell you on screen, when and where to write. Alternative: send off for a generalised application form used to apply for a broad range of shows. Try: BBC Game Show Contestants Department, Wood Lane, London W12 8QT. And: Action Time Limited, 2 Whitworth Street West, Manchester M1 5WX.

4. **Don't be daunted by the form** – it is extensive because they want to find out about you. In particular: your general knowledge and your personality. Wanted: the correct degree of general knowledge for the show. And: a confident extrovert with a sense of humour who won't panic under studio pressures.

5. **When answering quiz questions, fill in the ones you know from memory and leave the rest blank.** Don't use reference books to answer all of them correctly. Why: it's possible to be too clever for a particular show – get everything right, and you could be knocked out.

6. **Mention you've done amateur dramatics – even if it was only in a school play – as this marks you out as an extrovert.** And: say if you've been on television or radio before – this gives you a head start too. Also: expect to have to describe an amusing or embarrassing experience – the more hilarious or unusual the incident, the better. Important: give an appropriate answer for the show – for example, don't tell a risqué story if this is a family programme.

7. **Send in a recent photo which makes you look happy and outgoing.** Ideal: a head and shoulders close-up showing you with a natural, smiling expression. And: it should be crystal clear and less than a year old. Avoid: passport booth photos – they look too stagey for this purpose.

8. **'Sparkle' at your audition.** Your natural adrenaline will do this

– adding lustre to your eyes and an edge to your reactions. Never: have a drink to calm your nerves – it makes you look 'deadpan' on screen.

9. **Speak a little more slowly and clearly than normal.** Raise your vocal volume a bit higher than usual, and make your pitch a touch lower. This will make you sound attractive and confident.

10. **Smile frequently** – it lights up the screen and makes you look as though you're enjoying this terrific show.

11. **Stand up straight without swaying** – and keep your mannerisms under control, especially nose-rubbing and desk-tapping which make you seem nervous.

***PFC* bottom line:** enjoy the audition for its own sake, even if you're not selected this time. It will give you an insight into what happens behind the scenes. You can refer to it in future applications and even make an amusing or unusual story out of it.

(Source: Kathy Kantypowicz is the editor of Winner's *Friend published by Agora Lifestyles. Call 0500 523 499 for a free copy of the latest issue.)*

TURN A TAX INVESTIGATION TO YOUR ADVANTAGE

The chances of being subjected to a tax investigation were always remote – the Revenue aimed to look at around 1% of company returns each year, and even fewer from ordinary taxpayers. But the availability of increased resources for investigations and the introduction of random auditing has made the prospect of an in-depth examination of your financial affairs much more likely. But it's not all bad news – here's how you can make the most of it:

1. **Minimise the risk of investigation.** Submit your tax return, accounts and paperwork on time – those that are sent in late will attract attention. The Revenue always targets taxpayers who are behind with their affairs because this may indicate that their paperwork may be

incorrect; it's that much easier to find mistakes. Explain anything which appears inconsistent with earlier years – any aspects of your income, expenditure and/or profit which have changed noticeably will catch the inspector's eye. Tell them about it before they start asking questions. Detail anything which seems out of the ordinary – if you have a lower income, more expenses or a smaller profit margin than other people in comparable circumstances, state the reasons why.

2. **Handle the investigation professionally.** Treat the inspector with respect – many convey the impression that they have no knowledge of business nor of you; this is never the case. Fact: they will have studied all available paperwork and may have driven by your home to see if declared earnings match your lifestyle. Obey the golden rule – never give misleading answers, and if you don't know an answer, say so. Don't be tempted under pressure to guess or elaborate. Important: every question has a purpose, especially friendly and innocent ones. Example: 'Do you have any hobbies?' is designed to see if you can afford to pursue them on your stated earnings. Be as open as possible – admit any underlying problems straightaway; this minimises the risk of prosecution, and makes it much easier to negotiate a reasonable settlement with the inspector. Fact: wrong-doing will almost certainly be uncovered – the inspector will calculate your incomings and outgoings for each week; any unexpected changes, and they'll want to know why.

3. **Learn from the investigation.** Weaknesses in your book-keeping and accounts may be identified; and advice given on how to keep them in future. Ask the inspector to explain and show you what to do – it's the best free advice you'll ever get; no-one knows more. Find out about the tax system, and check you've claimed all possible allowances. The inspector is there to ensure you pay the correct (not the most) amount of tax; they are obliged to tell you what you've failed to claim, if asked. Note: after an investigation, your next two years' returns will be studied more closely than normal – so take extra care with them.

(Source: David Pooler, a former Inspector of Taxes, now working in investigation

services for Moores Rowland. The full version of this feature first appeared in PFC *September 1997, No. 12.)*

HARNESS THE POWER OF CHANGE – MAKE IT WORK FOR YOU

We live in an era of radical change; to family relationships, working patterns, technology – everything. It's natural to feel sometimes that we're being left behind. But change can be good for us if we embrace it – and learn to make the most of what it brings with it.

1. **Accept change as part of everyday life.** Fact: no matter how much we hanker for a safe and solid past, change is ongoing and is taking place even faster than before. And: we are all going to experience some dramatic changes in our lives; family breakdowns, step-relationships and career moves, as examples. Warning: it is unrealistic and unhealthy to imagine that life will always be the same, and that we will control it. Best: be prepared for success, but also realise that some circumstances are beyond your control and can turn against you. Example: accepting that your job will end one day enables you to handle it better when it does.

2. **Discover your anchor points.** Why: these give you something to hold onto during periods of change, now and in the future. Example: a woman lost her job and separated from her partner at the same time. Her anchor was religion – it gave her the strength to develop a new life and relationships. Most people can identify some anchor points that act as solid foundations for periods of change; such as a strong partnership, family ties, a comfortable home, friendships, hobbies and interests. Look for the constant themes that run through your life.

3. **Be prepared to abandon outdated ways of thinking, perceptions, ideas and beliefs.** Note: some changes will destroy these – so be ready to replace them and create something new and different so that you can move on. Example: a man in his 50's is made redundant. His plan to retire comfortably at 60 and travel the world is no longer

financially viable. He has to let go of that idea and replace it with another, more achievable one if he is to accept and manage change successfully. Instead: he might decide to move to a new part of the country, and explore it. Important: always maintain a personal sense of direction, even if it is a revised one. Having an achievable goal helps to sustain your stability and provides you with the momentum to go forward.

4. **Seek out the opportunities that come with change.** Fact: the way that you handle change depends largely on your approach to it. Bad: too many people see themselves as victims, subject to the actions and conspiracies of others. Result: they have a negative outlook, seeing only closed doors – and they don't even have the mental strength to go and knock on them! Good: you should look for ways to progress and develop as a result of change. Outcome: you will have a positive outlook, seeing open doors – and you're going to walk straight through them. Example: a woman was left on her own to bring up two children. Her immediate reaction was one of despair; a house to run, children to care for, and no money. Later, she saw the opportunities: she was free of a domineering husband, could become closer to her family who would help her, and could go on to enter higher education as she'd always wanted to do.

5. **Help others to manage change.** Adage: 'You really learn a subject when you have to teach it'. Helpful: identify five people who are experiencing personal change of a similar nature of your own; talk to them, share your thoughts, and hear what they have to say. Bottom line: studying something, thinking through new concepts, interacting with learners and sharing their perspectives adds to your understanding of the change process, and how to make the most of it.

(Source: Terry Wilson, director of Items Consulting Associates, a human resources consultancy specialising in change programmes, and author of Changing Your Spots – A guide to Personal Change, *published by Gower Publishing Group. Phone 01252 331551 for more information about the book. The original version of this feature first appeared in* PFC *April 1998, No. 19.)*

GET RID OF INDIGESTION FOR GOOD

Indigestion is a persistent or recurrent abdominal pain or discomfort in the upper abdomen. Many people believe this is caused by what they eat or drink. Fact: indigestion is rarely caused by food intolerance or allergy; in most cases it results from over-eating or eating too quickly. The best ways of avoiding indigestion are to:

1. **Eat meals at regular times so your stomach becomes familiar with your eating patterns.** Avoid: snacking on junk foods as you work; inevitably these are rushed, which leads to indigestion. Also: steer clear of any foods or drinks which seem to act as triggers to indigestion. Smoking often exacerbates the problem.

2. **Don't take aspirin for headaches, colds and coughs (or products which contain aspirin)** – this is a known trigger for indigestion. Reason: aspirin irritates the stomach lining. Better: paracetemol is kinder on the stomach.

3. **Don't take anti-arthritic painkillers if at all possible** – again, these have been known to trigger cases of indigestion. They too can irritate the stomach lining. Best: discuss your medication with your GP before starting or stopping a course of treatment.

(Sources: The British Digestive Foundation plus additional PFC *research.)*

ASK FIVE QUESTIONS – PICK A WINNING INVESTMENT TRUST

Selecting the best investment trust for your portfolio can seem a daunting task – there are more than 350 to choose from in the UK alone. But there is an easy way to make your selection decision. Simply ask and answer the following questions. When you've done that, you'll find you've chosen the most suitable trust for you.

1. **What are my investment objectives?** Typical: decide whether you are looking for capital growth or income growth. Example: someone

who has retired recently with a lump sum to invest will probably be seeking income to part-finance their retirement. Important: using your investment objectives to narrow down a list of trusts gives you the flexibility to constantly review those objectives and apply narrower definitions as you proceed.

2. **Which categories of investment trust match my objectives?** Categories: International (General/Capital Growth/Income Growth), UK (General/Capital Growth/Income Growth), High Income, North America, Far East (including Japan/excluding Japan), Japan, Continental Europe, Emerging Markets, Property, Commodity and Energy, Smaller Companies, Venture & Development Capital, Pan-Europe, Split Capital Trusts, Closed End Funds. Example: if you are looking for capital growth, you might consider those funds in the 'International Capital Growth' and the 'UK Capital Growth' categories. For income to fund a retirement, you might look at 'International Income Growth', 'UK Income Growth' and 'High Income'.

3. **Which of the possible categories offer the best performance potential?** Best past performance: 'Pan-Europe' and 'North America' feature most regularly at the top of the one-year, three-year, five-year and ten-year performance tables. Worst past performance: 'Far East Including Japan', 'Far East Excluding Japan' and 'Japan' feature most often at the bottom of the performance tables. Anticipated future performance: 'Europe' and the 'UK' sectors look to have the most potential for growth.

4. **What other investment criteria do I have?** Typical: you may want to establish a target for capital growth or your required gross income yield. And with income, you may want a trust that pays a quarterly dividend. Again, this will slim down the number of trusts available to you.

5. **How will I finance the purchase?** Usual: a lump sum or a regular monthly amount. Most investment trusts are now available through regular savings schemes, but not all of them – so check. And:

do I want to place my holdings in an Isa? Some trusts are not eligible for inclusion in these savings vehicles. Again, check.

(Source: Roddy Kohn, principal of Kohn Cougar Independent Financial Advisers and a member of the Board of the Personal Investment Authority.)

HOW TO BECOME A SUCCESSFUL HOME-WORKER

First, let's dispel some myths about becoming a home-worker. Myth: lots of home-working opportunities are advertised in the back pages of national newspapers. Fact: most of these advertisements are placed by rogues who will disappear with your deposit or (at best) will provide poorly paid, hard work, often for less than £1 per hour. Myth: reputable companies looking for home workers are listed in directories that are offered for sale through the press. Fact: this is another money making scam by con artists – respectable employers offering worthwhile work do not recruit in this way. Bottom line: if you want to obtain work and do it from home, you'll need to approach this task in the same way you would try to get any other job. Here's how:

1. **Create a complete package for yourself.** Important: identify your skills, knowledge and expertise as tightly as possible. Worst: an 'I can do anything' approach. Best: a short list of skills of specific benefit to particular employers. Why: this makes it easier for you to identify prospective employers and to convince them you're the right person to meet their needs. Helpful: ask yourself what type of job offer you'd like to receive from which company. Then think why they should come to you. If you can answer this, you should be able to produce that all-important short list.

2. **Offer good reasons why a company should employ you.** Key question: what can I do to fulfil a need, save them money, and add value to their goods and services? Examples: 'I can work out of normal business hours', 'I can provide cover during heavy workloads.' Know the

benefits – for them – of having you work from your home. Pointers: you can work odd hours, provide your own equipment and can offer an unbiased, outsider's view of problems. Be prepared to raise these benefits with potential employers.

2. **Don't sell yourself cheap.** Fact: an employer will use you only if your service is needed and will save money. But: this doesn't mean you should be the cheapest. Someone who can translate a million-dollar contract at midnight can charge an appropriate price for that special service. Tip: offer a package deal of benefits rather than an hourly rate – this always sounds more professional – and you can build some room for negotiation into your overall price.

4. **Be seen to supply a professional service.** Fact: to make money from home-working, you'll need regular repeat orders and long-term business. How: be easy to deal with – make sure you can be contacted at all times, be reliable and efficient, and deliver on time. Note: employers want two things from you – a professional approach and results.

(Source: Sophie Chalmers, editor of Better Business, *the monthly magazine for people working alone or from small offices. Call 01291 641222 for further details of the magazine. The original version of this feature first appeared in* PFC *January 1998, No. 16.)*

MAKE THE MOST MONEY WITH A CLEAN PENSION

A clean personal pension is one with a low and flexible charging structure. Benefit: with low and no hidden charges, more money is left in the pot for investment. For this reason, a clean pension always has greater potential for growth than an unclean one. Also: a flexible contract which allows you to increase, reduce, stop and re-start premiums to suit your changing needs offers the greatest likelihood of the contract term being completed, and the maximum profits being taken from the accumulated pension fund. To identify clean pension providers, ask six key questions before entering into any agreement:

1. **Is there a 'capital' unit or 'initial' unit structure?** Note: this is a popular way of taking commission out of a policy on an up-front basis. Initial – or 'capital' – units are bought within a timescale called the 'initial earnings period', determined by the term of the contract and the amount of commission taken. Required answer: 'no' – ideally, there will be no initial earnings period in the contract.

2. **Is there a 'reduced allocation period'?** Meaning: this is another way of extracting commission out of a policy up-front. It simply means that there is a period when less money is invested directly into your pension. Answer needed: 'no'. Why: a reduced allocation period will make early transfer values quite low.

3. **Are penalty-free premium holidays allowed?** Essential: this is especially relevant if your future employment pattern is uncertain. Desired answer: 'yes'.

4. **Can a penalty-free early retirement be taken?** Important: again, this is crucial if an earlier than expected retirement is a possibility. Answer wanted: 'yes'.

5. **Can I make the contract 'paid up' without penalty?** Explanation: 'paid up' refers to the state of regular premium policy when premiums have ceased. Ideal: clean companies reduce or even stop the regular administration charge in this event. Satisfactory answer: 'yes'. Do: look for a company that will allow a paid up policy to be restarted at no extra cost. This is vital if your work is of a stop-start-stop nature.

6. **Is there a surrender charge for regular premium contracts?** Usual: some companies levy a surrender charge as high as 10% to 20% of the fund's value. Answer required: 'no'.

(Source: Jon Briggs is an independent financial adviser at Chartwell Investment Management Limited, the Money Management *Investment Planner of the Year in 1996 and in 1997.)*

READ BETWEEN THE LINES OF A JOB ADVERTISEMENT – AND BE INVITED TO AN INTERVIEW

You can win a job interview if you know how to read a recruitment advertisement and respond to what it does – and doesn't – state. These are the little-known secrets to look for:

1. **Read all the job advertisements.** It is natural to look only for the titles of the jobs you are seeking. Better: get into the habit of reading all advertisements placed by organisations you're interested in joining. Just because they're not seeking someone like you in one advertisement doesn't mean they wouldn't welcome a cold approach from you. And you will have the advantage of learning about them from their advertisements, and can make a needs-orientated approach.

2. **Use a telephone number to make contact.** The golden rule of job hunting is to find out about an organisation before applying to it. This can be time consuming and difficult – unless a name and phone number is given in the advertisement. Use these to learn all you can and to establish a rapport with the person advertising. This will help when applying officially; 'You'll remember my skills are...'. Ask questions to establish their precise needs. Most people aren't brave enough to take this step – by doing this, it will single you out.

3. **Visit their website.** A growing number of organisations and recruitment agencies have web sites which are referred to in their advertisements. You simply must score points over your rivals by visiting the site to find out all you can and commenting on it when you apply. The same goes for an e-mail application. This will put you in the fast stream to success.

4. **Match up all the stated requirements.** Many advertisements list the attributes that the successful applicant needs to possess. Examples: 'You will have management experience in the computer industry', 'You like taking responsibility for a project'. Extend your covering letter by an

extra page, list the required qualities in one column and what you have to offer in another one. This demonstrates you have read the advertisement carefully, thought how best to help the organisation, and that you are ideally suited to it as well.

5. **Suggest the skills that are required.** Never assume an advertiser knows the precise details of the job and exactly who they want to employ – it's rarely the case. If the job description is vague, build your own job by suggesting the skills needed and demonstrating how you have them. What you're doing is making them realise that you, with your extra skills, can bring more to the appointment than they first thought.

6. **Use their language.** Identify the style of the advertisement and reproduce it in your covering letter and CV. Go through it, underlining words and phrases that are out of the ordinary. Pick out any jargon used too. If they've used bullet points, do the same in your application. It's like 'mirroring' in a job interview, when you subtly copy the interviewer's body postures. 'People like people who are like them' is an old saying, and a true one.

7. **Sidestep requests for salary information.** An elementary mistake made by many job applicants is to reveal their current salary or financial expectations. Too high, and you may be excluded automatically from the shortlist. Too low, and you may sell yourself short. If an advertisement asks you to give details of your present earnings, use a phrase such as 'I am confident that, if you agree we are well suited, salary will not be a problem'. Let them keep their options open.

8. **Ask a friend to apply to a box number.** Be wary of these – people have applied inadvertently to their existing employer in this way. Ask a trusted friend or relative to apply instead. A reply to them should contain details of the vacancy and you can then make a cold approach without revealing that you knew about it.

9. **Go for every job that appeals to you.** Don't be put off by a lengthy list of requirements if you are attracted to the job on offer. The

longer the list the better, because it is more likely that the organisation will fail to find the perfect match. Even if they do, they may have another opportunity arising soon for which you are well matched – and they'll save money, time and effort by not having to advertise it.

10. Adjust your application to the job advertisement. Emphasise your skills and suitability for this job by featuring achievements in your career that could solve the organisation's current problem. An achievement is something you did which used your skills, produced measurable benefits, and which you enjoyed doing. In your covering letter, draw attention to these achievements and show, point-by-point, how they are relevant to the advertised appointment.

11. Be enthusiastic and positive at all times. Why: a job often goes to the one person who states 'I really want to work for you!' These are wonderful words because they mean you are offering commitment and feel real excitement at the prospect of making a contribution to the company. Enthusiasm is a key quality as it makes a huge impact on the recipient. In your covering letter show with enthusiasm that you understand what they want; then demonstrate in your CV how you can deliver. And: every employer wants upbeat, 'can do' employees. So even if you don't have all the qualifications that they are looking for, give it a go. Don't use phrases like 'although I have no experience of contacting customers...'. Turn it around and say how quickly you learn new skills, how much you relish a challenge, and how you enjoy talking to people; then prove it in your CV. Think like a winner and you'll become one.

(Source: John Dunne, author of The London Evening Standard Action Guide to a New Job.*)*

LOOK RICH – WITHOUT SPENDING A FORTUNE

That's right – you really can look rich without having or spending a fortune. It's the little things that set the rich apart. Here they are:

1. **Keep an all-year round sun tan.** Only working stiffs are pasty faced – the really wealthy upper crust follow the sun at whim and maintain tans the whole year. A cosmetic tanning cream will bronze your face, and nobody will be the wiser.

2. **Wear natural-fibre clothing,** like cotton, wool and linen – and don't worry about the wrinkles. Rich people love them on their clothes.

3. **Wear neutral colours.** The rich love white, beige, black, cream and mauve.

4. **Don't wear gaudy baubles.** They are too tacky for wealthy people. All jewellery should have the appearance of quality – so stick with gold and silver fakes.

5. **Stay away from hair gels and garish hair colour dyes** – simple hairstyles are the hallmark of class.

6. **Drop names.** If you need to know which names are worth dropping, check out leading trade magazines and newspapers.

7. **Drop places.** Not Paris or Rome, but out-of-the-way spots only a well travelled, rich person would know about.

8. **Carry a book with you** – but nothing juicy. The rich are into self-improvement, business and philosophy. Or carry a foreign newspaper – you're checking on the political situation because your family has property there.

9. **Don't carry cash.** Top cats never have any liquid funds – they charge everything or use credit cards.

10. **Buy small items in prestigious shops** – top stores like Harrods

have stationery and cards that cost little more than other places. It'll make people think you shop there regularly.

11. Talk about spas or new health treatments like the garlic-oil and papaya-enzyme pills you've been advised to take.

12. Speak softly – rich and successful people don't need to raise their voices to get attention, because they're used to being listened to automatically.

13. Be eccentric – the richest people around can afford to be. Go sockless and wear boating shoes: everyone will think you own a boat too; a sure sign of wealth.

(Sources: Nicholas Reed, author of Making Money Made Easy, *published by Take That Limited, plus additional research amongst US and Australian lifestyle experts. Call the publishers on 01423 507545 for details of the book. The full version of this feature first appeared in* PFC *July 1997, No. 10.)*

BE A PORTFOLIO WORKER – AND MAKE MONEY IN TODAY'S WORKPLACE

A portfolio career is one where you have an income from a number of sources; perhaps several jobs, or a job and a business, or any combination of activities. As full-time, permanent employment declines over the next few years, more and more of us will become portfolio workers managing our own careers. Here's what to do:

1. Identify the key technical skills required by employers. We all have some technical skills that we can put on our CV, whether carpentry, pattern-making, or whatever. But: in an evolving workplace, the demand for such skills changes all the time. Note: many technical skills are often unusable outside of a particular work area or industry – and may be of limited use to portfolio workers. Core skills: numeracy, literacy, the ability to work with new technology, the ability to keep abreast of change in a trade or industry. Employer's quote: "The main thing we look for is multi-tasked people. If they have keyboard skills we can teach them the rest of it: switchboarding, typing faxes, letters, word processing, sales order processing, and so on."

2. **Recognise the important personal skills needed in the workplace.** Fact: the common thread that runs through most recruiters' requirements is personal skills. These often offer portfolio workers the best way into many companies. Definition: personal skills are our abilities – but not as we apply them in a technical sense. Example: it is not a matter of whether we can read a balance sheet, but whether we can communicate its salient points to our boss. Core skills: adaptability – the flexibility to work with anyone, to learn new skills and to move location if appropriate; resourcefulness; the tolerance of uncertainty; team-working skills; time management skills. Portfolio worker's quote: "People need to eliminate the divide in their minds that technical skills are work skills and personal skills are for their personal life. It's not like that. More and more, personal skills and work skills are one and the same."

3. **Spot the essential transferable skills wanted in a changing work environment.** People with those technical and personal skills that can be transferred easily to a variety of situations will always be in demand. But what do employers want most? 1: they don't necessarily want 'knowledge' – that hard-earned technical skill. Instead, they prefer to see the ability to gain knowledge. This is the key skill because it gives us access to any information that we want. 2: attitude. Have you ever been outraged by the rudeness of a shop assistant, or the failure of a service engineer to show up at the agreed time? Their attitude is wrong. Portfolio workers need an attitude that teams an industrious approach with a willingness to progress as an individual and to serve their clients well. 3: the ability to adapt to change. Portfolio worker's quote: "Change is only construed as bad if you're fully wedded to the old idea of a job for life. The nature of work changes all of the time – you have to be ready to change with it if you're to succeed."

4. **Acquire the new skills needed for your portfolio career.** You need a mix of readily transferable skills to succeed as a portfolio worker. Why: it spreads your risk and makes you more marketable and employable – you can use and develop whichever one of your range of skills is in demand at any particular time:

5. **Technical skills – find yourself a mentor; someone who knows how to impart the skill you need.** Example: perhaps ask a colleague to share their ideas or technical expertise with you in a 'skills exchange'. Warning: be wary of learning new technology on training courses at colleges and other educational establishments. Why: it takes most colleges two years to get a course up and running, by which time it is often out-of-date. And: it takes about six months to get a budget approved to buy any equipment – by which time the equipment that was specified has been overtaken. Bottom line: technology is moving too fast – by the time you've trained for something, it's already outdated. Tip: concentrate on learning keyboard skills rather than how to operate specific packages. Idea: you can often pick up an inexpensive computer from upgrading offices that would otherwise be throwing them away. It won't give you state-of-the-art knowledge, but lets you learn the basics of operating a computer and using technology.

6. **Personal skills – put yourself into situations that enable you to acquire those key skills that you feel you're missing.** Portfolio worker's quote: "When I was unemployed and trying to kick-start my portfolio career, I knew I needed to become more resourceful, more proactive in order to get work from strangers. So I signed up as a door-to-door collector for a charity. My wife said: 'How can you go knocking on doors knowing what people are going to say to you'. But I think to myself, I will not succeed at that house unless I knock on that door. That's a certainty. But if I knock on it, I might just succeed." Best: this strategy can be particularly effective if you're not naturally comfortable in the circumstances – it can enable you to learn more quickly and efficiently.

7. **Transferrable skills – watch how people interact with each other, both successfully and unsuccessfully, and identify what it is that makes them succeed or fail.** Then apply it to your own circumstances. Quote: "I learned most of what I need to know by watching my brother-in-law at work. He's a plumber, and when someone asks him how much a job will cost, he says '£50 – but £80 if you're going to sit and watch me'. He just can't work with people unless it's on his terms. He's damn near unemployable because of it. The thing I learned most from him was to smile – whoever you're talking to and whatever's going on, just smile. It works wonders." Truth: you'll often learn as much from other people's shortcomings as you will from their strengths.

(Sources: Joanna Grigg, business books author.)

UNLOCK YOUR SUBCONSCIOUS MIND – AND GET WHATEVER YOU WANT

The one thing about high achievers that stands out above everything else is that each and every one of them has used their subconscious mind to achieve greatness in their field. Here's how you can do it too:

1. **Construct your goals.** To achieve, you must start by conditioning your thinking to be goal-orientated, to become outcome orientated – in essence, to begin with the end in mind. How: write down your goals in the first person, present tense, and in a positive, emotional frame. Example: 'I am free to do the things that excite me now that I own my own house outright.' Vital: your goals must be personal – you can't set them for other people. And: they have to be in the present tense – install the goals as if they have already occurred. Also: they need to be positive and emotional – think what you want, not what you want to avoid. Helpful: you should record how you want the goals to make you feel.

2. **Overcome your fear.** Warning: fear – about finances, career, about attaining anything you desire – is caused by many things; but

most of all by the gap that appears to exist between the present reality and the reality we desire, and how – indeed if – we will close it. Idea: visualise a giant rubber band, with your present reality at one end, and your desired reality at the other. If the two move apart, tension builds in that band. View that tension not as stress or as pressure but as stored energy. You don't want to get rid of this tension; you want to convert it into energy that moves you towards the desired reality. And you'll help to do this by viewing your goals as if they were already present; and this will close that gap between the present and desired realities.

3. **Record your achievements.** Fact: the process of writing out your goals creates a commitment to them at a deep subconscious level. Experiment: a study of Harvard University graduates over many years divided them into two groups – those who achieved more than they set out to do, and those who achieved less. The high achievers shared one thing in common – they all recorded their life experiences on a regular basis. They each left Harvard with a written life plan – although not one of them kept to it! Instead, they rewrote that plan every time they changed direction. They wrote about their successes and their learning experiences. They noted when they were moving towards what they wanted, and when they were moving away. They analysed what they were doing; recording and commenting on their experiences all of the time. Bottom line: writing everything down is a fundamental key to success – use and amend a life plan of where you wish to go; and the marker points along the way.

4. **See – and then believe.** You need to install your goals emotionally in your subconscious, rather than intellectually in your conscious mind. Just saying your goals out loud or writing them down again and again is not enough – you've got to get them into the deepest levels of your consciousness. Example: the best method for you could be to create a very powerful, internal visualisation of what it is that you desire. Close your eyes and imagine what this might be like. Generate a vivid dream inside your head of how it would look, what you would be doing, and so on. Allow yourself to live it as though you are there – here

and now. Essential: live it as if it were real and happening at this moment. See it through your own eyes, hear it, smell it, taste it. Favourite saying: 'Successful people have already been where they want to go.'

5. **Unlock your resources.** Truth: everything you need to achieve success is sitting out there, somewhere in the world – your job is a simple one; you just have to find it. How: by visualising what you want to happen, your subconscious mind will start searching for whatever it is you need to succeed. Quite simply, it acts as a set of antennae. Proof: let's say you're going to have a baby and like the name 'Joel' – all of a sudden you start hearing that name all of the time. Or you're thinking of buying a classic car, perhaps a 1960s Triumph Herald – and you then start seeing these everywhere. Of course, there were always lots of Joels and Triumph Heralds out there all the while, but you just didn't notice them. Now that they have become significant to you, your subconscious mind has automatically begun to look out for them. Bottom line: awaken your subconscious mind and ask it to find what you need – and it will do it for you.

6. **Sow the seeds of success.** Important: write down the resources that you may need, and the people that might help you to achieve success, and then work out how to unlock them. Never: just write out a list – you have no emotional attachment to it. In the back of your mind it's just a wish list; and it's fruitless. Best: use your conscious mind to construct the list and then bring in your subconscious mind to gather up your resources.

(Source: Adrian Gilpin, chairman of the Institute of Human Development and the Transformational Leadership Forum and author of Unstoppable People – How Ordinary People Achieve Extraordinary Things, *published by Century Business Books. This feature first appeared in* PFC *May 1998, No. 20.)*

EARN 15% RETURNS AND WINDFALL BONUSES WITH TEPS

Most people with money to invest consider unit trusts and

investment trusts as investment vehicles; but few think about putting their money into Teps – yet traded endowment policies are an ideal choice for those people seeking maximum returns with minimal risk from their investments. Here are the main facts:

Definition: a traded endowment policy is one which is being sold by the original policy-holder; typically because they cannot afford to keep up the premium payments or their circumstances change – a couple may separate and need to sell and divide their assets. The new owner pays an agreed purchase price (of about 25% more than the surrender value), takes over the payment of premiums for the remainder of the term, and benefits from the policy's full maturity value. Example: a Royal Insurance Group policy purchased for £4,200 at an auction in April 1991 matured in February 1995 for £7,921 – an approximate annual compound yield of 16.5%.

Benefits: Teps offer a low-risk investment with a guaranteed value below which they will not fall (assuming premiums are maintained until maturity) – consisting of the basic sum assured plus yearly revisionary bonuses which cannot be removed once they have been added. And: by buying a second-hand policy, most of the onerous upfront charges have already been incurred by the original policy-holder – so greater profits can be generated for you.

Time to buy: the Tep market is growing – as a simple consequence of supply and demand, and improved public awareness. Fact: some people with endowments cannot maintain premium payments and switch to repayment mortgages, whilst others are faced with unemployment or negative equity and need cash. Result: approximately 70% of all with-profit endowment policies are cashed in early. Research findings: it is estimated that more than 300,000 individual policies are surrendered each year, representing £5.4bn. Indpendent actuaries assess that around 25% of these policies could be traded. With the traded endowment market currently at £200m per annum, there is huge scope for growth.

Best Buys: pick second-hand endowments from companies tipped to be demutualising or involved in takeovers in the near future. Why: by purchasing a with-profit endowment policy from these insurance companies, you become a member and stand to gain from any windfall bonuses – automatically adding value to your investment. Prediction: the life assurance sector will undergo massive restructuring in the next two years which will lead to the number of with-profit life offices reducing dramatically – mainly as a result of a series of acquisitions which are likely to take place during this period.

Caution: never cash in an endowment policy early – surrender values are often poor, and any attempt to get money out before the full term means you'll be penalised. Example: a 30-year-old man taking out a 20-year endowment policy and investing £50 per month with one office could expect to get back £1,828 if he surrendered it four years later; by which time, he would have paid in £2,400, taking account of initial policy charges and commission. Typical: an investor needs to hold a policy for around seven years before it is worth more than the premiums paid into it. Note: in extreme cases, 25-year term with-profit endowment policies being surrendered after 24 years can result in 27% of the final maturity value being lost!

Where to go: auctioneers who sell policies on a weekly basis to the highest bidder. Contact: H.E. Foster & Cranfield, 20 Britton Street, London EC1M 5NQ, (tel: 0171-608 1941). Brokers/trawlers who offer policies around the market with a view to achieving the best price for a policy by matching the buyer and the seller. Contact: The Insurance Policy Trading Company Limited, 22 Church Street, Godalming, Surrey GU7 1EW, (tel: 01483 427575). Market makers who buy and sell policies for their own account; buying and selling them on later when they own the policies. Contact: the Association of Policy Market Makers, Holywell Centre, 1 Phipp Street, London EC2A 4PS, (tel: 0171-739 3949).

What to pay: consider three factors when buying a Tep. A: your total outlay – this comprises the purchase price and future premiums to the end of the term. B: the period between the date of purchase and maturity – most Teps should be considered as long-term investments; five years plus. C: the sum you are likely to receive – consisting of the basic sum assured, annual or reversionary bonuses, and a terminal bonus. Note: future rates of bonuses are unknown; so stick with those insurers likely to be demutualising or involved in takeovers to maximise value.

***PFC* recommendation:** obtain Teps literature from auctioneers, but do not buy at an auction unless you know exactly what you are looking for; know the price you are prepared to pay, and don't go beyond it. Why: auction sale prices vary enormously and only experts are able to spot bargain buys. Best: approach a broker or market maker when you know what you want; and negotiate. The Teps market is a cut-throat one, and we found that most sellers were prepared to offer discounts of up to 5% to those people buying direct rather than through IFAs.

(Source: Richard Orme is the Sales Director of Securitised Endowment Contracts, the UK's largest market maker of traded endowment policies and European Endowment Traders of the Year in 1996.)

SLASH 33% OFF YOUR HOUSEHOLD BILLS

You can stay warm and save money on your electricity and gas bills if you follow our tricks of the trade:

1. **Insulate your home.** Double glazing can reduce heat loss by as much as 50%. But: it is expensive. Alternative: sheets of polythene are sold in different sizes, can be cut as required and attached to windows by heating it with a hair dryer. Or: clingfilm may be used. Helpful: adding polythene or clingfilm can prevent glass shattering everywhere if the window is broken. And: Apply sealant to the inner frames of windows. How: open window, apply sealant to inner frame, close window to ensure sealant fits well, open window and allow sealant to dry. Tip: check the tightness of windows (and doors) by moving a lighted candle around their frames – if the flame flickers, you need to add more sealant. Plus: thick and lined curtains are essential for winter warmth.

Place a 2" insulating roll on the floor of the loft. If you live in an older property, check with the local council to see if you might be eligible for a grant for insulating your home. Put a jacket on your hot water tank. Cost-cutter: two layers of cardboard wrapped around it is effective. Insulate key heat loss areas. Problem spots: loft hatches and pipes to and from the hot water cylinder. Also: put a jacket around the cold water tank to reduce the risk of freezing. But: do not insulate the space below the tank – rising heat helps prevent freezing.

2. **Use central heating economically.** If you're planning to have central heating installed for the winter, consider its layout carefully. Avoid: placing radiators below windows – this leads to excessive heat loss through those windows. And: curtains funnel heat away from the room and up towards windows. Also: fit radiator foil to prevent heat loss through windows and thin walls. Cheaper: fix kitchen foil behind radiators and beneath shelves immediately above them – this reflects heat back into the room. Essential: make sure the shiny side faces inwards towards the radiator and the room for maximum heat retention. Turn down the heating by 1°c. Fact: this can cut your heating bills by as much as 10%. Best: when cold, wear extra thin layers of clothes to stay warm. Reduce the heating at night. Note: a steady low heat is less costly and often feels more comfortable than short bursts of on-off heating throughout the day. Have your heating system tested and serviced annually – now is the time to do it. Important: a 2% increase in efficiency will cover the cost of this outlay. Ideal: replace your central heating boiler every ten years – you can save up to 10% on your fuel bills overnight.

3. **Monitor lighting.** Basics: turn off lights in rooms you are not using at that time. But: keep stairways well lit for safety purposes, especially with younger or elderly people in the home. Tip: keep a jam jar near to light switches and fine people who leave a light on in an empty room – they'll soon stop doing it. Plus: have dimmer switches installed – they'll soon pay for themselves. Reason: they reduce running costs by up to 75%, and allow bulbs to last longer too.

Use fluorescent tubes rather than ordinary bulbs where possible – they are half as expensive to use, and last up to ten times longer as well. Wise: leave fluorescent lights on rather than continually turning them on and off – it costs more to keep switching on and off. Dust fluorescent tubes and light bulbs at least once a week. Why: dust can reduce the light generated by as much as 50%. Outcome: more lights are turned on, at greater expense. Put 'heat and light' bulbs in the coldest areas of your home. Examples: toilets and extension rooms. Why: these bulbs can add sufficient warmth to create a comfortable atmosphere.

4. **Watch your hot water.** Why: heating water takes up an average of 20% of fuel bills. Best: heat water with a central heating boiler rather than an immersion heater – it's usually less expensive that way. And: Keep the thermostat at around 60° Fahrenheit or slightly less. Because: it's wasteful to have water so hot that you need to add cold water to use it. And: excessive steam will damage bathroom walls and fittings. Shower when possible to minimise costs. Fact: four people can shower in the same amount of water used to fill a bath!

5. **Economise when cooking and eating.** Always: use your microwave whenever possible – it uses far less energy than a standard oven. Alternatives: slow cookers and deep fryers are also more economic to use than a normal oven. Other money-saving ideas include: when using a conventional oven, cook several items at the same time to minimise cost. And: clean the oven regularly – clean walls maximise the reflective heat. Boil only as much water in a kettle as you need for your purposes. Always: measure out the right amount with a cup or mug. But: ensure the heating element is covered to prevent possible damage when boiling.

6. **Use your appliances carefully.** Do: get into the habit of using your washing machine, tumble dryer and other appliances in the most economic way. Use your washing machine only when you have a full load. First: soak grubby clothes in cold water for a few hours before washing – this is a cheap way of loosening dirt. Ignore: pre-soak and hot

wash cycles. Better: wash on a shorter cycle at a cooler temperature – it's less expensive and less damaging to your clothes. Then: turn off the machine when water and washing powder have mixed thoroughly, and leave the load to soak for an hour – this helps to dissolve dirt. Last: switch on again, and complete the cycle. Outcome: clean clothes, at half the price. Hang clothes up to dry instead of using a tumble dryer. Alternative: when using a tumble dryer, turn it off halfway through the suggested drying time and leave the load to dry in the warm drum. This way, you're using up all the available heat, and at around half of the normal cost. De-scale kettles and irons regularly. Why: those appliances which contain built-up, hard water scale cost up to twice as much to use. How: de-scale a kettle by half-filling with an equal mix of water and vinegar. Boil, cool and rinse. De-scale an iron by pouring warm vinegar into the steam channel. Wait until the scale dissolves, then drain and rinse with boiled water. Important: make sure you unplug the iron during this process. Tip: keep a marble in your kettle to prevent further build-up.

(Source: PFC *editor Iain Maitland.)*

HAVE A BETTER ORGASM – JUST STOP URINATING

Improve male orgasms by doing fifteen Kegel exercises, three times a day – simply contract your muscles whilst urinating so that you stop and withhold the flow mid-stream. Note: as men grow older, the pelvic muscles that control orgasm become weaker and orgasms become less intense – but these exercises have a rejuvenating effect. Also: during love-making, stop as you approach orgasm, ease off and start again; this further strengthens the pelvic muscles.

(Source: Al Cooper, clinical director at the San Jose Marital and Sexuality Clinic, California.)

UNCOVER THE HIDDEN SECRETS OF YOUR PATIENT NOTES

Patient notes used to be a mystery to everyone outside of the health professions. And their contents were a closely guarded secret. But as a patient of a General Practitioner or a hospital Consultant, you're legally entitled to read your notes in full. Here's the best way to obtain access to your patient details; and how to read them:

1. **Ask permission to access your notes – and you'll get to see them more easily.** Fact: a GP or a hospital Consultant is the legal protector of the contents of patient notes. And: anyone outside of the medical professions who wishes to read the notes must first obtain permission in writing from that legal protector. Action: write a polite letter to your GP or your hospital manager requesting permission to access your notes. Include: your full name, date of birth, full address and your patient number (if known). Important: state the reason why you want to see your records and ask for a response within two weeks – some practices and hospitals don't give priority to these requests and will not deal promptly with them unless they are given a deadline.

2. **Understand how your notes are organised – so that you know how to read them properly.** Tip: the organisation of patient notes can be very confusing. Usual: patient notes consist of four different sections. One: your essential details – name, address etc; visits to or by your GP; past and present medications prescribed to you; previous referrals to hospital; out-patient clinic appointments; operation details and dates; details of any care you have received at home by community nurses. Two: treatment details for each of your visits to your GP or hospital – information about the reason for your visit; how your illness was managed; and the medications given and/or operations carried out. Three: letters – copies of communications between healthcare workers such as GPs and hospital Consultants regarding your past and present care; including referral letters from your GP to a Consultant, and discharge letters from a hospital to your GP. Four:

investigations – a full record of blood tests, X-rays and scans, and full reports from the health departments involved.

3. Take a witness with you when you visit the practice or hospital – this protects you in case notes go missing later on. Typical: you will usually have a member of the practice or hospital staff sitting with you as you read your notes – to ensure that you do not tamper with or remove any of them. Vital: ask your partner or a trusted friend or relative to sit in as well – this covers you against the possibility of a complaint by the GP or the hospital management. Example: if some of your notes are subsequently mislaid, you'll find it easier to prove that this was unrelated to your visit.

4. Check that you're given the correct notes – and avoid potential confusion and even alarm. Why: there may be more than one patient with the same name as yourself at that practice or hospital; Smith, Jones and Patel are very common names. Example: at present, there are ten 'David Jones' living in the town of Guildford in Surrey – a source of confusion if one of them asks for his medical records at the nearby hospital. How: check that the cover of the notes has your correct name, date of birth and address. Also: double-check that each page of the contents has your details on it – notes are sometimes re-filed in other files in error.

5. Have a plan of action – so that you can read your notes quickly and easily. Helpful: before reading, be clear about the exact information that you want to obtain from these medical records. Example: you may have had a growth removed from your bladder and want to see if the explanation given to you by the hospital Consultant matched the information detailed in Consultant – GP correspondence. Useful: write down a list of questions that you want answered on a piece of paper; then tick off each question as you find out what you want to know. Vital: if in doubt, ask. Typical: medics are renowned for their illegible handwriting and for using abbreviations. Example: FBC means full blood count; a routine, basic blood test used to screen for such disorders as anaemia, infection and blood clotting abnormalities. Other common abbreviations include:

- ac – ante cibum; before food
- AXR – abdominal X-ray; an investigation carried out if you have had abdominal pain
- BP – blood pressure
- Ca – carcinoma
- CI – contraindications
- CNS – central nervous system
- CSF – cerebal spinal fluid
- CT – computerised tomography; a scan similar to an X-ray to visualise internal organs
- CVP – central venous pressure; an indication of cardiac health
- CVS – cardiovascular system; comprising the heart and blood vessels
- CXR – chest X-ray
- DM – diabetes mellitus
- D&V – diarrhoea and vomiting
- DVT – deep vein thrombosis; a blood clot typically in a vein in the lower leg
- ECG – electrocardiograph; a means of monitoring cardiac health with a tracing of its electrical activity
- ENT – ear, nose throat
- GB – gall bladder
- GI – gastrointestinal

GU – genito-urinary; the reproductive and urinary systems

Hb – haemoglobin; a basic blood test, typically for anaemia

IM – intramuscular; for example, injections into a muscle

IV – intravenous; as an example, injections into a vein

JVP – jugular venous pressure; another sign of cardiac health

LFT – liver function test; blood test carried out to assess the health of a liver

MSU – midstream urine; the least contaminated urine, used to test for kidney infections, for example

nbm – nil by mouth; before an operation

NSAID – non-steroidal anti-inflammatory drug used for pain and to reduce inflammation

PO – per orum; by mouth

PR – per rectum; rectal examination

SC – subcutaneous; for example, injections given into the tissue just below the skin.

SE – side effects; of a drug

T – temperature

TPR – temperature, pulse and respirations; basic observations of a patient's condition, after an operation, for example

U&E – basic blood test to screen for the abnormality of the natural chemicals in the blood; abnormal levels of potassium and sodium can contribute to ill health

URTI – upper respiratory tract infection; laryngitis, for example

UTI – urinary tract infection; an infection of the kidney or bladder, as examples

Note: a medical dictionary is essential if your notes are likely to be extensive and/or complicated. Recommended: *The Oxford Concise Medical Dictionary* (Oxford University Press) – it's used by the professionals and provides clear, understandable definitions.

7. **Make notes about your records – this way you'll have a permanent, written record of them.** Unfortunate: although you have a legal right to read your patient notes, you are not allowed to remove any of their contents, write comments on or deface them in any way. Motto: look but don't touch. Hint: take in a pen and paper to write notes for future reference about what you've read – document times, dates, which medical professions were responsible for your treatment, investigations etc.

8. **Stay calm – so that you avoid being rushed.** Fact: medics are busy people and may want to speed you through as quickly as possible. But: you have the right to take as long as you wish. Caution: if you wish to make a complaint about the management or treatment of an illness, put it in writing on an official basis. Don't: complain verbally there and then. Reason: the best way to get the desired results from any future official action you may take is to be methodical; this increases your chances of receiving co-operation from within the medical profession.

(Source: Dr Jeremy Sims is a hospital doctor. The original version of this feature appeared in PFC *July 1998, No. 22.)*

THREE SECONDS TO SAVE A LIFE

Reduce the risk of whiplash and neck injuries – check the position of the head restraint each time you get into a car; and adjust accordingly. Fact: less than 50% of car drivers and passengers have their head restraints positioned correctly, and run an increased risk of unnecessary injuries in an accident. And: less than 10% check the position of their head restraint when they sit down. Details: the top of the restraint should be level with your eyes and ears, and adjusted forwards so that it just touches the back of the head. Vital: head restraints should be readjusted when different people occupy the seat; they may be shorter or taller than the previous occupant.

(Source: Tim Rogers, PFC *subscriber and breakdown patrolman.)*

SIX QUESTIONS TO IDENTIFY A BUSINESS OPPORTUNITY SCAM

Many people want to make extra money working from home – and that leaves them vulnerable to the charms of smooth-talking con artists. But you can spot a home-working scam simply by asking these questions before proceeding:

1. Is this an offer of work? Fact: the most popular home-working cons involve persuasive letters and glossy leaflets that invite you to discover how to find work – but they don't actually provide real work of any kind. Important: see these offers for what they are – typically, booklets produced at home on someone's computer, advising you in general terms how to be a successful entrepreneur. And: you're paying £10 or more for something that won't tell you anything you didn't already know – and it's probably written by someone who's failed to do it themselves! Otherwise: they'd be earning money from that work rather than sharing this information with you. Wiser: don't waste your money on over-priced booklets by business failures and deadbeats – the market is awash with them. Instead: walk into the local branches of the main high street banks, say you're thinking of running your own home-based business, and leave with armfuls of useful books, pamphlets and leaflets; and all for free.

2. Does this claim to be a big money work opportunity? Tip: most con artists draw in their victims with offers of £300 a day, £100,000 a year, or even 'unlimited earnings'. Why: nearly everyone wants to be a big earner so these crooks pitch the stated potential earnings at such a level that they nag away at you until you give in and decide it's worth a £20, £50 or £100 'registration fee' to find out more. You take a gamble, and you lose – every time. Reality: home-workers don't make big money The majority carry out routine work that pays between £2.50 to £5.00 per hour on average. Guideline: check out what you'd earn doing this type of work on an employer's premises – your local job centre should help you here. Theory: you might expect to earn a little more as a home-based worker because the employer will not have to pay national insurance contributions, provide equipment, heat and light premises, and so on. Practice: you'll earn the same or less than the going rate as the employer will want to pocket these savings rather than give them to you. So: if this so-called opportunity offers more than average earnings, it's almost certainly a scam.

3. Does this sound like an easy way to make money? Tactic: charlatans want you to think the work is simple – so simple that anyone can do it, straightaway, and earn an immediate, lucrative return. Alarm bells: 'simple', 'easy', 'instant'. Unfortunate: there is no such thing as a simple work/big money combination – simple work/little money and skilled work/big money deals are realistic but simple work/big money works only for con artists who prey on their naive victims. Warning signs: 'no education needed', 'no training required' – you don't make big money for easy work, unless you have a special talent, skill or training. Proof: a successful business offering genuine work will have lots of satisfied workers around, so ask for a list of their home-based workers and approach half a dozen chosen at random from that list. Evidence: crooks won't produce a list – either because there aren't any workers or they're working long hours for little money and wouldn't speak well of the organisation.

4. Is this an out-of-the ordinary, home-based opportunity? Note: con artists lure in their victims by offering easy and big money – and then adding a twist. Technique: most people realise they won't make good money stuffing envelopes, painting figures, doing ironing or typing – so the crooks promote work such as home publishing and mail order opportunities that people have heard of but know little about. These sound as though they're lucrative and might just pay off. Note:

money can be made in home publishing and mail order; but they usually require substantial upfront investment in terms of equipment, time and money. And: the chances of failure are high. Statistic: one in three businesses fail within the first year; and only one survives for five years or longer. Remember: if you're not fully familiar with something, you cannot expect to understand and master it, and turn it into a money-spinner. Bottom line: if you don't know what you're getting into, get out fast.

5. Does this involve me sending off money in advance? Truth: scams always involve payments in advance somewhere down the line – this is the money that's going to be stolen from you. Typical: some home-based work involves you buying materials from a business, putting them together and returning completed units for payment. The chances of you selling those electrical components or whatever to someone else is remote – you're obviously going to complete and hand them in for payment. So: to pay anything upfront should be unnecessary; and is certainly unwise. Crucial: if this is a genuine and profitable business, someone, somewhere will have heard of it – the representative association of the industry and/or a regulatory body, as examples. Always: ask around – check the local phone directory and call the nearest chamber of commerce and the small business and/or local trading standards officer at the council. If no one's ever heard of this business, avoid it at all costs.

6. Is this a believable work opportunity? Fact: home-working cons just don't add up, if you think carefully and do your sums. Sensible: never take facts and figures at face value – verify them with reputable sources such as the relevant trade association or the trading standards officer at the local council. Common example: many scams involve mail order – 'send off this circular and you'll get a 50% response rate'. Check: anyone involved with direct mail will tell you that the average response rate is between 1.5% and 5% – and that's a great return. 50% is unheard of – unless you're a con artist. Helpful: take the details of this offer and show it to someone else; a partner, an adviser at the Citizens' Advice Bureau, a small business adviser at the local bank. Tell-tale sign: if you're embarrassed to do so, then you already know it's a scam.

(Source: PFC *editor Iain Maitland and his team of researchers. This feature first appeared in* PFC *October 1998, No. 25.)*

EASY WAY TO AVOID THRUSH

Eliminate thrush easily – maintain your vaginal pH. Problem: vaginal thrush is caused by a yeast organism that lives naturally inside humans and doesn't normally create problems because numerous body factors keep it in check – but if you alter any of these factors, the organism multiples rapidly and thrush develops. Solution: wear cotton underwear – avoid nylon knickers and/or tight jeans that create warm and humid conditions. And: use panty liners rather than tampons. Plus: keep cool – bathe or shower immediately after exercise. Also: avoid perfumed bath or shower products – these are notorious for upsetting the vaginal pH. Avoid: sunbeds – ultraviolet exposure causes yeast to multiply rapidly.

(Source: David C. Harcombe, freelance community pharmacist.)

THREE STEPS TO FANTASTIC FEET

The simplest way to keep your feet in tip-top condition is to choose and wear the right shoes. Here's the all-important information:

1. Know how to buy shoes – this way, they'll be a perfect fit. When: buy shoes in the late afternoon. Why: feet spread slightly during the day – if you bought shoes in the morning, they'd become uncomfortable by the evening. Choose: soft, malleable shoes, with cushioning and support. How: fit shoes with your hands – look for an index finger's width between shoe tip and toes. And: when standing, the shoe should not be taut or pushed out of shape. Important: wear the right shoe for the right occasion – one pair of shoes can't do everything.

Do: have a pair of trainers to wear to and from work – to make your feet feel comfortable. And: ration the amount of time you wear shoes – take them off at your desk, to give your feet a chance to breathe and relax.

2. Wear low-heeled shoes that feel balanced – to support your feet effectively. Best: those with heels below 1½ inches – these enable wearers to walk properly, and protect the feet from unnecessary wear and tear. Unfortunate: higher-heeled shoes increase the curvature of the spine, compress vertebrae, and strain muscles. And: these lead to foot problems, including dropped arches, claw toes, and corns and calluses. Useful: ankle straps and wide-based heels aid stability and balance, and help reduce these problems. Guideline: check that you can stand comfortably when wearing them; you shouldn't feel as though you're struggling to stay steady.

3. Wear fashion shoes in the evenings and at weekends only – and keep your feet in excellent condition. Worst: court shoes – these are a size smaller than regular shoes so that they won't fall off when walking. The foot is squeezed into too small a space. And the big toe will bend in and over the other toes. And: mules – these allow the foot to slide forward. Toes are rammed into the front of the shoe. This results in corns, calluses and bunions. Also: stilettos – the tall, narrow heels make them unstable to walk in. And the muscles have to work hard to keep the body balanced. This leads to tired, damaged muscles. Plus: wedges – these do not offer ankle support. The wearer can't follow the normal, 'heel-to-toe' walking action. This can cause sprained ankle ligaments, and even lead to fractured ankles.

(Source: Laurence Kirk of the British College of Naturopathy & Osteopathy (BCNO). The full version of this feature first appeared in PFC *April 1999, No. 31.)*

DON'T LET MEDICINE BURN YOUR SKIN

Avoid sunburn – check your prescription drugs and over-the-counter medicines. Fact: all drugs and medicines have side-effects of some kind; and many common drugs cause photosensitivity, which leads to sunburn even in cloudy weather. Main culprits: amiodarone, azapropazone, chlorpromazine, ciprofloxacin, doxycycline, frusemide, nalidixic acid, ofloxacin, quinidine, tetracyclines. Symptoms: skin rashes and/or an exaggerated sunburn. Remedy: talk to your GP or pharmacist about switching to different medications.

(Source: PFC *health experts.)*

GET THE MONEY YOU'RE OWED IN SEVEN DAYS

If you're owed more than £750 and can't get paid, don't waste your time with letters, phone calls and threats of county court summons. These are often ignored by reluctant payers. Instead, serve a little-known statutory demand – and get paid fast. Here's how this works in practice:

1. Get to know the insolvency law – so that you understand how to short cut the system. Fact: you don't need to issue a summons to recover a debt of £750 or more. Instead: by-pass the small claims and county court systems, and issue a notice under section 122(f) of the Insolvency Act 1986. Details: these 'statutory demands' can be served against all types of debtor – limited companies, partnerships, even individuals operating as sole traders. And: if the debt is not paid within seven days, you are then entitled to issue proceedings to close down the debtor's business – they either pay up now or cease trading in one week's time.

2. Issue the correct form properly – and the debtor will know this is serious. Information: to issue a statutory demand, complete form 4.1 for an individual or a partnership or form 6.1 for a limited company. Where: obtain these from a law stationers – see your local *Yellow Pages* for details. Note: you don't need to employ a solicitor to prepare these forms; they're easy to complete yourself. They include clear instructions for you, and tell the debtor what they must do along with the consequences of ignoring the demand. Vital: for a limited company, the statutory demand must be served at the registered office; not necessarily the same place as the head office. Check: the company's letterhead; by law it must state the registered office. For an individual or a partnership, the form must be served personally on the debtor; or debtors if it is a partnership. How: this can be done by you, a process server or a bailiff, but not through any other third party. And: before serving the statutory demand, it must be confirmed that the recipient is named on the form. Best: hand it over yourself in a nondescript envelope, and say, 'I think this is for you. Are you Martin Smith?'

3. Act convincing – and frighten the debtor into paying up. Statistic: a statutory demand scares 95% of bad debtors into settling their debts; but only if they're convinced that you will follow through and close them down if they withhold payment. Wise: serve the demand with a simple covering letter – no threats, no bluster, no swagger. To be effective, this needs to appear to be a routine procedure for you. Warning: a loud and embarrassing approach makes it look as though you're bluffing. Caution: if you are convincing, and the debtor still doesn't pay, this indicates that they're in serious financial trouble and are likely to close down anyway. Unfortunate: consider cutting your losses now, saving further time and effort pursuing a debt that probably cannot be paid.

4. Quote the law – it's the easiest way to show you mean business. Why: it will make them think you've done this successfully many times before. Useful: section 122(f) of the Act permits a company to be wound up if it is unable to pay its debts as they become due. And: section 123(e) of the Act states 'a company is deemed to be unable to pay its debts as they fall due, by forwarding a final notice to the company's registered office, giving it seven days to pay the account in full'. So: this provides sufficient proof for you to initiate proceedings to wind up their firm in seven days' time. Bottom line: convince them you mean business, and you'll get your money.

(Source: Roy Hedges is a former collections manager for a leading trade finance company. The original version of this feature first appeared in PFC *November 1998, No. 26.)*

WHY YOU SHOULD PUT HAEMORRHOID CREAM ON YOUR FACE

Look good – for the lowest possible price. How: The cheapest and most effective way to reduce puffy eyes, eliminate undereye bags, tighten skin and provide an instant face lift is to apply haemorrhoid cream. Why: this cream contain shark's liver oil and yeast – exactly the same ingredients that are found in firming creams sold at expensive cosmetic counters. Useful: mix haemorrhoid cream with moisturiser to produce your own personalised firming cream, at a fraction of high street prices.

(Source: Diane Irons, US model and image journalist.)

HOW TO SPOT A MIRACLE CURE THAT REALLY WORKS

There's a simple way to identify a genuine cure amongst all of the wonder drugs, potions and remedies on the market. Just follow this five-step guide, and you'll make the right choice:

1. **Seek an independent assessment – it's the best way to get the facts.** Sources: a peer-reviewed journal, a university or other academic establishment, a health association or self-help group. Why: they're most likely to test products and claims most thoroughly. Tip: your GP or local Citizens' Advice Bureau should provide contact details for relevant bodies. Note: information that's available only from a manufacturer, distributor and/or promoter may be unreliable; it's in their interests to overstate or report medical information inaccurately. Example: claims are based on so-called proof from testimonials provided by individual patients; but these may be employees or business associates. And: in worst cases, manufacturers just make up information about their products.

2. **Be wary of multi-cure claims – they almost certainly won't**

work. Example: 'this product is effective for all (100) forms of arthritis' – it's just not possible. Truth: very few medical treatments work on more than a few, related conditions. And: be sceptical of any 'special' or 'secret' formula claims – these rarely exist in practice. Fact: if something truly works, manufacturers are the first to tell everyone about it. So: they can take credit for its success; and establish a strong brand name and reputation in their field. These generate more sales and profits.

3. **Look for a full list of ingredients – so that you know what's really in it.** Warning: beware of the word 'complex' if specific amounts aren't listed. Reason: it's usually a cover-up for cheaper, less potent ingredients. Example: a chondroitin/glucosamine complex in arthritis drugs sounds like a powerful combination. But: it may contain 95% glucosamine and only 5% chondroitin. And: glucosamine is much cheaper; chondroitin is far more effective. Best advice: ask your GP to explain each of the contents; their role, and their side-effects.

4. **Be cautious of cut-price products – they're usually less powerful than similar brands on the market.** Scam: some manufacturers can produce cheaper products containing the same, basic ingredients as rival products. How: the bulk of the product is so impure that it has little therapeutic effect. But: be aware that substantially higher-priced products are not necessarily purer or better though. Unfortunate: some manufacturers over-price their products because some people will pay more; typically, for the best-known brands.

5. **Search for two or more scientific studies with comparable, positive results – this suggests this product really does work.** Ideal: one scientific study that produces evidence, with an independent organisation duplicating that study, and generating the same or similar findings. Important: all studies should contain a control group with members who are monitored physically on an ongoing basis. Because: this produces hard evidence. Pointless: simply asking people how they feel generates inaccurate data. Why: a proportion will always think they feel better just because they've taken something that ought to improve

their health. Wise advice: refer to *The Lancet* (0171 436 4981); a weekly magazine that publishes latest study findings. Bottom line: ask your GP to show you recent issues

(Source: Dr Jason Theodosakis, Assistant Clinical Director at the University of Arizona College of Medicine in Tuscon, USA.)

WARNING! HIGH STREET CON ALERT

Don't be ripped off by high street electrical stores – be very wary of extended warranties. Tip: extended warranties on household electrical items are a waste of money. Details: salespeople in electrical stores use hard-sell, scare tactics to persuade customers to purchase these warranties – because they earn higher commission on these than the goods themselves. But: most manufacturers offer 12 months' free parts and labour guarantees anyway. And: the Sale and Supply of Goods Act of 1994 makes a retailer responsible for repairing faulty goods without charge within a 'reasonable' period from the date of purchase – and major items such as washing machines should last for much longer than a year without developing faults. Plus: Consumers' Association research shows it's almost always cheaper to pay for repairs as required rather than buy an expensive warranty.

(Source: PFC *consumer researchers.)*

ADVERTISE ANYTHING TO ANYONE, ANYWHERE – FREE

If you've got something to promote or sell, get in touch with your local radio station. They're always looking for interviewees for their shows. And you can use this opportunity to put over your message to a captive audience, completely free of charge. Anyone can do this successfully if they have that all-important, inside knowledge. Here it is:

1. **Know your subject well – this way, you'll maximise your chances of an effective interview.** Why: you won't be given any

questions in advance, so you need to be able to talk off-the-cuff about anything connected with that topic. Tip: the presenter is unlikely to be an expert, and will take the role of an interested and intelligent member of the public. Useful: write down the types of questions they might ask – and think how you'd respond to them. Wise: try to compose a separate list of questions you couldn't answer – if you succeed, you're probably not ready to be interviewed on this subject.

2. Say you're available only when the show is off air – they'll then have to pre-record the interview which is less stressful for you. Tactic: never admit you want to pre-record because of nerves – they'll try to talk you out of it, as this is more time-consuming for them. But: a pre-recorded interview gives you greater control. Example: if you don't like what you've said, you can stop by saying, 'I'm sorry, I'd like to do that again'. And: you can go on doing this until you're happy with your performance. Note: be aware that a technician may subsequently edit out anything that's considered boring or irrelevant – even though this might have been something important to you. But: they cannot do that with a live interview – so once you've gained plenty of experience, go live in future.

3. Be well prepared – finding out as much as possible about the interview enables you to approach it with total confidence. Fact: success is 99% preparation and 1% inspiration. Do: double-check where and when the interview will take place – and if you've time, do a dry run the day before and allow an extra 30 minutes for your journey on the day. Important: radio shows are scheduled tightly – if you're late, you won't go on. Helpful: get dressed up, tidy your hair and go to the toilet before going on air – these all help you feel more relaxed. Outcome: you'll perform better.

4. Rely on the presenter – they're there to help you to succeed. Because: they want to create an entertaining and informative conversation for the listeners – and that's easiest to do if you're working together. Sensible: sit where they suggest, and accept their offer of headphones – these allow you to hear what's being transmitted. Unfortunate: without them, you'll not be able to tell when the music ends and the conversation starts. Trick: put on your headphones immediately to familiarise yourself with them as soon as possible. Unexpected: you'll be able to hear your own voice which can be disconcerting.

5. **Use bullet-point notes – these ensure you put across all of the key points.** Idea: jot down soundbite expressions on a postcard. These are short and catchy comments that can be used regularly to emphasise what you want to say. Avoid: lengthy notes and written quotes – you'll sound like you're reading from an unfamiliar script. Advisable: look at the presenter and talk naturally as though you were having a one-to-one conversation with them; hesitate, cough, wave your hands and arms about – do whatever you'd do normally. Never: concentrate on thinking about what you're doing and saying. That's the quickest way to start making mistakes.

6. **Paint mind pictures for the listeners – it's the most powerful method of conveying your message.** Meaning: give full rather than one-word answers, and provide visual examples. Typical: saying you've raised £47,000 for your local hospital sounds impressive. But: explaining that this is enough to buy an extra four kidney machines which will save ten lives over the next year is more graphic, and successful. Bottom line: radio pictures are better than those on television because they happen inside listeners' minds – and there's no limit to their imagination.

(Source: Nigel Catlow, freelance broadcaster for BBC Radio Lancashire and BBC Radio Merseyside. This feature first appeared in PFC *March 1999, No. 32)*

ONE QUESTION REVEALS HOLIDAY HELL-HOLE

Boost your chances of choosing a good holiday hotel – just ask your travel agent one simple question. Query: what does the ABC

Agents Gazetteer say about this hotel? Explanation: unlike the glossy brochures, this trade directory reveals the whole truth about hotels around the world – including the nasty bits that the tour operators haven't mentioned. Examples: if your hotel is surrounded by wasteland, is adjacent to a noisy disco or is separated from the beach by a busy road, the Gazetteer should expose these drawbacks. Caution: some travel agents are reluctant to let you have this inside information – so make it clear that your booking (and their commission) is dependent upon you seeing the relevant entry.

(Source: PFC *travel writers.)*

FIND YOUR TRUE SOULMATE FOR 35p

One of the easiest and most popular ways of meeting a partner is through the classified ads in your local newspaper, or a favourite magazine. But to find your true soulmate, you'll need to use these little-known tricks of the trade:

1. **Look in a publication that you enjoy reading – this increases your prospects of meeting someone suitable.** Why: people who read the same newspapers and magazines tend to share certain characteristics and outlooks. And: they're much more likely to have something in common.

2. **Ensure your ad is read – so that you maximise the number of replies received.** How: start with an 'A' if the ads run alphabetically – nearly everyone looks carefully at those first few ads. And: make the opening words as distinctive as possible – this way, they'll grab the readers' attention, and make them want to read on. Example: 'A Match Made in Heaven' is an eye-grabber. 'A Single White Female' isn't.

3. **Be as original as you can – this makes you seem special and encourages people to respond.** Do: make every word punch its weight. How: avoid meaningless words like 'attractive' 'warm' and 'good sense of humour' – they're pointless because everybody uses them. And they

don't really tell the reader anything about you. Instead: look through a thesaurus for alternative, descriptive words for yourself. Exception: 'assertive' is a good word for women to use because they're then less likely to meet any men who feel threatened by a self-confident woman.

4. State precisely who you're looking for – it helps readers to screen themselves, and guarantees a higher proportion of potentially suitable replies. Example: if a non-smoking partner is important to you, say so. Also: you can state what you're not looking for. Example: '9-5-ers need not apply'. Useful: an age range is a good idea, but don't make it too narrow, as you may exclude the right person for you. Suggestion: a ten-year age range is often ideal.

5. Describe yourself – this ensures that only the most interested people apply. Best: select a few words that sum you up most accurately. Caution: don't overstate your qualities though – the biggest complaint from people who answer ads is that advertisers exaggerate. Unfortunate: this wastes everybody's time. Helpful: deal with reality – give your age, and mention if you have children and/or animals. That way, there'll be no surprises later on. Tip: if you state your height, put your weight too – otherwise, it implies you have a hang-up about it.

6. Send brief replies to any ads you see – and boost your chances of being chosen. Because: on average, men receive 25-50 replies to their ads; and women receive 50-150 – so they'll not need or want to read through reams of paper. Guideline: the longer the reply, the more likely it is to be put to one side. Wise: say who you're looking for and what you're like. Avoid: the life history.

7. Be creative – so that your reply makes it to the top of the pile. Idea: do or say something unusual. Example: one woman replied to an ad by writing on an airline napkin, 'I'm 35,000 feet up over France. The pilot took a right instead of a left over Greenland. Thank goodness I had this month's *X-Cel* to read with your personal ad in it.' Trick: look for the twist in the ad itself. Example: one man responded to a woman who said she liked ice cream, by writing a reply on the back of a (clean) ice cream carton. Worst: don't use notepaper torn from a student's notepad – lots of people do, and it looks cheap and tacky.

8. Show your sense of humour – this is the quickest way to succeed. Example: one man saw an ad including the words 'photo appreciated', and sent photos of famous people such as Liam Neeson and Brad Pitt with the message, 'You asked for a photo. I'm not sure who you prefer, so I've sent you a selection of different ones.' Vital: if the other person simply doesn't appreciate your personal sense of humour, then you're probably not right for each other. Your reply will be eliminated straightaway – and that saves everybody's time.

(Source: Sheila O'Connor, a specialist in personal and relationship issues. The full version of this feature first appeared in PFC *February 1999, No. 29.)*

SMEAR CAT LITTER ON YOUR FACE

Cleanse your skin successfully – spread cat litter all over your face. Con: some spas and health centres that charge hundreds of pounds for 'herbal wraps' are actually using cat litter costing less than £2 per bag. Details: these 'mud' or 'clay' treatments are ideal for detoxifying the skin but they're made from simple 'fuller's earth'; the 100% natural clay that is free from chemicals, additives and clumping materials – and is used by cost-conscious pet owners as the cheapest cat litter on the market. Tip: take a tablespoon of the dried clay and mix it with a little water for a refreshing face-mask; or detoxify your whole body with a £2 bag – and save yourself hundreds of pounds.

(Source: PFC *health and beauty contacts.)*

SIT DOWN, PUT YOUR FEET UP – AND EARN MONEY

If you're looking for well-paid, home-based work with flexible hours, and all without needing any equipment or cash outlay, become a freelance proof-reader. All you need to do is to read the proofs – prepublication copies – of books and spot any errors in them. And you get paid for it! Here's how to succeed:

1. **Understand what proof-reading involves – so you can decide if it's right for you.** Fact: to be a successful proof-reader, you need two key skills. One: the ability to read and see everything. Examples: the missing letter, the extra space between two words, the comma instead of a full stop. Note: top proof-readers are those who are always spotting mistakes in whatever they read. Helpful: train yourself to proof-read by looking constantly for errors when reading. Two: the ability to correct spelling, punctuation and grammar as they relate to the material. Meaning: the style of a sports biography may be much looser than an academic textbook; and any grammatical corrections should reflect this.

2. **Aim to proof-read books that you enjoy reading – you'll find you're tuned automatically into their particular style.** And: it makes the job easier. Useful: look for appropriate books in the book shops – and make a note of their publishers. Next: refer to a copy of *Writers' & Artists' Yearbook* or *The Writer's Handbook*; these are the two main reference sources in the publishing industry and include contact details for leading publishers. Tip: save money by using an older copy in your local library – most publishers' details remain unchanged year after year. Useful: some libraries stock *The Bookseller*, a weekly publication listing new books. And: it is also published as a twice-yearly directory detailing books for the next six-month period. Use these to identify new and existing publishers entering your areas of interest.

3. **Seek work successfully – telephone the publishers, and ask for the name of the 'desk editor'.** Reason: this is the person who is responsible for taking authors' manuscripts through to publication. Important: never send a general letter of enquiry to a publisher. It will go unanswered – nobody will take responsibility for dealing with it. Also: don't waste time approaching any 'director', 'publisher' or 'editor' listed in *Writers' & Artists' Yearbook* or *The Writer's Handbook* – they're rarely involved in commissioning proof-readers and probably won't pass

on your details. Note: in larger publishers, there will be many desk editors responsible for different categories – so check you've got the right desk editor's details.

4. Write to the named desk editor – and sell yourself effectively. Wise: use discreet, headed paper that appears stylish; garish, 'look-at-me' paper shows you're trying too hard to impress. Helpful: make sure you spell their names correctly – mistakes can cause offence. Avoid: stating your features – 'I've enjoyed reading maths books for 20 years', for example. Why: the desk editor doesn't care. Better: sell the benefits to them of employing you – 'I've been a maths teacher for 20 years – so I can double-check all the calculations and equations for you'. Reason: desk editors want an easy life; tell them how you can help them achieve it. Check: make sure the letter is accurate in all respects; particularly your spelling, punctuation and grammar. Proof-readers must prove they have a keen eye for detail at all times. Advisable: show your letter to someone else – few people can spot their own mistakes. Timing: most desk editors use a small team of regulars; your best chance of breaking in is when someone may be unavailable; Christmas, New Year, Easter, summer holidays.

5. Act like a professional proof-reader – and profit from your new-found business opportunity. Do: be prepared to negotiate a fee and submit invoices for payment. Guidelines: expect to earn between £10 and £15 per hour, submit invoices with the work, and chase payment just before the 30-day payment period falls due. And: to correct proofs, you need to highlight errors using universal marks in the text and in the margins. So: make sure you're familiar with these – see *Writers' & Artists' Yearbook* and/or *The Writer's Handbook*. Bottom line: as a freelance proof-reader, you'll be self-employed so tell the Inland Revenue and the DSS. And: set any writing expenses against this freelance income – if writing expenses (heat and light at home, travel costs, book purchases for research purposes etc) exceed any writing income, the resulting 'loss' can be used to reclaim tax paid on your other income.

(Source: Tracey Maitland, a freelance proof-reader for UK publishing houses.)

CAR TRADERS' TRICKS EXPOSED!

Cut £750 off the price of a new showroom car – just follow the insiders' tricks of the trade. Do: negotiate by telephone; there's less pressure than in the showroom. How: dealers have a new car profit margin of up to 10%, and receive further manufacturers' bonuses for meeting sales targets; worth up to £500 per car. Ask them to split this 50-50 with you; if not, find someone who will. Helpful: wait until the end of the month when dealers are close to achieving sales targets; they'll be more inclined to cut prices. Useful: pick a car that's been in stock for two months; dealers will be keen to sell at a discount to release money. Caution: avoid buying 'add-ons' such as credit insurance, mechanical breakdown insurance and accessories; these are always over-priced because they're used by dealers to claw back discounts and increase profits on the deal. Bottom line: if you want them, shop around via insurance companies and other dealers – you'll save up to 25% on the prices.

(Source: PFC *consumer specialists.)*

FIVE WAYS TO BUILD A STRONG PARENT/TEENAGER RELATIONSHIP

Almost all children struggle for power against their parents during their teenage years. But if you know what to expect and how to handle it, you can enrich and even enjoy that parent-children relationship. Here's what to do:

1. **Stand firm on your convictions – and help your teenagers to develop theirs.** Fact: children push constantly against any boundaries imposed on them. But: subconsciously they want those boundaries to exist. Why: if you give in whenever you're challenged, your teenagers never have a strong foil against which to test their own convictions. And: they will interpret your lack of resistance as simply not caring about

them. It will seem you didn't feel strongly enough about the issue or your teenagers to take a stand. Proviso: learn to distinguish between when you're acting unreasonably and acting responsibly. Unfortunate: subconsciously, a power struggle is often triggered by a parent's natural fear of letting children grow up – and they then take an entrenched position. So: if a difficult issue arises, ask yourself whether you're acting out of true conviction or simply protecting your own power. Key question: does it really matter?

2. **Learn to compromise on non-conviction issues – and enable children to grow as individuals.** Note: emotional scenes over apparently minor issues occur frequently in adult-teenage homes. But: although the apparent issue seems trivial, the underlying issue isn't – it's about power, and who is the strongest. Important: these scenes will continue and worsen if you feel you must defend your position of authority above everything else. Better: decide which issues do not allow for room for compromise; and those that do. Examples: their choice of schools, a healthy diet, and good manners may be non-negotiable in your home; whereas their choice of friends, clothes and room arrangements may be subject to negotiations. Which issues fall into which category is a matter of personal choice; and will always vary from one home to another.

3. **Acknowledge your teenagers' points of view – and side-step damaging confrontations with them.** Understanding: for teenagers, their opinions and sense of identity often merge. They take a rejection of their opinions as a personal rejection of them – and confrontations end up bigger than they needed to be. Guideline: some younger teenagers of 13 and 14 years often disagree with their parents just for the sake of disagreement. They don't really know what they want – except that they need to have their opinions valued. Older 16 and 17 year olds usually have greater powers of reasoning, and these need to be acknowledged too.

4. **Encourage children to identify different remedies to**

problems – this is often the quickest way to agree on a solution. Tip: many power struggles arise because most teenagers don't yet realise the world is composed of shades of grey. Instead: they see everything in black and white, good and bad, winners and losers. But: differences over chores, curfews and expectations normally offer some room for different approaches – and encourage children to realise that shades of grey exist. And: your teenagers' attitudes often change when they're able to think things through from both sides, and come up with a solution. Unexpected: parents are often surprised at the fairness of their childrens' proposals.

5. Increase their decision-making powers – and develop trust with your teenagers. Truth: children need opportunities to test their ideas and develop responsibility if they're to grow into well-balanced adults. Wise: concentrate on discussing those negotiable areas that exist in your household. Because: as long as adults issue final decisions without sharing the decision-making process, teenagers will react badly. Reality: teenagers' self-evaluation is often an effective way to increase responsibility. Benefit: as their defensiveness is reduced, the possibility of trust grows greater – and this builds that strong parent-children relationship.

(Source: Betty Staley runs parentcraft workshops at the Rudolf Steiner College in the USA. The original version of the feature first appeared in PFC *February 1999, No. 29.)*

ACNE-BUSTING SECRETS

Beat acne – rubbing ice cubes over your face for three to five minutes before applying medication can minimise this problem. Tip: Benzoyl Peroxide is an effective treatment available in various formulations and strengths. Warning: don't buy acne washes – they're largely ineffective. Note: alcohol based gels are more effective than lotions and creams of the same strength – but they can cause skin irritations such as dryness, redness and peeling. Best: apply and try –

reduce frequency of application if irritation occurs, increase application to twice a day if no side effects are visible. Caution: Benzoyl Peroxide bleaches clothing and towels – wash your hands after use and dry them thoroughly.

(Source: PFC *medical advisers.)*

WATCH OUT, THIEF ABOUT!

Protect yourself against pickpockets – don't reach for your wallet or purse when someone cries 'stop thief!' Trick: pickpockets who are about to strike often call this out in the middle of a crowd. Why: it makes people feel automatically for their money and look towards the noise. And: the pickpocket's accomplices now know where wallets and purses are – and can attack from behind whilst everyone is looking in the opposite direction. Warning: get ready to be jostled if you hear this cry, or something similar. Bottom line: put money in a front or inside pocket secured with a large safety pin. And: carry a bag with the strap placed diagonally across your body; left shoulder to right hip, or vice versa.

(Source: PFC *travel researchers.)*

NATURAL, SAFER ALTERNATIVES TO HORMONE REPLACEMENT THERAPY

Many women sail happily through the menopause without any difficulties. They're the ones who know about natural treatments instead of relying on the Hormone Replacement Therapy (HRT) offered by their GPs. If you or your partner are approaching the menopause, try this life-enhancing approach:

1. Understand hormone replacement therapy (HRT) – so you know what it is, and what can happen to you. Definition: HRT involves synthetic female hormones being given for the menopause or after a hysterectomy. Fact: 70% of women come off HRT within one year. Because: HRT has many side effects including fluid retention, muscle/joint pain, headaches and migraines, weight gain, mood swings and depression. And: HRT is associated with an increased risk of strokes, heart disease and cancer. Alarming: GPs continue to routinely prescribe synthetic HRT. Unfortunate: HRT is relatively new – and many doctors are poorly educated on this complex subject. Worse: there is no real evidence to support the use of synthetic HRT. Research: according to Dr John Lee – the world authority on natural hormones – major trials on synthetic hormones have been poorly designed and/or have shown no benefit at all.

2. Recognise why synthetic treatments are provided for you – and it's all to do with money, and nothing to do with your health. Unbelievable: synthetic hormones are often made from natural ones. Example: pharmaceutical companies buy natural progesterone – derived from soya or wild yam – and chemically alter its molecular form to produce synthetic hormones. Why: synthetic hormones have molecular structures not seen in nature. And: these new molecules are patentable and can be sold for more than natural hormones; which means increased profits for everyone concerned. Bad news: Unnatural molecules often interfere with metabolism. Example: synthetic progesterone acts more like oestrogen, and increases fluid retention.

3. Recognise the natural alternatives – and consider taking them if you want to go through the menopause more smoothly. Choice: natural oestrogens and natural progesterone, herbs, vitamins, plus complementary therapies – a combination that suits your body will see you safely through the menopause. Sensible: seek medical advice appropriate to your personal circumstances. Warning: if you are currently on HRT, do not stop taking it immediately – this could be harmful to you. Instead: ask your GP how to reduce your HRT under medical supervision. Idea: if necessary, shop around to find a doctor willing to offer natural alternatives.

4. Take natural, herb-based oestrogens – your body will tolerate

these far better than their synthetic counterparts. Best herbs: Dong Quai, Siberian Ginseng, Garden Sage, Chaste Berry, Sasparilla, Black Cohosh, Unicorn Root, Wild Yam, St John's Wort. Note: these are available from health food shops, and are most effective in combination. And: take natural progesterone too – again, this is kinder on your body. Additional benefits: improved skin/hair condition, and weight loss. Source: natural progesterone is only available by medical prescription. Caution: despite claims, wild yam products from health food shops don't contain natural progesterone. Unfortunate: most GPs are unaware that natural progesterone exists – and are ignorant of its advantages over synthetic hormones. And: natural hormones are unlisted by medical pharmacies. Reason: the pharmaceutical industry has such a huge profit incentive to promote synthetic hormones that few doctors are exposed to natural products. Also: most doctors believe that unless a drug is widely accepted by their peers, it should be avoided.

5. Adopt the holistic approach – and ease through your menopause more successfully. Do: take supplements – especially 100mg vitamin C, 300mg calcium and 350iu vitamin D a day. Important: monitor your diet. Eat more: fruits and leafy green vegetables. Drink less: alcohol, fizzy drinks, coffee and tea. Wise: go organic, especially with meats. And: cut back on processed foods. Avoid: plastic-wrapped food – plastics contain molecules that are similar to oestrogens. Also: cut down your intake of fluoridated tap water – this is bad for your bones. Recommended therapies: aromatherapy, homeopathy, reflexology – these all help to promote less stress and more balance in your body.

(Source: Dr Sanjay Chaudhuri is a strong believer in complementary healthcare and preventative medicine. This feature first appeared in PFC *May 1999, No. 32)*

DANGER! PERMANENT ERECTIONS

Enjoy a safer, more comfortable bicycle ride – check your bicycle seat, and replace if necessary. Problem: a narrow, one piece seat often causes discomfort to men – and in some cases leads to temporary impotence and even priapism; a painful, permanent erection. Because: the design puts pressure on the internal chambers of the penis. Remedy: fit a split seat; with one side to support the left buttock; and the other to support the right buttock.

(Source: PFC *medical specialists.)*

FUN BETS FOR FAMILY OCCASIONS

Here are some amazing bets that will fascinate and infuriate your family and friends at holiday times. And if you don't mind falling out with them, you can offer these bets for money – and recoup the cost of any birthday or Christmas presents!

1. **Match the Birthdays. Bet: offer an even-money bet that at least two people in a group of just 26 will share a birthday** – most people will accept, because it seems so unlikely with 365 days in a year! However: the actual odds are nearly 2-1 in your favour. Explanation: establish the probability of finding no matching birthdays. How: the chance of the second person's birthday differing from the first is 364/365, the chance of the third person having a different birthday is 363/365 and so on – until the chance of the twenty-sixth person not having a matching birthday is 340/365. And: all these conditions must be met for no-one to have matching birthdays – so for your bet to fail, multiply these fractions together. This produces a figure of 0.37. Subtracting this from one gives a probability of 0.63 – or 63% – that two people will have matching birthdays. Guidelines: with 23 people, the odds are only just in your favour; with 34, the chances of a match are 80%.

2. **Double Sixes. Bet: tell your friend or colleague that the chances of rolling a double six with two dice are one in 36** – that's a proven fact! And: offer an even-money bet that they cannot roll a double six in 20 throws. Fallacy: the odds appear to be in their favour – they have more than half of 36 attempts to roll a double six. But: this

automatic assumption is based on the belief that a double six is certain to come up once in 36 throws – but it's not. Reality: the true odds can be calculated by taking the odds of not rolling a double six – 35/36 – and multiplying this by 20; the number of throws. This produces a figure of about 0.57, or 57%. Subtracting this from one gives a probability of 0.43 – or 43% – that a double six will occur. So: you have a 'house advantage' of 14% – five times the advantage that a casino gets from a roulette table. Note: for this bet to be really fair, you'd need to offer an even-money bet on 25 rolls of the dice.

3. Spot the Matching Pair. Bet: place two packs of cards side-by-side. And: offer an even-money bet that if you go through the packs turning up the top cards simultaneously, you'll find a matching pair by the time you reach the bottom. Helpful: this sounds like a good bet for the other person – each time you turn over a pair of top cards, the odds are 51/52 against a match. But: in order to fail to find a match through the entire pack, these 51/52 odds must be multiplied 51 times. Result: this gives you a total probability of missing a match of 37% – and the probability of success is 63% in your favour.

4. On the Bottom. Bet: cut one pack of cards into three piles and offer an even-money bet that there will be a picture card on the bottom of one of them. Reaction: it appears to be a great bet for the other person. But: there are 12,220 possible three-card combinations that contain at least one picture card – and only 9,880 combinations that do not contain any at all. So your chances of success are 12,200/(12,200 + 9,880) = 0.553. That's just over 55% in your favour against a probability of losing of just under 45%. – a winning edge of over 10%. Bottom line: as with all these bets, you'll need to offer a series of wagers to turn that edge into success, and hard cash.

(Source: Nick Daws, the editor of British Gambling News. *The full version of this feature first appeared in* PFC *December 1998, No. 27.)*

WHY UNLUBRICATED CONDOMS ARE BETTER

Minimise the risk of female urinary tract infections – make sure your partner wears unlubricated condoms during love-making. Research: recent US studies reveal that those condoms lubricated with spermicide destroy both sperm and healthy, protective bacteria within the vagina – and allow infection-causing bacteria to multiply. Alternative: condoms lubricated with non-spermicidal lubricants, such as KY jelly.

(Source: PFC *medical contacts.)*

HOW TO CAPTURE THOSE HAPPY MEMORIES FOREVER

If you want to remember children's birthdays, weddings and other family occasions more easily, video them. And if you want a video that everyone will enjoy watching again and again, follow these tricks of the trade:

1. Plan a story – this makes it easier to film, and more enjoyable to watch. Example: Dad wants to video the family holiday. But: most people get no further than filming the odd swim or day out. Result: a video of limited interest. Fact: most audiences like a story. Better: Dad gets the children to explain where they want to go and why, and what they're doing. Outcome: personalities and places are portrayed, and a story develops. Wise: draft a loose storyline with a beginning, middle and end, and what you want to see within each of them.

2. Pay attention to the lighting – so that the right mood is created on video. Do: try filming in different lighting situations beforehand, to see what works and doesn't. And: lock the exposure for the duration of a shoot, rather than using the automatic exposure feature. Why: this controls how much light is let in, and can change whilst filming and ruin the shoot. Example: if a white van went through your picture. Also: make certain the overall colour balance is correct.

How: if your camcorder has a white balance switch, point the camcorder at a piece of white card that fills most of the frame. And: position the card so that the light is falling on it. Next: check your colour monitor – looking in particular at flesh tones – and redo the white balance until you're happy with it.

3. Think about the sound – offscreen noise and sounds can distract from your story. Unfortunate: a camcorder microphone records all the sound presented to it; including sounds you don't want to hear. Outside: putting a baby's mitten over the microphone can minimise noise on a windy day. Indoors: filming the source of any noise can help to reduce viewers' irritation later; when they would otherwise hear but not see where it was coming from. Note: background chatter often sounds better than an embarrassed silence – and it also helps to relax anyone who is being filmed.

4. Put participants at their ease – so that the video seems natural and real; rather than staged and acted. Important: getting a good 'performance' from your stars means making sure they don't become self conscious, perform or act up. General: keep your filming as unobtrusive as possible. Useful: try to film them doing something they normally do, so they don't have to think about it. Example: you want to film a child opening a present. So: give them the present and let them get on with unwrapping it – don't tell them where to sit and how to open it.

5. Vary your shots – to add variety and interest to the story. Tip: high angle shots – from the top of a ladder or a roof – can create a feeling of detachment or space. And: moving sideways to follow a person can add a sense of depth to a scene. Also: low angle shots – from a small tripod known as 'baby legs' – can convey a child's eye view. Plus: moving the focus from one person to another or zooming in or out can liven up a lengthy shot. But: resist the temptation to do this more than once or twice. Too often, and it becomes a distraction. Guideline: practise in advance. See what interests you – and when these tricks begin to irritate.

6. Work with both eyes open – to make sure the story unfolds successfully. Explanation: a camcorder's viewfinder usually comprises a small monitor with an adjustable viewing lens. And: most first-timers keep one on that, and the other one closed. Wiser: train that other eye to stay open to observe the 'real' scene; what's happening nearby, who's coming into shot etc. And: this can enable you to shoot some unexpected, magical scenes. Examples: a baby's smile, a child's funny walk, a dog chasing its tail.

7. Let the story speak for itself – and increase the viewers' enjoyment of your video. Always: bear in mind that the eye takes precedence over the ear. So: an exciting visual event will have far more impact than any commentary. And: if you've a clear storyline – beginning, middle, end – a commentary should be unnecessary anyway.

(Source: Nick Hale, a member of the British Academy of Film and Television Arts. The original version of this feature first appeared in PFC *April 1999, No. 31.)*

THE FASTEST WAY TO CLIMB THE CAREER LADDER

To succeed at work, just get yourself known by influential people. The reason's very simple – most companies prefer to employ and promote people on the 'better the devil you know than the devil you don't' principle. These are the right ways to get noticed:

1. Draw up a 'hit list' of people you need to know – anyone that can help you to get ahead. Wise: sit down, analyse your organisation and decide who can promote your career – either directly or indirectly; by putting in a good word for you. Also: look outside your organisation – at competitors, suppliers, customers, and other firms and people in your industry. Note: they may be prospective employers – or may praise you to people higher up in your own organisation. Guideline: these are the people who need to notice you.

2. Be visible – so you're on greeting terms with as many key

players on your hit list as possible. Fact: being visible means being in the right place at the right time – but it doesn't involve being the loudest or most noticed person in the room. So: decide which are the most important meetings and gatherings and be there – even if it's to hold someone else's notes. Why: people will see you, and automatically assume you're a major player. Do: attend all leaving and Christmas functions – and mingle and talk to as many people as you can. Good news: once you're labelled as 'someone going somewhere', there is little to stop you achieving it.

3. **Assume the role of a more senior manager – and you'll fill it that much sooner.** Fortunate: most people make great assumptions on the basis of very little evidence. Proof: you've probably been to an event and seen someone you didn't know who had an air of importance – and assumed they were important. It's a natural thing to do. So: be seen with the right people – mix with senior managers at a conference, and other delegates will assume you're at that level. And: adopt the bearing and gestures of those people above you on the career ladder – walk tall and be confident. Also dress the part – look at someone you admire within the company, and wear what they wear. Note: this all confirms visually that you're a confident person capable of doing your current job, and the one above.

4. **Look out for go-ahead opportunities – and use them to progress within the organisation.** Typical: if you overhear someone discussing a project, ask about it. If the project hasn't yet started, ask when they'll be selecting the team for it. And if you enjoyed a seminar and thought the speaker was someone worth knowing, go and introduce yourself at the end; ask a question, start a conversation. Otherwise: you'll spend the rest of the day regretting it. Best advice: be around when decisions are being made, use every opportunity to introduce yourself and make that all-important impression.

5. **Find out where hit list people can be found in social situations – and initiate conversations with them.** Tip: it's easy to

contrive a business introduction – simply walk up and introduce yourself. But: it's hard to take the conversation on from there; especially if they're overloaded with work. Better: meeting socially provides a lead and a ready-made follow-up – 'would you like a game of squash?', for example. And: when they're at leisure, they'll be more inclined to chat to you. Bottom line: this isn't cheating – it's just speeding up what would have happened anyway given time.

(Source: Karen Mannering, personal development expert who specialises in helping people build up a portfolio of career-enhancing skills. This feature first appeared in PFC *May 1999, No. 32.)*

HOW TO MAKE YOUR MP SIT UP AND BARK LIKE A DOG

If you need help of almost any kind, your local MP can enable you to achieve whatever you want – because they know how the system works, and how to work the system. Get your MP working for you with these little-known tactics:

1. **Write to your constituency MP about personal issues - this is the one member of parliament who will really help you.** Why: the letter comes from one of their own constituency addresses – other correspondence receives short shrift. Note: by convention, MPs do not take up cases for other MPs' constituents. Where: write to the House of Commons, London SW1A 0AA. Important: never write direct to a Government Department – you'll receive a non-committal reply drafted by a civil servant. If you write to your MP, you'll get a reply that's at least signed by a minister. It may be the same reply - but you can then contact the MP again to ask if they or the minister read the letter before sending it to you. Tip: this is really effective - it attracts the MP's interest who'll pass on your comments to the minister who'll refer it to that civil servant who drafted the reply. This increases the attention given to your problem.

2. **Telephone the House (0171 219 3000) for urgent matters and leave a message for your MP to call you back – this way, you'll get a faster response.** And: when you speak, ask for a personal meeting to discuss the issue.

Location: MPs hold regular surgeries in their constituency where they meet constituents. Unfortunate: surgeries are not publicised widely so you'll need to contact your MP or local constituency office. Look in the telephone book under the appropriate political party's name to find out when the next one is being held, and make an appointment Helpful: you'll get a more practical response from the MP if you supply some background details before your meeting.

3. **Lobby 200 MPs if you represent a pressure group – this is the most effective way to get action.** Reason: ten constituency letters sent to one MP on the same subject discloses a serious issue that should be followed up by that MP. And: if 200 MPs each receive ten letters on the subject from their constituents, the Government is alerted to the matter. Best: those letters that are written in constituents' own words. Worst: printed forms distributed by an organisation to its members for signing and forwarding to MPs. These are usually treated with contempt by MPs. Because: printed forms suggest that these people have such little interest in the matter that they cannot be bothered to write for themselves.

4. **Always ask your MP if they're prepared to table a Parliamentary Question (PQ) about a serious private or public matter – this can have an electrifying effect on resolving your problem.** Because: the request will almost certainly be passed to a minister who will ask a bureaucrat to deal with it. And: nothing disturbs a civil servant more than having to prepare a PQ for oral answer - it's not only necessary to provide an initial reply, but to counter every conceivable supplementary question as well. Evidence: this is why ministers bring such big books to the despatch box at Question Time; there may be several pages of notes and comments for each PQ that's been tabled. Bottom line: civil servants are the same as everyone else; they're not keen on extra work. When they're faced with a constituent who knows how the system operates, they'll usually do all they can to bring matters to the speediest possible conclusion.

(Source: Robert S. Redmond is a former MP, and has been involved in politics for more than 50 years. The full version of this feature first appeared in PFC *January 1999, No. 28.)*

A TREASURE-TROVE OF INSIDE INFORMATION FOR YOU

• Always ask an independent financial adviser for a cashback on any financial products bought through them – and suggest you'll be doing business together again soon. Our research indicates that most IFAs are willing to return part of their commission to regular customers – if your one doesn't, consider shopping around.

• Write to your mortgage lender informing them that you're planning to move your mortgage elsewhere – it can encourage them to offer you a trade-secret discount off their official mortage rate.

• Request a no-claims discount if you haven't made a claim on your buildings or contents insurance policies in the past year – we've discovered that the majority of insurance companies will agree rather than risk losing your custom.

• Change your shampoo and conditioner every two months – if you use the same ones for too long, they'll lose their effectiveness for your hair.

• Clean your teeth before eating – this destroys the plaque that would otherwise combine with sugar in food to produce acids that damage your teeth.

• Add baked potatoes, bananas, spinach and orange juice to your diet if you want to lower your blood pressure – these common foods and drink are rich in potassium which helps you to achieve this.

• Sniff a fresh lemon to eliminate seasickness – it'll get rid of morning sickness too if you're pregnant.

• Avoid using headache tablets every time you experience headaches – repeated use can aggravate the pain. Instead, try natural alternatives such as heat, ice packs, massage and relaxation treatments.

• Chew gum to alleviate heartburn – this produces saliva that washes away the stomach acid that creates pain if it rises up into your gullet after you've eaten.

• Smear a little vaseline on a small cut before covering it with a plaster or bandage – minor cuts heal faster if they're kept moist.

• Keep nits out of a child's hair by brushing conditioner through it with a nit comb three times a week – nits cannot hold onto conditioned hair and will go elsewhere. Avoid head lice shampoos with organophosphates that can be absorbed into and damage the nervous system.

• Pause regularly when speaking – this emphasises your comments. Filling silences with 'actually', 'as a matter of fact' and 'you know what I mean' detract from what you're saying.

• Lighten a bad mood by writing down everything you're unhappy about on a postcard that you're going to send to yourself – by the time you've finished, you'll feel much happier, and will have decided not to post it.

• Get rid of cat and dog fleas in your home by putting a flea collar in your vacuum cleaner – they'll be sucked up and killed as you clean around.

• Make rooms smell fresh and appealing by wiping a dab of perfume or essential oil onto cold light bulbs – they'll generate a wonderful scent as they heat up.

• Add a sparkle to windows by cleaning them with a vinegar/water mixture – the vinegar removes grease and gives a terrific shine too.

• Keep your children's drawings forever by spraying them with hairspray – this stops colours fading and being rubbed away.

• Rub the side of a cut-in-half onion across your car windscreen in cold weather – this stops it freezing over.

• Remove rust spots from your car bodywork by rubbing them with aluminium foil that's been soaked in coca cola – it's easy, effective and works every time.

• Keep e-mail messages clear and succinct to ensure they're understood fully – humour of any kind is often overlooked or misinterpreted; especially if you're corresponding with people from other countries.

• Succeed at a job interview by listening for the interviewer's breathing patterns and matching them – this puts across the subliminal message that you're on the same wavelength.

• Maintain good relations with your employer by admitting to a mistake and saying sorry – avoid providing detailed reasons for the error; they sound like excuses. Best: remedy the mistake yourself without having to be prompted.

• Calculate the true value of a mortgage cashback offer – divide the cashback by the length of the redemption penalty and deduct this from the standard mortgage rate. Example: 6% divided by six years cuts 1% off the usual variable rate.

• Tackle insomnia – force yourself to yawn over and again; by the sixth or seven yawn, you'll start to feel sleepy. Alternative: try a lettuce sandwich – the laudanum in the lettuce helps you to go to sleep.

• Make young children feel grown-up and secure when shopping – attach a whistle to their clothes; and tell them to blow it if they become separated from you.

• Improve a jobsearch or business letter – add a handwritten touch. Best: a personalised greeting and a PS stick in the memory – and are essential if you're looking to impress a would-be employer.

• Protect eyeglasses when decorating – wrap cling film around the lenses, and replace as and when necessary.

• Rev up your diet – mix in chilli peppers, mustard and ginger. Details: US research shows that these raise your metabolic rate so that you burn up calories much faster than before; and lose more weight.

• Prevent lightweight vases being knocked over easily – fill the bottom with sand; or use marbles if the vase is used for flower arrangements.

• Keep cats away from furniture and household plants – spray the area with lemon scented polish; cats hate the smell and will go elsewhere.

• Clean your computer screen effectively – use a soft, lint-free cloth dampened with water; anything stronger can strip off the antiglare coating on the screen.

• Reduce painful headaches - wear shoes with soft soles and heels; these minimise the impact of walking, and the knock-on effects on your skull.

• Obtain free small business advice – approach the business schools of local universities; most MBA students (many of whom are experienced business people) will be interested in tackling real problems as part of their coursework.

• Cure hiccups – swallow a teaspoonful of sugar; US studies suggest that this is effective in 95% of cases.

• Dry flowers quickly and effectively – heat them in a microwave; within three minutes they'll be ready to put into an attractive arrangement.

• Save spending cash on unsuitable cosmetics – ask for free make-up samples at cosmetic counters in larger stores; most keep a wide range of samples under the counter and will provide these on request.

• Move a washing machine more easily – squirt a little washing-up liquid beneath the rubber feet; it will then slide out smoothly. Use the same trick for fridges and freezers.

• Reduce your overdraft charges – ask your bank to explain how they were calculated. UK research indicates that 80% of all overdraft charges are calculated incorrectly. If your bank cannot justify them, you should be entitled to an appropriate refund.

• Stop your dog chewing your belongings and household objects – give it only one toy; too many, and it will think it can chew everything. Avoid: a shoe-shaped toy and anything else that resembles your possessions.

• Demolish a colleague's bad idea sympathetically – say 'That's a good idea. Can I just ask one question about...?'. This way, you'll sound positive, and allow your colleague to conclude this is a bad idea whilst they're explaining it.

• Check if you're overweight – calculate your body mass index; simply divide your weight in kilos by your height in metres squared. Example: 70kg divided by 1.75 metres multiplied by 1.75 metres equals 22.87. Note: a total of 25 to 30 means you're overweight.

• Re-instate accidentally deleted text on your computer screen – hold down 'Alt' and press the backspace key. Alternative: hold down the 'Ctlr' key and press 'z'.

• Find out what's happening in your firm – mix with the smokers at break times. If they're banned from smoking at their desks, employees from all departments and levels will meet in a corner, exchanging information that wouldn't normally circulate around the company.

• Stop children going off with strangers – have a family password; only trusted friends and relatives will be given it in an emergency.

• Have a healthier heart – give blood regularly. Why: UK studies indicate that male blood donors have a lower risk of heart attacks than those who do not donate at all.

• Spot a liar – just ask a simple, direct question. How: listen for the giveaway response; generalised comments accompanied by vague speech patterns such as 'yeah', 'well', 'you know'. And: watch for the tell-tale body language; loss of eye contact, hands over the mouth.

• Beat that cold – take a large dose of vitamin C at the first sign of a cold. Details: UK research reveals it will reduce the length and severity of a cold. Fact: vitamin C cannot prevent colds but its antioxidant properties alleviate the symptoms.

• Take control of business meetings – be the first person to extend their hand for a handshake. Tip: this boosts your confidence, and gives you control of the situation. Remember: keep your right hand free whenever you're approaching hand-shaking scenarios.